THE OLD
TESTAMENT FOR
LATTER-DAY SAINTS

THE OLD TESTAMENT FOR LATTER-DAY SAINTS

ALEX DOUGLAS

SIGNATURE BOOKS | 2023 | SALT LAKE CITY

For Celeste,
whose sacrifices made this work possible

Join our mail list at www.signaturebooks.com for details on events and related titles we think you'll enjoy.

Design by Jason Francis

FIRST EDITION | 2023

LIBRARY OF CONGRESS CONTROL NUMBER: 2023947415

Paperback ISBN: 978-1-56085-468-5
Ebook ISBN: 978-1-56085-485-2

CONTENTS

INTRODUCTION

When I was in high school, my LDS seminary teacher challenged each of us to read the entire Old Testament before the end of the year. As a dedicated student, I gave his challenge my best effort, but if you've ever tried to read the Old Testament from cover to cover, you probably know how this story ends. I don't remember much from my seminary lessons or the Bible reading I did that year, but I vividly remember my confusion and boredom as I slogged through chapter after chapter of ancient Israelite laws and dietary regulations.

As I have come to find out, my experience was hardly unique. Whenever I discuss the Old Testament with someone, I usually hear some variation of the same story. They tried to read it all the way through but petered out not far into the opening books.

The confusion and boredom many people experience as they read the Old Testament are understandable but also unfortunate, for it is a truly remarkable book. It serves as the foundational text of both Judaism and Christianity; the Qur'an draws extensively from its pages, as well. More people consider the Old Testament to be inspired by God than any other book in the world. It is epic, insightful, beautiful, and profound.

But it is also difficult. Right when the story gets interesting, the narrator is likely to pause and give a lengthy genealogy of the characters involved. At the climax of the exodus narrative, when Moses has led the Israelites to freedom and they see God's presence descend onto Mount Sinai, the reader is treated to chapter upon chapter of Israel's legal code, discussing everything from making restitution for theft to determining guilt in cases of manslaughter. The narratives themselves are often outlandish, with stories of superhuman strength, talking donkeys, and people living for more than 900 years. God is sometimes presented as vengeful and vindictive, wiping out entire populations to prevent unbelievers from tempting the Israelites. But sometimes God is portrayed as a loving, caring parent who yearns to comfort his people. The juxtaposition can be jarring; the tender verse, "The Lord is my shepherd, I shall not want" (Ps. 23:1) lies only two chapters away from the celebration of God's treatment of his enemies: "You will destroy their offspring from the earth, and their children from among humankind" (Ps. 21:10).[1]

The difficulty of reading the Old Testament is compounded by the fact that its world is so far removed from our own. Twenty-first-century readers don't have the cultural understanding or background knowledge that the Old Testament's original authors took for granted. For example, how many of us know what a cherub actually is? What does it mean to "devote" your enemies (Lev. 27:29)? What does it mean when Manasseh practices "soothsaying" and consults "mediums" while making a "sacred pole" and a "carved image of Asherah" (2 Kgs. 21:6, 3, 7)? Most of us recognize that these practices have something to do with magic and idolatry, but that is about as far as we can go.

If you are as perplexed as I was by the Old Testament, you might go looking for clarification. Indeed, the fact that you are reading this book suggests that you are doing just that. But outside sources are sometimes more confusing than enlightening, mainly because an author's assumptions about the Old Testament unavoidably color their interpretation. Some authors may see the Old Testament as myth, considering it akin to any other culture's stories of gods and heroes. Others may see it as God's dictated word. Some LDS apologists are likely to scour the Old Testament's pages looking for parallels to modern Mormon practice or for prophecies of the Latter-day Restoration; authors from other denominations will use its passages to prove their own worldviews.

To show you just how deeply our assumptions can impact our reading of the book, consider why we even call it the Old Testament. In Judaism, this book is often referred to as the Tanak or *Torah*, a

---

1. All quotations are taken from the New Revised Standard Version of the Bible, unless otherwise noted. The only exception is that when the divine name יהוה (*Yhwh*) is used, the NRSV translates it as LORD in small caps, whereas I usually render it as Yahweh.

Hebrew word meaning "law" or "instruction." But Christians call it the Old Testament, where the word "testament" is used in its older sense of "covenant." By calling it the *Old* Testament, Christians imply that the text is correctly understood as being replaced by the *New* Testament—"the new covenant in [Christ's] blood" (1 Cor. 11:25). In LDS discourse, the term "testament" has come to be understood particularly as a reference to how the book testifies of Jesus Christ. Thus, the Book of Mormon compares itself with the Old and New Testaments by calling itself "Another Testament of Jesus Christ." However, those of a more academic bent prefer none of these names, and they usually refer to the Old Testament as the Hebrew Bible—a name that respects the sacred place this text holds in various religious traditions while also acknowledging that these writings are not fundamentally Jewish or Christian, but rather ancient Hebrew.

Thus, authors with different worldviews can easily come to very different conclusions about the interpretation of a single verse, making the interpretation of the Old Testament overall seem like a lost cause. Despite these difficulties, there is much to be gained from taking time to explore the Old Testament, whether you want to understand your own religion or that of others, whether you are a trained historian or a newcomer, whether you want to appreciate the book's literary beauty or its history. This book lies at the foundation of Western civilization—from the Renaissance to the Reformation, from the Christianization of the Roman Empire to the Holocaust. The work you put into understanding the Old Testament will be endlessly rewarding.

My goal in this book is to help make the Old Testament a little less daunting and a little more relatable. As much as I would love to say that I can offer an unbiased look at the Old Testament, such a claim is unrealistic. Like every other author, I understand the Old Testament from my own life's perspective. I was born and raised a member of the Church of Jesus Christ of Latter-day Saints, and my interests have always been influenced by that community. Questions about the ancient temple or the historicity of the Book of Mormon, for example, matter to me, and they affect the way I read the Old Testament—often in ways I am not even aware of.

Though the impetus for exploring the Old Testament stemmed from my membership in the LDS Church, it has been shaped by years of secular academic training. I once pored through Leviticus looking for parallels to modern temple practice, but after earning both a master's and a PhD specializing in the Old Testament, I now read those passages with an eye toward understanding ancient Israelite religion on its own terms. I have gained an appreciation for the way many interpretive traditions bring the scriptures to life, and I have come to care much more about what the text actually says than about what that text can prove or disprove. The approach I take in this book mirrors my background. For example, I usually refer to the text as the "Old Testament," and I will touch on many issues relevant to the LDS community. Yet this book is academic, not devotional. Thus, my primary goal is to show you the wealth of scholarship created during the past few centuries, and along the way we will explore what this scholarship can mean for modern LDS belief and discourse.

The Hebrew Bible has many parts, some of which can be understood as history, prophecy, law, or advice. Yet each category falls short if we use it to define the Bible's entire essence. Even the word "Bible" itself denotes this plurality, as it derives from the Greek word βιβλία (*biblia*), meaning "books." When people in the ancient world spoke about the Bible, they did not refer to it as a single entity; they literally talked about "the Bibles."

Each chapter of this book examines the Hebrew Bible from a different perspective. Chapter one looks at the Old Testament as myth, chapter two as legend, chapter three as story, chapter four as law, chapter five as history, and so on. These chapters also progress through the Old Testament roughly in the order we now find it. So chapters one through three deal with Genesis–Deuteronomy, chapter four with Joshua–2 Kings, and so on until the end of the Old Testament.

In chapter one, we see that the concept of myth can help us understand the stories of Genesis and Exodus—not in the sense that the stories are not true, but in the sense that they serve the same purpose that foundational myths fulfill in other societies. In other words, the Old Testament opens with Israel's mythic origin story, beginning with the creation of the world and climaxing with the birth of Israel as God's covenant people. Chapter two examines the Old Testament as legend, particularly in the stories of Abraham, Isaac, Jacob, and Jacob's twelve sons. Chapter three looks at the Old

Testament as story, focusing on how different voices and viewpoints are incorporated into one coherent story about God and Israel.

Chapter four looks at Exodus–Deuteronomy and examines the Old Testament as law. We explore the ancient Near Eastern precursors to the law of Moses and what these rules mean for modern religious communities. We also look at ancient Israelite religion on its own terms, including the temple and priesthood, followed by a look at the ways the Old Testament does and does not function as a rulebook.

Chapter five turns to Joshua–2 Kings, examining the Old Testament as history. As we see, much of the Old Testament recounts the history of Israel, but not in the way that we understand history today. These stories were compiled in reaction to the most traumatic event in Israelite history, and they were shaped primarily to ensure that the reader would draw particular lessons from that history.

Chapter six considers 1–2 Chronicles, and the Old Testament at large, as revisionist history. At some point after Babylonian exile, Israelites began to reexamine their history and update it to fit their changing world. This chapter looks at how fluid the concept of scripture was in ancient Israel and offers a glimpse at some of the ideological battles fought over scripture's contents.

Chapter seven moves to the books of Isaiah–Malachi and considers the Old Testament as prophecy. We often think of the Old Testament as predicting future events, whether it be the coming of Jesus or the Restoration. Since prophets and prophecy had a unique function in the ancient Near East, we look at the context that shaped their messages.

The book of Isaiah plays a central role in the Old Testament, early Christianity, and the Book of Mormon. For this reason, Isaiah is the sole focus of chapter eight. Being a complex work—and its authorship a thorny problem—Isaiah raises a host of issues related to the composition of the Old Testament and its relationship to the Book of Mormon.

Chapter nine examines many of the books known in the Jewish tradition as "the Writings," such as Job, Psalms, Proverbs, Ecclesiastes, Esther, and Ruth. Here we consider the Old Testament as advice and show the myriad ways biblical authors wrestled with the issues of their day.

Finally, chapter ten looks at the Old Testament as scripture in a Jewish, Christian, and LDS context. We see how the Hebrew Bible is transformed when it is brought into these three traditions—and how it changes these traditions in turn.

An afterword then discusses how to interpret the Book of Mormon in light of what we know of Old Testament scholarship.

My hope is that these various perspectives will help you appreciate the Old Testament's beauty and complexity as much as they have helped me. The Old Testament comes from a completely different time and culture, but once you find a foothold, it becomes accessible and exciting in ways you could never have anticipated.

While I am listed as the author of this book, in truth, it is the product of an entire community, and I would be remiss not to mention the many people whose help made it possible. My wife and children have been patient with me beyond measure, both in helping me through graduate school and in allowing me the time to complete this project. Every hour I have spent immersed in the world of biblical scholarship has been an hour I could not spend with them, and they deserve all the love and appreciation I possess.

I also owe an immense debt to the countless men and women who have devoted their life to the study of the Bible. This book draws extensively from the world of biblical scholarship, and I have benefitted from excellent teachers. I would never have pursued a PhD in the Old Testament had it not been for David Bokovoy, whose engaging LDS Institute classes ignited in me a passion for bridging the worlds of faith and scholarship. Throughout graduate school I was given the chance to work with some of the greatest minds in the field: Andrew Teeter, Jon Levenson, Peter Machinist, Michael Coogan, Richard Saley, Shaye Cohen, Piotr Steinkeller, and Larry Stager. I truly feel that if I have seen anything, it is because I have stood on the shoulders of giants.

Finally, this book would not exist were it not for the editorial team at Signature Books. The long journey from initial manuscript to finished product would never have happened without their encouragement and direction, and their sharp eye has improved the writing immensely. Any mistakes in this book are my own.

1

THE
OLD TESTAMENT
AS MYTH

(Genesis 1–11)

If you look at any society, past or present, you are likely to find that the people of that society tell stories they consider foundational. Passed down through the generations, these stories describe where that society came from, what its values are, and how it sees itself in relation to the wider world.

For at least two centuries in the United States, the dominant version of our foundational story began with the Pilgrims fleeing religious persecution in Britain and coming to the New World. These pilgrims came to establish a city on a hill, a beacon of freedom and social mobility. When Britain's rule grew oppressive, these colonies rose up and defied all odds by defeating the English superpower. Then the founders crafted a government both by the people and for the people. This story is retold in our schools and homes, and many of our public rituals are shaped by it. We pledge allegiance to the flag; our sports events begin with "The Star-Spangled Banner," commemorating how narrowly we won our independence; tourists in the Northeast walk the Freedom Trail and visit the Liberty Bell; school children recite "Paul Revere's Ride"; and each 4th of July Americans gather to watch the fireworks in celebration of the Declaration of Independence.

The stories underlying these rituals and celebrations are myths. But let me be clear: To say that a story is "myth" is not a judgment on how factual the story is. Instead, the term "myth" refers to the *function* the story plays in society. In the United States, the founding myth I just described attempts to bind us together as citizens of the United States, even though we come from all kinds of backgrounds—first-generation immigrants, descendants of enslaved people, refugees, European migrants, and the list goes on. Only a tiny fraction of the population can trace its ancestry back to the pilgrims on the Mayflower or to the Revolutionary army, yet in each public commemoration, this story ties us all together as if it were in some sense *our* story. Our founding myth gives us a sense of identity and purpose: We believe in equality. We defend freedom. We can prevail against all odds. The myth gives us a way to understand our past.

The opening books of the Old Testament certainly contain sections that read like history. But if we look at the *function* these stories serve, at why they were included in an ancient Israelite collection of sacred writings, it is hard to escape the conclusion that these stories work in much the same way that America's founding myth does. If we read these chapters only as histories, we miss the primary purpose for which they were written. We might say that Genesis and Exodus contain not history, but History with a capital H—the kind of story meant to unite the ancient Israelites, to give them a sense of identity and purpose, and to provide them with a way to understand their past. Myths make the world look a particular way, and, in that sense, Genesis 1–11 are deeply mythic. To see how this is true, let us look at some of the stories in Genesis.

The Creation and the Garden of Eden

Genesis begins with chaos—the earth is "a formless void" (Gen. 1:2) and everything is blended together. Then God steps in. He separates light from darkness on day one; he creates a dome to separate the water above the sky from the water beneath it on day two.[1] On day three he separates the dry land from the water. Then he begins populating these environments. Corresponding with the light he created on day one, God creates the sun, moon, and stars on day four, each with the job of separating and marking off distinct times

---

1. The Hebrew word here is רקיע (*raqia'*), which translates to "dome," but the word is rare in Hebrew. Ancient Greek translators were not quite sure what to make of this word, so they translated it as στερέωμα (*stereoma*), which literally means "a firm thing." The translators of the King James Version (KJV) appear to have been equally perplexed, which is why they render the Hebrew as "firmament."

and seasons. Corresponding with the dome he created on day two that separates sky and sea, he creates the birds and fish on day five. And just as on day three he created the dry land, on day six he creates animals and humans. Now that the world is ordered, God's crowning act of creation is to bless and hallow the seventh day.

The strict order of the creation story is no accident. Genesis 1 is not so much a story about creation *per se* as it is a story about order. Over and over again, God separates out, names, and places his creations in their proper sphere. God "separated light from darkness"; the dome "separates the waters from the waters"; the sun and moon "separate the light from the darkness" and "rule over the day and over the night"; and humans "have dominion over ... every living thing." Every plant has its own seed, every animal its like descendant, every being its proper dominion. Even the text is strictly ordered, each day beginning with "God said," continuing with "God saw," and ending with "there was evening and there was morning, the [number] day."

This story arranges the world in the way that Israelite culture was ordered. Notice, for example, how much the story emphasizes the separations that lie at the heart of the law of Moses. As we will see in chapter four, according to Mosaic law, clean animals are the ones that fit neatly into their proper place; anything that transgresses those boundaries is considered unclean. Thus, cattle are considered clean because they have split hooves and "chew the cud" (Lev. 11:3), but animals that mix these categories are off limits, such as badgers (which chew the cud but do not have split hooves, Lev. 11:5) and pigs (which have split hooves but do not chew the cud, Lev 11:7). Similarly, fish that do not have fins or scales are off limits, as are birds that eat meat and winged insects that walk on all fours (Lev 11:12–20). Fish without scales and birds that eat meat cross too many boundaries. Israelites were likewise forbidden to crossbreed animals (Lev. 19:19), yoke donkeys and oxen together (Deut. 22:10), or even wear garments mixing wool and linen (Deut. 22:11). Cross-dressing was also seen as a transgression of natural boundaries (Deut. 22:5). All these divisions—including, most importantly, the division between holy days and working days—have their foundation in the creation story.

Myths, remember, are told not to recount history, but to arrange the world in a particular way. The Genesis creation story helped ancient Israelites create a mental map of their world much the same way that the LDS temple endowment ceremony helps contemporary Saints make sense of their world. Both are used mythically.

However, when we hear the word "myth" today, most of us do not think of stories such as America's founding narrative. Instead, we tend to think of Greek and Roman myths: fantastical stories about gods and goddesses, magic, and heroic struggles. Or perhaps we think of something akin to the Sioux myth where a white raven warns the buffalo that hunters are coming, until one day a hunter takes the raven and thrusts it into the fire, thus turning the raven black. Myths like these purport to explain why ravens are black, why the seasons change, why sacrifices are offered to the gods, or why the sun moves across the sky. Scholars refer to these explanatory elements of myth as etiologies.

The next major story of Genesis, the Garden of Eden, bears all the hallmarks of more traditional myths, complete with etiologies. A man and woman are placed into a garden of delights (the Hebrew word for Eden, עדנה [ʿednah], literally means "pleasure") with two supernatural trees, one that bestows immortality and one that bestows knowledge. A talking serpent convinces the couple to eat from the tree of knowledge, and they are banished to a life of hard work as a result. The story explains the origin of marriage (Gen. 2:24), why people wear clothes (3:7), why snakes do not have legs (3:14), why women bear children (3:16), and why farming the land is so difficult (3:18). The etiological elements of the Eden narrative are not side notes; they pervade the story. Indeed, the narrative seems purposefully shaped to convey these explanations.

Like any good myth, the Eden story gives readers a way to understand their place in the cosmos. Immortality is presented as belonging exclusively to the divine realm, while the ability to discern between right and wrong makes us nevertheless godlike. It casts the difficulty of life as being part of the natural order of things. The story helped justify why men held so much power over women in Israel's patriarchal society: according to Genesis, God explicitly told women, "Your desire shall be for your husband, and he shall rule over you" (Gen. 3:16). Indeed, Genesis 3 was used as justification for the subordination of women for millennia, from the early Christian church (1 Tim. 2:12–14) to modern Christian denominations, and even in LDS temple ceremonies.

Later interpreters, living well after the Old Testament period, infused the Garden of Eden story with significance beyond what is found in the story itself. For example, at the time the Eden myth was established, Israelites did not believe in a Satan or devil figure (more on that later), but by the New Testament period, belief in Satan was widespread. Thus, later interpreters came to identify the snake in the story as Satan, even though the text itself only refers to it as "the serpent." Adam and Eve's actions came to be seen as the origin of sin and humankind's sinful nature. Similarly, Eden came to be seen as the place where the "fall" of humankind took place. But nothing in the story suggests that human nature itself was changed or that Adam and Eve are responsible for sin entering the world. In fact, not a single verse in the Old Testament refers back to the Garden of Eden story as an explanation for sin. The Eden story held a much different significance for ancient Israelites than it does for most contemporary Christians.

Cain and Abel

After being driven from Eden, Adam and Eve bear two sons: Cain, who is a farmer by trade, and Abel, who is a shepherd. Both offer sacrifices, but for unknown reasons God prefers Abel's offering over Cain's.[2] Cain kills his brother in anger, and when God discovers the murder, he banishes Cain and places a mark on him.

Throughout the ancient Near East, farmers and nomads were constantly fighting. The book of Joshua describes how the Israelites—who

---

2. The text says that Abel brought "the firstlings of the flock," while Cain brought "the fruit of the ground." Both types of offerings were accepted in ancient Israel, so most commentators seize on the fact that Abel brought the firstborn of his flocks, whereas Cain is not mentioned as having brought the first of his crop. As one prominent biblical scholar notes, however, this line of reasoning is tenuous at best. "If we are to rationalize the rejection of Cain's offering and the acceptance of Abel's by reference to a word or two in the text and on the basis of an argument from silence, we could just as easily rationalize the reverse result, for whereas Cain brought his sacrifice 'to the LORD' (v 3), Abel, on this sort of microscopic over-reading, did not" (Jon D. Levenson, *The Death and Resurrection of the Beloved Son: The Transformation of Child Sacrifice in Judaism and Christianity* [New Haven: Yale University Press, 1993], 72).

were at that time nomads living in the desert—came in and wiped out all the Canaanite settlements. Then the Israelites spend much of the rest of their history fending off other nomads who try to invade the land. Cain and Abel perfectly fit the roles in this stereotypical feud, so it is hardly surprising that the story ends in violence. Indeed, the story seems designed to explain the origin of this animosity. After God discovers the murder, he banishes Cain specifically to the life of the nomad, cursing the ground against any farming he might attempt: "When you till the ground, it will no longer yield to you its strength; you will be a fugitive and a wanderer on the earth" (Gen. 4:12). Cain responds by complaining of this very animosity between nomads and farmers: "I shall be a fugitive and a wanderer on the earth, and anyone who meets me may kill me" (Gen. 4:14).

The explanatory, or etiological, nature of the story does not stop there. Cain's descendants are presented as giving rise to various aspects of ancient society. Jabal is "the ancestor of those who live in tents and have livestock" (Gen. 4:20); Jubal is "the ancestor of all those who play the lyre and pipe" (Gen. 4:21); and Tubal-cain "made all kinds of bronze and iron tools" (Gen. 4:22).

Two other oddities in the story further lend credence to the idea that it is usefully understood as myth. First, the brothers' names: Abel literally means "emptiness," "breath," or "nothingness," so it should surprise no one when he dies a mere eight verses into the story. Cain also happens to share a name with a group of nomads to the south of Israel called the Cainites (or Kenites in many Old Testament translations).[3] Aside from the occasional mention, we do not learn much from the Old Testament about the Cainites/Kenites, but they do appear to have been antagonistic toward the Israelites, much like the Amalekites and Midianites around them. In fact, from the few references we do have, they seem to be the kind of nomads who, if you killed a member of their tribe, they would kill seven of your people in retaliation.[4]

This helps explain the second oddity in the story. After Cain complains that anyone who finds him will kill him, God responds by

---

3. Though the names Cain and Kenite look different in English, the Hebrew is identical: both are spelled קין (*qayin*).

4. For a much more detailed discussion, I recommend James Kugel, *How to Read the Bible: A Guide to Scripture, Then and Now* (New York: Free Press, 2008), 63–67.

placing a mark upon him. Most English translations gloss over the odd wording here and have God saying, "Whoever kills Cain will suffer a sevenfold vengeance" (Gen. 4:15), but the Hebrew says כל הרג קין (*kol horeg qayin*), which is literally "every killer of Cain," or "every killer of a Cainite." How could we speak of *every* killer of Cain unless the story is, in fact, the origin myth of the Cainites? In other words, the distinctive mark God places on Cain seems to be his tribe's exemption from the usual law of eye for an eye and tooth for a tooth. Contrary to Israelite law, Cain is not put to death for killing his brother, and God ordains that the Cainites can take seven-fold vengeance when a member of their tribe is killed. This is the "mark on Cain, so that no one who came upon him would kill him" (Gen. 4:15).

I should stop here to point out that I am not suggesting the Cain and Abel story—or indeed any of the stories in Genesis and Exodus—is best read *only* as myth. Later interpreters have gained much from reading these stories literally, allegorically, or spiritually. There are thousands upon thousands of pages interpreting the Cain and Abel story, from rabbinic midrash to early Christian readings, from Thomas Aquinas to LDS general authorities. The few paragraphs I have included here about the Cain and Abel story are not meant to wave all that interpretation away, as if my few paragraphs contain the one true interpretation. These other readings are valuable, too. In fact, it is this very act of interpretation that keeps the scriptures alive for the communities that treasure them.

What I am suggesting is that the Cain and Abel story was understood much differently by ancient Israelites than it is by modern Jews and Christians. While modern believers look to this story to understand God, grace, justice, or redemption, ancient Israelites would have heard a story explaining the origins of their neighbors to the south, as well as a way to make sense of these neighbors' nomadic and violent lifestyle. That does not mean modern readers should limit themselves to this ancient understanding, but it does help us make sense of an otherwise difficult text. In a lifetime of talking to people about the Old Testament, I have never heard anyone say, "I enjoy the Old Testament because it makes so much sense." Much of this discomfort and confusion stems from the fact that we so often do not understand the original context.

Noah and the Flood

After Cain, the world degenerates deeper and deeper into sin, until finally God decides to wipe out humanity and start over. But before the flood narrative begins, Genesis 6 provides a fascinating story that sheds light on the story's genre. According to Genesis 6, as humans multiply across the land, the gods see these humans as desirable and begin to have intercourse with them. Human women then bear giant children known as the Nephilim.[5] God, distraught at the mixing of humans and divinities, decrees that the human lifespan "shall be one hundred twenty years" (Gen. 6:3), thus explaining why humans do not live for hundreds of years. Describing these half-human, half-divine offspring, the story notes that "these were the heroes that were of old, warriors of renown" (Gen. 6:4).

The story turns on the term בני אלהים (bene 'elohim), or "sons of God." In Hebrew, the term bene can refer to sons, as in a person's biological offspring, or it can be used to describe the members of a group, as when the Old Testament uses the term "sons of Israel" (i.e., Israelites), "sons of man" (humans), "sons of rebellion" (rebels, Num. 17:10), or "sons of the prophets" (prophets, 1 Kgs. 20:35). The "sons of God," therefore, would be the gods, hence the reason their offspring are giants and heroes. While the idea that Genesis 6 tells a story of gods and giants may sound bizarre to modern ears, this interpretation was widely accepted in the ancient world, as seen in numerous ancient sources.[6]

With the stage thus set, God wipes out all of humanity save Noah and his family, who escape by building an ark. After the flood subsides, Noah offers a sacrifice to God, who establishes certain regular signs to guarantee that he will never send a flood again: he places his hunting bow in the sky, now turned safely away from the earth (Gen. 9:13), which explains the origin of rainbows, and he sets "seedtime and harvest, cold and heat, summer and winter, day and night" (Gen. 8:22). Once again, one of the central purposes of the narrative appears to be etiological.

---

5. The Hebrew term used in Gen. 6:4 for this offspring is נפלים (nephilim), which the NRSV renders as "Nephilim" and the King James Version renders as "giants." These giants make later appearances in the Old Testament as well, such as in Num. 13:33.

6. See, for example, 1 Enoch, Jubilees, 2 Baruch, and Targum Pseudo-Jonathan.

The Curse of Canaan, The Table of
Nations, and the Tower of Babel

The next three stories all share a similar focus: explaining the origin of the nations around Israel. The first begins immediately after the flood when Noah gets drunk and passes out naked in his tent. Ham, one of his three sons, enters the tent to find his father naked and runs out to tell his brothers, Shem and Japheth. The latter two dutifully cover their father with "their faces ... turned away" (Gen. 9:23). When Noah wakes up and realizes what has happened, the curse he utters is odd, for he does not actually curse Ham. Instead, he curses Ham's son, Canaan: "Cursed be Canaan; lowest of slaves shall he be to his brothers." Then he goes on to say of both Shem and Japheth, "let Canaan be his slave" (Gen. 9:25–27).

Why would Noah curse Canaan for something his father had done? True, in some places the Old Testament does embrace the idea of punishment crossing generations, as in the Ten Commandments,[7] but Ham had many sons—why single out Canaan?

To answer this question, we need to skip ahead one chapter. Genesis 10, which scholars call "the table of nations," gives the genealogies of Noah's three sons. It lists individuals named Egypt, Canaan, Cush, and Aram, which, as you might have guessed, also happen to be names of nations. In other words, the reader is not so much getting a lesson in genealogy as a lesson in geography. The descendants of Shem are the Israelites and their immediate neighbors to the east, with individuals including Asshur (Assyria), Sheba (whose queen will one day visit Solomon), Aram (the people who speak Aramaic), and Ophir (a region renowned for its gold). The descendants of Ham are Egypt, Cush (the biblical name for Ethiopia), Put (the biblical name for Libya), Canaan, Sidon (the home of Jezebel), and Heth (where the Hittites live). The descendants of Japheth are Madai (Media/Persia), Rhodanim (Rhodes), and a number of other places that play minor roles in the biblical narrative. The modern-day equivalent to Genesis 10 would be a story about a woman named Europa who gave birth to children such as Italy, Germany, Britain, and France.

---

7. "I, Yahweh your God, am a jealous God, punishing children for the iniquity of parents" (Ex. 20:5).

Modern readers tend to see the genealogical lists of the Old Testament as pointless and boring, but for an ancient audience, these lists and stories helped map out the world around them. There were no actual maps circulating among the common people; instead, these stories gave them a mental picture of their environment. When a story was told about a man named Edom, ancient Israelites used this story to understand who the Edomites were, where they came from, and what their values were. (Edom, by the way, is the name given to Jacob's brother Esau in Genesis 25.) When Genesis 19 tells of how Moab and Ammon were conceived through deception and incest, it was meant to help the Israelites understand why the Moabites and Ammonites were so morally depraved.

All of this brings us back to our initial question: Why, if Ham was the one who discovered his father naked in the tent and told his brothers, was Canaan cursed to be a slave to Shem? Since Israel traces its lineage back to Shem, the story seems to be depicting Israelite righteousness and Canaanite depravity, reinforcing Israel's belief that it was superior to its Canaanite neighbors and justifying the later conquest, slaughter, and enslavement of the Canaanites in the book of Joshua.

The Tower of Babel serves a similar etiological function, only now the focus is on language. The world of the Old Testament is quite small; if you look at modern-day borders, to travel from the eastern edge of Egypt to the southern tip of Turkey is only about 350 miles by land, or roughly the height of the state of Utah. In biblical times, this area contained a dizzying array of languages, though most of these languages came from the same linguistic family. Thus, just as a native Spanish speaker can see a clear relation between her own language and Portuguese, so a speaker of Hebrew would have seen Moabite, Ammonite, or Aramaic as distinct languages, though still familiar.

Genesis 11 explains the similarities and differences among these local languages through a story about a tower in Babylon. Babylonia was known for its pyramid-like temples, called ziggurats. These ziggurats would have been the tallest buildings most commoners would have ever seen. The Genesis account describes how people went to the land of Shinar—the biblical name for the area around

Babylon—and built a tower "with its top in the heavens" (Gen. 11:4). The city is called בבל (*babel*), which is the Hebrew word for Babylon, and the play on words is perfect, for here God confounds (בלל, *balal*) the peoples' language.[8]

The stories we have covered so far, comprising Genesis 1–11, are together known among biblical scholars as the "primeval history," so called because they "create" the world inhabited by the ancient Israelites. These chapters teach the reader about the origins of the cosmos, marriage, clothing, farming, language, and culture. They are built on what we might call a traditional-mythic outlook because they share numerous similarities with origin myths of other cultures. In the Greek and Roman myths, for example, there are numerous gods and goddesses, and the primeval history likewise assumes the existence of multiple gods: in the creation story, God says, "Let us make humankind in our image" (Gen. 1:26), and in Eden God laments, "the man has become like one of us" (Gen. 3:22). Again, at the Tower of Babel God addresses some unnamed group of deities as he counsels, "Let us go down, and confuse their language" (Gen. 11:7), while Genesis 6:1–4 describes the physical union between gods and humans, a union that results in the birth of giants and warriors. The union in Genesis 6 likewise mirrors the many stories in other mythic traditions where gods and humans have relations and produce heroes, such as Zeus producing Hercules.

Not only do there appear to be multiple divine beings in the primeval history, but God is not portrayed as the omniscient deity we see developed in the New Testament. God fears the Tower of Babel, concerned that "this is only the beginning of what they will do; nothing that they propose to do will now be impossible for them" (Gen. 11:6). He asks where Adam and Eve are in the Garden. He asks Cain where his brother is. He expresses regret for having created humankind—as if he had not been aware of the evil they would commit. Neither is he always benevolent. Much like the Greek gods, the God of the primeval history is occasionally even antagonistic toward humankind. He confounds their languages to keep them from becoming too powerful, he curses the ground for Adam, he has no

---

8. The English pun between Babel and babble fortunately works, but it is purely coincidence.

regard for Cain's sacrifice, and he wipes out all of humankind. Adding all this to the constant etiologies—as well as stories of fallen angels, giants, and global floods—the stories of the primeval history look remarkably similar to the mythic traditions of other ancient Near Eastern cultures.

The Mythic Background of the Primeval History

Stories are not told in a vacuum. Any story, no matter when it is told, is suffused with the culture of its audience. Modern stories, whether fact or fiction, draw from an immense pool of common characters, tropes, institutions, and history. Our stories mention sour grapes and the lazy grasshopper, the hapless father and the rebellious teenager, Richard Nixon and Ringo Starr, the Vietnam War and Black Lives Matter, cell phones and fax machines, CEOs and janitors. When we see a movie with a hacker that is both female and socially adept, we take note of how that movie breaks a common trope. If someone from 2,000 years ago watched an American movie or read a modern novel, they would miss so much cultural context that they would be hard-pressed to figure out most of the author's intent.

The Old Testament is no exception: its authors drew extensively from ancient Near Eastern culture, so the similarity between Genesis 1–11 and myths from other cultures is not surprising. Yet the relationship between the primeval history and these other myths goes well beyond a surface similarity. In fact, the stories in Genesis 1–11 often incorporate and rework entire myths from the other cultures around ancient Israel.

Consider, for example, the Babylonian creation myth, which goes by the title *Enuma Elish*. The story begins "when the skies above were not yet named, nor earth below pronounced by name" (*Enuma Elish* I) and all that existed was a watery chaos.[9] Tiamat, the monstrous sea-goddess, gives birth to the gods, but the noise and disruption from these gods keeps Tiamat awake. As she grows more sleep-deprived, she vows to destroy the gods she has created. The gods plot to fight back, choosing as their hero Marduk, who agrees to save the gods if they will make him their king. "If indeed I am to

---

9. All translations taken from Stephanie Dalley, *Myths from Mesopotamia: Creation, the Flood, Gilgamesh, and Others* (New York: Oxford University Press, 2008), 228–77.

be your champion," he says, "if I am to defeat Tiamat and save your lives, convene the council. ... My own utterance shall fix fate instead of you!" (*Enuma Elish* II). The gods agree and Marduk is given power over the whole universe.

After gathering his weapons, Marduk confronts the sea goddess and attacks her with the winds he has harnessed. Tiamat opens her mouth to swallow the winds, but they thrash about inside her, stirring up the sea and forcing her mouth to open wider. Marduk uses the moment to deliver a fatal blow, piercing Tiamat with his arrow and slicing her body in half. He takes half of her corpse and forms it into the dome that we call sky. On top of the other half, he builds dry ground, thus providing for the rain that comes from above and the rivers and oceans that come from underground. He soon realizes that the gods will be endlessly occupied with taking care of this world, so he creates humankind to do their work for them. Thenceforth, humans are in charge of the care and feeding of the gods. As his culminating act, he creates Babylon—the location of his temple and the seat from which he will rule the world.

The parallels between *Enuma Elish* and the creation story in Genesis 1 are legion. Their opening lines are nearly identical, with both depicting a formless earth that existed only as a watery chaos. The same characters make an appearance, though they can be hard to see in the English translation. Genesis tells us that "darkness covered the face of the deep" (Gen. 1:2), but the word translated here as "deep" (תהום, *Tehom*) is actually the Hebrew name for Tiamat.[10] The verse continues on to note that "a wind from God swept over the face of the waters," just as Marduk had stirred up his powerful wind to defeat Tiamat.[11]

---

10. You can see that this refers to Tiamat in a few ways. First, Hebrew is like English in that proper names do not take a definite article ("the"); you would never say "the James" or "the Susan." *Tehom* here does not have a definite article, even though it would if it meant "*the* deep." You can also see *Tehom* appear in other places throughout the Old Testament, as when Habakkuk 3:10 says that upon seeing God's bow and arrows, "deep [*Tehom*] gave forth its voice. [It] raised high its hands"—which makes sense, given that Tiamat was slain with Marduk's bow and arrows.

11. The King James translation of Genesis 1:2 reads, "The Spirit of God moved upon the face of the waters," but this translation decision was influenced by the Christian translators' desire to see the Trinity at work in creation. The Hebrew term רוח (*ruah*) does mean either wind or spirit, but the flow of the story and its ancient context overwhelmingly favor "wind" here. Therefore modern scholars prefer the translation given above, which comes from the NRSV.

While in *Enuma Elish* Marduk slays Tiamat and splits her in two to create the waters above and below the earth, the Genesis God accomplishes the same feat without combat: he simply speaks, creates the dome, "and separated the waters that were under the dome from the waters that were above the dome" (Gen. 1:7). In fact, according to Genesis 1:21, rather than slaying the sea monsters, "God *created* the great sea monsters" (emphasis mine).

Marduk's power over the universe is shown when he creates simply through the power of his word. *Enuma Elish* reads, "He spoke, and at his word the constellation vanished. He spoke to it again and the constellation was recreated. When the gods ... saw how effective his utterance was, they rejoiced, they proclaimed, 'Marduk is king!'" (*Enuma Elish* IV). Likewise, in Genesis 1, God creates through his speech, and every creative day begins with some variation on the phrase, "God said, 'Let there be light,' and there was light" (Gen. 1:3). Finally, the Babylonian creation myth culminates in the creation of Babylon as the religious center of the world and seat of Marduk's power. The Genesis story likewise builds up to the setting apart of a religious space as sacred, but in Genesis this space is temporal: God hallows the Sabbath as holy rather than hallowing a physical location.

The list of parallels could go on, but for our purposes we can see that the similarities between the Babylonian story and the Genesis account are too specific and numerous to be the result of chance. One of these stories was familiar with the other and deliberately incorporated language and themes from it. So which direction does the dependence go? Did the biblical story rely on the Babylonian account, or did Babylonian authors mimic the Old Testament? The answer to this question lies in the mention of Tehom/Tiamat.

To understand the full significance of the biblical story, we need to be familiar with the backstory of a deity conquering Tehom/Tiamat with his wind, but one can understand the Babylonian account perfectly well without ever having heard the biblical creation story. While we do not have an exact date of composition, the Babylonian account was written as early as 1,000 years before the Old Testament. Babylonia was a major world power in the first millennium BCE whose culture had profound influence throughout the ancient

Near East. Meanwhile, Israel was a minor province. In other words, all the available evidence points to the creation story in Genesis being a deliberate reworking of the Babylonian creation myth.

Recognizing this dependence helps us understand why Genesis 1 is constructed the way it is. What would it have meant for an ancient Israelite audience, particularly after Babylon had destroyed Jerusalem and carried the Israelites away captive, to hear their creation story told as a reworked version of Marduk's story? How comforting would it have been for Israelites to hear that, even though their temple had been destroyed, God had sanctified the Sabbath day as their sacred space? Or that while Marduk was fighting sea monsters, the Israelite God was so powerful he was *creating* sea monsters? The exalted place of humankind in Genesis, being given dominion over every living thing, is highlighted all the more by its stark contrast with the Babylonian story where humankind is created to serve the gods. To modern ears it may sound odd that every created object in Genesis 1 is called by its proper name, with the sole exception of the sun and moon, which are only called "the greater light" and "the lesser light" (Gen. 1:16). This makes sense, however, when we consider that in the Babylonian story the gods were created only when "their names [were] pronounced" (*Enuma Elish* I) and that Babylonians worshiped the sun and moon as gods. The biblical account thus leaves no room for the worship of the sun or moon as deities.

The next mythic tradition behind the Genesis stories comes from an account known as *The Epic of Gilgamesh*, which originates some 1,500 years before the Old Testament. The story begins in the city of Uruk, where Gilgamesh reigns as king. The gods create a wild, feral man named Enkidu who does not wear clothing or participate in civilization. Gilgamesh ponders how to bring Enkidu into civilized life and decides to bring a harlot out to him and have them sleep together. This plan is successful, and after sleeping with the harlot, Enkidu loses his wild nature. He puts on clothing, and, as the text relates, he "had become wiser" (*Gilgamesh* I).[12] On seeing him afterward, the harlot notes, "You have become like a god" (*Gilgamesh* I).

Similarly, in the story of the Garden of Eden in Genesis 2–3, Adam and Eve live naked, forbidden from partaking of the fruit of

---

12. All translations taken from Dalley, *Myths from Mesopotamia*, 39–135.

the Tree of Knowledge of Good and Evil. In modern interpretations we tend to cast this tree as containing moral knowledge, as if it can convey the ability to distinguish between right and wrong. But in an ancient context, the phrase "good and evil" was most likely understood as a merism, where the two extremes stand in for the whole. Thus, when you say that you searched "high and low" or "far and wide," what you mean is that you searched everywhere; likewise, the knowledge of "good and evil" most likely meant, "all knowledge."

What, then, did all this knowledge entail? In the Old Testament, "to know" someone is a euphemism for sex. Adam and Eve were like children in the garden—not needing clothes or civilization. But once they partook of "knowledge," they were forced to grow up: God curses Eve with childbearing, which is obviously a direct consequence of sex, and Adam is cursed with having to work for food, thus establishing the beginnings of civilization. And what is the first thing they do after they are driven out? "Adam *knew* his wife; and she conceived" (Gen. 4:1). The Tree of Knowledge of Good and Evil looks very much like a stand-in for sex.

What is only implied in the biblical story is made explicit in the story of Enkidu. Enkidu gains wisdom and judgment through his sexual encounter with the harlot, and this encounter takes him out of nature and makes him civilized. This view of sex as a civilizing impulse stands in stark contrast to modern notions of sex as debasing or as an animal instinct. It is also noteworthy that the harlot tells Enkidu the same thing that God tells Adam and Eve: "You have become like a god." Sex, in an ancient worldview, was not animalistic. It was what made humans like the gods.

Gilgamesh and Enkidu go on a series of adventures until one day Enkidu dies. Grieving for his friend and faced with the prospect of his own eventual death, Gilgamesh sets off to discover the secret to eternal life. He travels across the world until he finally comes across Ut-napishtim, the legendary survivor of the great flood. Since Ut-napishtim had been granted eternal life by the gods, Gilgamesh asks him how he also can achieve immortality.

Ut-napishtim tells Gilgamesh the story of the flood, which sounds similar to the story in the Old Testament. In Ut-napishtim's version, the gods decide to destroy the earth, but the god Ea warns

Ut-napishtim of the coming disaster and commands him to build a boat. Ut-napishtim builds it according to the dimensions revealed by Ea, and he lines it with bitumen and pitch. Ut-napishtim gathers "all the seed of living things" onto the boat (*Gilgamesh* XI), and after the flood, the boat comes to rest on a mountain. Not knowing whether the ground has dried yet, Ut-napishtim releases a dove, a swallow, and a raven. The first two return without having found anywhere to perch. When the third does not return, it is a signal that the family can disembark. After leaving the boat, Ut-napishtim offers sacrifice to the gods, who "smelt the fragrance" and decide that they will no longer use a flood to punish sinners (*Gilgamesh* XI).

The parallels to the Noah story are striking. Just as in the Ut-napishtim version, the biblical God decides to destroy the world by flood but commands Noah to build a boat. Noah builds it according to the revealed dimensions and lines it with bitumen and pitch—just as Ut-napishtim did—after which he brings every animal on board. After the flood, the boat rests on a mountain and Noah releases birds to see whether the water has subsided. The third bird does not return, so Noah disembarks and offers sacrifice. "When Yahweh smelled the pleasing odor" (Gen. 8:21), he vowed never to destroy humankind with a flood again.

Many people, when they see how closely these two stories line up, respond by saying that if there was a global flood, we should expect multiple civilizations to have a record of it, so the Babylonian account is confirmation of the historicity of the Old Testament. While this line of reasoning is appealing on its surface, it does not account for the close literary connection between *Gilgamesh* and the Old Testament. For example, there are many Native American, African, and Chinese flood myths, but their similarities to the Old Testament essentially begin and end with the simple fact of a flood. If all cultures carried a remnant of a historical memory, why should the culture that just happens to be closest to Israel not only share the rough outlines of the same story, but intersect with the biblical account over and over again, even on issues such as what God/the gods were thinking? *Gilgamesh* and the Old Testament cannot simply be two cultures' recollections of the same event. One is literarily dependent on the other. Given that *Gilgamesh* was written hundreds of years before Moses lived, it is hard to avoid the conclusion that the Old Testament's flood story is patterned after the Gilgamesh story.

After Ut-napishtim recounts the story of the flood, he tells Gilgamesh that his immortality was granted by the gods after the flood, so Gilgamesh will not be able to follow that same path. Dejected, Gilgamesh prepares to leave, but Ut-napishtim tells him that there is yet hope: a plant grows deep in the sea that can make the old young again. If Gilgamesh can get this plant, he too can have eternal life. Gilgamesh finds the plant, but as he is returning home with this treasure, he stops to wash in a pond. While he is washing, a snake steals the plant, shedding its skin in the process and robbing Gilgamesh of his chance at immortality.

Here we can see parallels to the Eden story once again, where humankind is robbed of a plant that grants immortality by the trickery of a snake. And once again the direction of dependence can be seen in the details that make sense only if we know the other story. Why a snake should steal immortality from Gilgamesh is obvious; with their ability to shed their skin and renew themselves, snakes were believed to possess some secret to immortality. Why a snake should be the antagonist in the Garden of Eden is less obvious, however, and the story would work just as well with any other animal.

These ancient Near Eastern myths tell us something important about the stories in Genesis. Modern readers, particularly in more fundamentalist branches of Christianity, tend to read Genesis 1–11 as history, but these instances of literary dependence on the myths of other cultures—not to mention the mythic elements within the Old Testament itself—should give us pause. Is it possible that there was an ancient flood, a tower at which languages were confounded, or a garden with magical trees that granted immortality and knowledge? Of course. Virtually anything is possible. But the analysis in these past few pages would suggest that these stories were not meant to be taken as history, nor were they understood as such by the Israelites. When we read these stories as history, as if they were a factual account of events that actually took place, we should be aware that we are most likely misinterpreting them.

Historically, the LDS tradition has tended to favor a strictly literal interpretation of these stories. If the story of the Tower of Babel did not actually happen, the Book of Mormon's claim to historicity may be cast into doubt, since the Brother of Jared's story begins at Babel. If we take away Babel, we need to grant that either Moroni (as abridger of Ether's story) or Joseph Smith (as translator) changed Jared's story to make it fit with ideas they had about the Tower of Babel, even though Jared and his family experienced no such event. Such a reconception of Moroni or Joseph's role in the writing process is possible, but I suspect many believing Latter-day Saints would find it uncomfortable. Likewise, traditional LDS interpretations of the Atonement have depended on a literal Adam partaking of a literal fruit in the Garden of Eden, thus setting up the Fall from which Jesus subsequently redeemed humankind.

Despite this literalist bent in LDS tradition, there is nevertheless some room for understanding these stories as non-historical, even among orthodox believers. Bruce R. McConkie, for example, cites multiple pieces of the Garden of Eden story as being figurative, including the very existence of the Tree of Knowledge of Good and Evil.[13] Brigham Young likewise never felt bound to interpret the Old Testament literally. On the question of how to interpret portions of the Eden story, he states, "You believe Adam was made of the dust of this earth. This I do not believe, though it is supposed that it is so written in the Bible.... What is the reason I do not? Because I have come to understanding, and banished from my mind all the baby stories my mother taught me when I was a child."[14] According to Young, many stories in the Bible are comparable to morality tales or fables—stories that are not literally true but which teach true principles. Such a position is the minority view in current mainline LDS thought, but we see that some church leaders have carved out at least some theological space for it.

---

13. McConkie writes, "Again the account is speaking figuratively. What is meant by partaking of the fruit of the tree of the knowledge of good and evil is that our first parents complied with whatever laws were involved so that their bodies would change from their state of paradisiacal immortality to a state of natural mortality" ("Christ and the Creation," *Ensign*, June 1982, 15).

14. Brigham Young, "The Gospel," Oct. 23, 1853, *Journal of Discourses*, 26 vols. (Liverpool, Eng.: Latter-day Saints' Book Depot, 1854–86): 2:6.

2

THE
OLD TESTAMENT
AS LEGEND

(Genesis 12–Exodus 15)

After the primeval history, we come to the second main section of Genesis, comprising chapters 12–50, known as the patriarchal narratives. Now that the biblical world has been set up, this next cycle of stories describes the chief ancestors of Israel: Abraham and Sarah, Isaac and Rebekah, Jacob and his wives, and Jacob's twelve sons. For many Jews and Christians, the rough outlines of the stories are familiar: Abraham nearly offering Isaac as a sacrifice, Jacob cheating Esau out of his birthright, Joseph's brothers selling him into slavery in Egypt. But if we want to get beyond the basic plot summaries and truly understand these stories, there are two sets of myths from the ancient world that we need to know.

The Greek Myths

The first is the set of Greek myths surrounding the figure of Hellen. In the sixth century BCE, Greece had not yet been unified into one empire. The area was made up of numerous city-states that constantly vied for control of the Greek-speaking peoples. As these states began to come together, they referred to themselves as "Hellenes." Around this time, a series of myths began to coalesce around the Greek tribes' ancestors. One particular work, the *Catalogue of Women*, offers a snapshot of this process. In the *Catalogue*, the progenitor of all the Greek tribes is a man named Hellen—after the Hellenic people. Hellen had four descendants: Dorus, Aeolus, Achaeus, and Ion, who represent the Hellenic tribes: the Dorians, Aeolians, Achaeans, and Ionians. Other individuals mentioned in the genealogy are presented as being related to, but not directly descended from, Hellen, such as Macedon and Magnes, who were Hellen's nephews. During the period when the *Catalogue of Women* was written, Macedonians and Magnetes were considered as related to the Greek tribes, but not "Hellenic" in the sense that tribes such as the Dorians were.

The myths surrounding the eponymous ancestors of the Greek tribes illustrate several important points. First, they show that in the ancient world it was common for groups of people to pass along stories about their putative ancestors. The Hellenes told stories of Hellen, the Romans told stories of Romulus, and the Israelites told stories of a man named Israel. That is not to say that these stories were necessarily made up or completely ahistorical (as we will see, there are indications within Genesis that some elements of its stories are quite ancient), but as the Hellenic myths show, such stories were not primarily about preserving history. Rather, the characters and their relationships were indicative of the relationships between groups at the time the account was written. Indeed, anthropologists have long noted that in modern oral cultures, genealogies still fulfill this function today. A genealogy in an oral culture is not a fixed list of ancestors; it is a living reflection of current-day relationships and power dynamics.

Because genealogies are meant to reflect the present rather than the past, when present-day relationships change, the relationships between members of the genealogy are amended to reflect that shift. The Greek account of Hellen and his offspring, for example, came from the sixth century BCE, when the Hellenes still consisted of a loose coalition of only a few city-states—the Macedonians and Magnetes were still considered outsiders. But over the next few centuries, these tribes were incorporated into the new Greek empire, so the myths had to be amended to include them.[1]

This same process played out in Israel starting from its origin around the thirteenth century BCE and continuing through the height of its power from the tenth to eighth centuries BCE. Israel

---

1. See, in particular, Herodotus's *Histories* 5.22.1–2 and 9.45.2, where King Alexander I of Macedonia's standing as a Hellene is challenged. Macedon was not considered a descendent of Hellen in the *Catalogue of Women*, yet in both passages Alexander appeals to his ancient "Hellenic" descent as proof that he should be considered a true Greek.

did not begin as a united kingdom; instead it was a loose confederation of tribes, as seen in the book of Judges. Just like the Greeks, these tribes eventually came together to form the state that would become known as Israel. But that unification took place over centuries, so the definition of who constituted "Israel" had to be updated. To see how this happened, consider three poems that, due to their archaic language and form, scholars largely consider to be much older than most biblical texts: Judges 5, Deuteronomy 33, and Genesis 49. In Judges 5, which seems to be the oldest of these texts, the tribes of Israel are commended or condemned for whether they came together to fight off a foreign enemy. What is odd is that the list of tribes does not match the twelve that we know from later sources. Simeon, Levi, and Judah are nowhere to be found, while the tribes of Gilead and Machir are mentioned as if they are part of Israel. At that early point in Israel's history, the other tribes that we typically identify as part of Israel either did not exist or were not considered descendants of Israel.

As we move later in Israel's history, we see the names and number of the tribes fluctuate. By the time Deuteronomy 33 is written, Levi and Judah are considered Israelite, Machir is known as Manasseh, and Gilead has been excluded altogether. Simeon is still not included as a tribe, though this is remedied in Genesis 49 (which appears to be the earliest place where the twelve tribes match the twelve sons of Jacob).[2]

This difference between the earliest lists of tribes and the story contained in Genesis 12–50 about Jacob and his twelve sons suggests that the narratives in Genesis are later creations meant to explain the relationship these twelve tribes would ultimately share as they forged a common identity as "Israelite."[3] This is not to say

---

2. Changing genealogies to reflect current relationships may seem far-fetched, but the Old Testament actually shows this process play out on numerous occasions. For example, the Calebites were originally considered to be non-Israelites; Numbers 32:12 lists Caleb as a Kenizzite. But over time, the Calebites joined in with the tribe of Judah, requiring a change in the genealogical relationship. Accordingly, 1 Chronicles 2:9–24 lists Caleb as a descendant of Judah.

3. Though we usually think of peoples and nations as being named after their ancestors (i.e., the descendants of the man named Israel come to be called Israelites), the reverse is most likely the case in Genesis. We can see this particularly clearly in a name such as Ephraim, which is grammatically a place's name, not a person's name. The suffix –aim in Hebrew denotes places, for example Egypt (*mitsraim*), the sky (*shamaim*), and

that the narratives are dishonest; rather, the stories in Genesis serve the same function that all such stories did in the ancient world: to explain the relationships and power dynamics current at the time they were written.

Take Reuben for example. By all indications, Reuben was a large and powerful tribe in early Israelite history, which is why he is listed as Jacob's firstborn son. In the stories of Genesis, Reuben is often presented as taking the initiative and trying to set things right, as when he tries to save Joseph from being killed by his brothers (Gen. 37:21). Yet within a few centuries, the tribe of Reuben seems to have essentially disappeared, and Ephraim comes to dominate the northern tribes of Israel. Reuben's position becomes so tenuous, in fact, that in Deuteronomy 33:6 the speaker prays, "Let Reuben live, and not die; and let not his men be few."[4] So how is this history reflected in the Genesis narratives? Despite Reuben playing a key role throughout the Genesis stories, in Genesis 35:22 Reuben sleeps with Bilhah, his father's concubine, and Jacob curses him: "You shall no longer excel because you went up onto your father's bed" (Gen. 49:4).

The characters of Simeon and Levi are likewise woven into the text in a way that explains their tribes' histories. As we saw earlier, both Simeon and Levi are missing from the list of tribes in Judges 5, which suggests that these two were latecomers to Israel. Such a history might be taken by some to mean that they were less than loyal to the broader Israelite community, but Genesis 34 says otherwise. Jacob's daughter Dinah is raped by a man named Shechem, and Simeon and Levi are so outraged by this affront to the family honor that they devise a scheme to exact revenge. They convince the Shechemites to become Israelites and be circumcised, saying, "Then we will give our daughters to you, and we will take your daughters for ourselves, and we will live among you and become one people"

Jerusalem (*yerushalaim*). To say that there was a person named Ephraim sounds the same as saying there once was a person named Jamestown. Benjamin likewise appears to derive from a place name, for Benjamin literally means "southerner," and the tribe of Benjamin was the southern-most tribe of Israel.

4. Even non-biblical sources attest to the disappearance of Reuben. The Mesha Stele, which comes from the ninth century BCE, mentions Moabite king Mesha's conquest of various Israelite cities, including those that the Old Testament lists as belonging to the tribe of Reuben. Yet the stele makes mention of only Gad, not Reuben, in its account of the conquest.

(Gen. 34:16). But once the Shechemite men undergo circumcision and are in bed recovering, Simeon and Levi go into the city, kill the males, and plunder their possessions. The tribes of Simeon and Levi are presented as being so loyal to Israel that they are willing to wipe out an entire city to defend the family's honor.

Much like ancestral myths of other cultures, the patriarchal narratives aim to explain what constitutes Israel: Where did Israel come from? Why did it settle where it did? Who are its neighbors? What relationship does it have with its god?

Israel's relationship with its god, land, and neighbors are central themes in these stories. The very first verse of Genesis 12 details God's call to Abraham, and over the next thirty-eight chapters we see how this call and promise are tested. God promises Abraham some land, but in Genesis 12:10 a famine drives him out of that land and down to Egypt. When he returns, his nephew Lot takes possession of the most fertile areas, which then leads to a multi-chapter diversion recounting how Lot's descendants lost their claim to God's favor and were driven out of the land of Israel. In this section, we hear of the destruction of Sodom and Gomorrah, the turning of Lot's inheritance into a salted plain, and how the Moabites and the Ammonites originated out of an incestuous relationship between Lot and his daughters. The stories hinge on a Hebrew play on words meant to denigrate Israel's neighbors, where Ammon (עמון, 'ammon) is understood to mean "inbred" (בן עמי, ben 'ammi), and Moab (מואב, mo'ab) is understood to mean "[born] from the father" (מאב, me'ab).

Israel's promised inheritance is later endangered by Jacob's brother Esau. Esau represents Israel's closest neighbors to the south, the Edomites. We can tell because, according to Gen. 25:25, when Esau was first born, he was red (אדמוני, 'admoni, a play off the name Edom) and hairy (שער, se'ar, a reference to Se'ir, the Edomites' homeland). Esau/Edom is portrayed as too interested in short-term satisfaction to inherit God's blessing, trading his birthright to Jacob for a pot of what the Old Testament calls "red stuff" (אדם, 'adom, another reference to Edom's name). Esau/Edom gets so angry at Jacob's trickery that Jacob is forced to flee to the land of the Arameans, who were Israel's closest neighbors to the north. There, Jacob tricks his Aramean uncle Laban into giving him wives, concubines, and wealth. The story of the Arameans ends with Jacob and Laban setting up a pillar to establish the northern border between Israel and Aram, with both promising, "I will not pass beyond this heap to you, and you will not pass beyond this heap and this pillar to me, for harm" (Gen. 31:52). Among the Israelites, Moabites, Ammonites, Edomites, and Arameans, these stories essentially complete the map of Canaan.

The stories of Jacob's sons, as we have seen, explain the relationships between the various tribes of Israel, with the Joseph story designed to explain the later prominence of the tribes of Ephraim and Judah. By the eighth century BCE, when Israel had split into two kingdoms, the other tribes had mostly faded from importance, and the northern kingdom of Israel came to simply be known as "Ephraim" (e.g., Isa. 7:1–9), while the southern kingdom was called simply "Judah." The Joseph story pre-enacts the failure of Reuben to protect Israel and the rise of Judah to the occasion. When the brothers travel back down to Egypt to ask for more food, it is Judah who offers to keep Benjamin safe, and when Joseph plants the silver cup in Benjamin's sack, it is Judah who asks to be imprisoned in Benjamin's stead. Similarly, once Jacob arrives in Egypt and is leaving his blessing on his descendants, he plays one final trick, crossing his hands to make sure that Ephraim receives the birthright blessing instead of Manasseh (Gen. 48:14–20).

The patriarchal narratives were not meant to be morality tales, nor were the patriarchs supposed to be understood as paragons of virtue. Rather, these stories are a founding myth, much like the myth of the founding of the United States. Their primary purpose is to explain Israel and its surroundings. Note, for example, how nowhere in the Old Testament are people told to "be like Abraham" or "act like Jacob." In fact, the patriarchs have a fairly loose moral code: Abraham lies twice about his wife being his sister; Jacob cheats Esau out of his birthright; Jacob manipulates his flocks to enrich himself at Laban's expense; Reuben sleeps with his father's concubine; Levi and Simeon deceive and then destroy an entire city; and Judah sleeps with his daughter-in-law and then condemns her to death. Of course, the patriarchs are not all bad, and they do show moments of impressive faith and trust. But we have to realize that these stories served a particular function for ancient audiences—one far removed from what modern readers expect.

The Ugaritic Myths

The second set of myths vital to understanding the patriarchal narratives is a series of stories that come from a small town called Ugarit, just north of Israel in modern-day Syria. The Ugaritic myths were produced just before Israel emerged, and they are striking for how closely they line up with the stories in Genesis 12–50. These Ugaritic "patriarchs" deal with the same type of problems that the biblical patriarchs do, and their interactions with the gods follow essentially the same script. One such character is Daniel, who seeks the gods' help because he has no offspring—the same problem that occupies Abraham in Genesis 12–22. As with Abraham, a messenger appears to Daniel telling him he will have a son, and the text even describes how Daniel laughs upon hearing the news, just as Abraham did.

Another Ugaritic "patriarch" named Kirta also seeks the gods' help because he has no son, and the gods eventually grant him children. But in a twist, they announce that his youngest child has firstborn status. This supplanting of the traditional order happens frequently in Genesis: Isaac inherits the blessing rather than his older sibling, Ishmael; Jacob tricks his older brother, Esau, out of the birthright; Joseph is favored over his older brothers; and the birthright blessing is given to Joseph's son Ephraim instead of the older son, Manasseh. Almost every one of these inversions of the traditional order sets off infighting and violence, as it does among Kirta's children in the Ugaritic myths.

The parallels between the Ugaritic myths and the patriarchal narratives go well beyond the examples just cited. As with *Enuma Elish* and *Gilgamesh*, the alignment also surpasses what would occur by chance. Scholars have long recognized that one of two explanations likely accounts for these parallels: either the Genesis stories were based on—and to a degree modeled after—the Ugaritic stories or both story sets drew from the same pool of oral traditions common across ancient Canaan.[5]

---

5. There is ample evidence that Israelite authors were familiar with these traditions; Ezekiel 14:14, for example, lists Daniel as a legendary figure from the distant past, and

While the literary relationship between the two story sets is fascinating, the Ugaritic myths also tell us much about the ancient Canaanite understanding of deity. According to the Ugaritic myths, the divine world was ruled over by the high god El, who was envisioned as an aged, grey-bearded king. El is described as "the father of years," a patriarch who presides over the other deities and who periodically calls them together in a divine council, along with his wife/consort Asherah. A cadre of other subservient deities, many of whom are El's children, inhabit the divine realm as well, including Mot (Death), Yamm (Sea), Nahar (River), Resheph (Plague), Leviathan, Tannin (the twisted serpent), and the storm-god Baal.

As high god of the Canaanite pantheon, El was widely worshiped in ancient Canaan, while each Canaanite nation claimed a different minor deity as their patron god. In Ugarit, for example, they primarily worshiped Baal, developing a whole series of myths about Baal's rise from being simply another member of El's divine council to becoming a powerful god with his own religious following and temple on Mount Zaphon. In Moab, the patron god was Chemosh, in Edom it was Qos, in Ammon it was Milkom, and in Israel it was Yahweh.

This history is relevant to the Old Testament because, as it turns out, the patriarchs in Genesis are overwhelmingly portrayed as worshiping the Canaanite god El. In Genesis 21:33, Abraham sets up a shrine to El Everlasting; in Genesis 16:13 Hagar worships All-Seeing El; in Genesis 35:7 Jacob builds an altar to El of Bethel (Bethel in Hebrew literally means, "the house of El"); in Genesis 33:20 Jacob builds an altar to El the God of Israel; in Genesis 18:19 Melchizedek blesses Abraham by El Most High; and Judges 9:46 refers to a shrine that had been set up to El of the Covenant.[6] The patriarchs' names reflect their worship of El, as seen in names such as IsraEL ("El reigns") and IshmaEL ("El hears"). In Exodus 6:3

Ezekiel tells the prince of Tyre that he is "wiser than Daniel" (Ezek. 28:3)—a comparison that would only work if both Ezekiel and the prince of Tyre were familiar with the same stories. The book of *Jubilees*, which is an apocryphal rewriting of the book of Genesis, actually lists Daniel as the grandfather of Methuselah, thus placing him among the biblical patriarchs.

6. The presence of El is mostly hidden by the King James translation, which invariably translates the Hebrew אל (El) as simply "God." The only exception to this is Gen. 33:20, where the name of the sanctuary set up by Jacob is simply transliterated from Hebrew as "El-elohe-Israel."

God tells Moses, "I appeared to Abraham, Isaac, and Jacob as El Almighty, but by my name Yahweh I did not make myself known to them."[7] In other words, while the Israelites would eventually come to worship Yahweh as their patron deity, the earliest stories we have about Israelite religion depict it as being centered on El—stories which, not coincidentally, mirror the Ugaritic myths about El in both style and content.

So, if the Israelites originally worshiped El, who was this god Yahweh that Israel eventually came to claim as its own? In all likelihood, Yahweh was a son of El and a member of the divine council, just as Baal and other national deities were. We can see this in Deuteronomy 32:8–9, where the text reads: "When the Most High (Hebrew: *Elyon*) apportioned the nations, when he divided humankind, he fixed the boundaries of the peoples according to the number of the sons of God; Yahweh's own portion was his people, Jacob his allotted share."[8] This verse envisions a "Most High" god creating as many nations as there are sons of God and giving each nation its individual god, with Yahweh—who is presumably one of these sons—receiving Israel as his portion. Other nations were assigned to other gods, an arrangement to which Jephthah appeals in the book of Judges when he asks the Moabites, "Should you not possess what your god Chemosh gives you to possess? And should we not be the ones to possess everything that Yahweh our God has conquered for our benefit?" (Judg. 11:24).

Psalm 89:6–7 likewise portrays Yahweh as a member of El's council. The verses read, "Who among the heavenly beings (Hebrew: בני אלים, *sons of El*) is like Yahweh, God feared in the council of the holy ones, great and awesome above all that are around him?" This "council of the holy ones," or divine council, appears frequently in Ugaritic myth, and in the Old Testament we even see scenes play out in that

---

7. The translation given here departs slightly from the NRSV.

8. I have changed the NRSV's "gods" to "sons of God" to better reflect the underlying Hebrew, בני אלהים, *bene 'elohim*. Later Jewish scribes were uncomfortable with the notion that God divided up nations according to the number of the sons of God, since it assumed the existence of divine beings other than Yahweh. So they changed the text to read "according to the number of the sons of Israel," which the King James translation follows. The original reading of "sons of God" is preserved, however, in both the Dead Sea Scrolls and the Septuagint.

council. Psalm 82, for example, begins: "God has taken his place in the divine council; in the midst of the gods he holds judgment" (v. 1). The psalm goes on to describe how these gods have been acting, and in verse six the speaker appeals to them: "You are gods, children of the Most High (Hebrew: *sons of Elyon*), all of you."[9]

Yahweh appears to have originally been considered a storm god, like Baal. When Yahweh appears to the Israelites on Mount Sinai, the top of the mountain is wreathed in a thick cloud roiling with thunder and lightning. Psalm 18 describes Yahweh in decidedly storm-like terms: "he came swiftly upon the wings of the wind. He made darkness his covering around him, his canopy thick clouds dark with water. Out of the brightness before him there broke through his clouds hailstones and coals of fire. Yahweh also thundered in the heavens" (Ps. 18:10–14; see also Ps. 29:3). Rain goes before Yahweh's presence (Ps. 68:8), and he is even described as "him who rides upon the clouds" (Ps. 68:4)—the same title given to Baal in the Ugaritic texts. When Elijah challenges the priests of Baal on Mount Carmel, the challenge is to see which god can send down fire from heaven (i.e., lightning) and then rain to end the drought (1 Kgs. 18:20–46). When Moses meets Yahweh, the Old Testament tells us that "Moses would speak and God would answer him in thunder" (Ex. 19:19).

As time went on, Yahweh, El, and Baal eventually merged in the Israelite mind to become one God. Yahweh came to inherit not only Baal's characteristics but even his enemies; just as Baal fought Yamm (Sea), Nahar (River), Resheph (Plague), Leviathan, and Tannin (the twisted serpent) in the Ugaritic myths, so Yahweh is praised: "You divided the sea (Hebrew: *Yam*) by your might; you broke the heads of the dragons (Hebrew: *Tannin*) in the waters. You crushed the heads of Leviathan ... you dried up ever-flowing streams (Hebrew: *Nahar*)" (Ps. 74:13–14; see also Ps. 148:7, Job 26:13, Isa. 27:1, and Isa. 51:9). Habakkuk 3:5 identifies Resheph as following Yahweh, and Psalm 48:2 actually places Yahweh's home on Mount Zaphon, just as Baal's home was.[10] El's consort was the goddess Asherah, and in 2 Kings 21:7 we learn that a "carved image of Asherah" was placed

9. For other divine council scenes, see 1 Kgs. 22:19–22, Job 1:6–12, and Jer. 23:16–18.

10. The KJV translates this as "on the sides of the North," since *zaphon* can also mean "north" in Hebrew.

in Yahweh's temple. Extra-biblical evidence also points to the fact that Yahweh and Asherah were considered a divine couple, as seen in a cryptic inscription from Kuntillet Ajrud that refers to "Yahweh and his Asherah."

The merging of Yahweh, El, and Baal was so complete that King David, the purported author of the book of Psalms and a man who was described as being after Yahweh's own heart, gave his son the name Beeliada, which means "Baal knows."[11]

As we will see, not everyone was thrilled with the commingling of Yahweh, El, and Baal, but the identification was strong enough that later scribes did not edit this connection out of the book of Genesis, even though it showed the patriarchs worshiping El.

Yahweh, Jehovah, El, and Elohim

As an LDS graduate student, I found myself particularly drawn to the question of God and God's names. Mormonism has a unique theology identifying Elohim as God the Father and Jehovah as God the Son, so, from an LDS standpoint, the origin of Yahweh as a son of El has provocative implications. How does biblical evidence both support and stand in tension with LDS theology?

The first point to clarify is that the Hebrew word אלהים, *'Elohim*, is not a proper name. It is simply the Hebrew word "god," and it can be used to describe Israel's god or any other god in the pantheon. The god worshiped by Israel went by the proper name יהוה, *Yhwh*. Most Hebrew texts are written with only consonants and no vowels. Since Jewish tradition held that the proper name of God should never be pronounced, the actual pronunciation of the name *yhwh* has been lost. Most scholars reconstruct it as Yahweh, which is the name I use here, but there is some uncertainty on this question. In keeping with the ban on pronouncing God's name, when ancient readers came across the name *yhwh* in the Old Testament, they instead said אדני, *'adonay*, meaning "Lord" in Hebrew, which is why most Old Testament translations render *yhwh* as Lord in small caps.

The reconstruction of *yhwh* as Yahweh is fairly recent. Before then, people tended to take the vowels from *'adonay* and combine

---

11. 1 Chr. 14:7; see also 1 Chr. 8:33–34 for Saul's son Esh-baal ("man of Baal") and Jonathan's son Merib-baal ("Baal advocates").

them with the consonants from *yhwh*, which gave us the name Yahowah. We can thank our German friends—for whom J is pronounced as an English Y and W is pronounced as an English V—for the transformation of Yahowah into Jehovah. Thus, Jehovah is an Anglicization of a Germanization of the combination of *yhwh* and the vowels of *'adonay*. Or to put it even more succinctly, Yahweh and Jehovah are different pronunciations of the personal name of God in the Old Testament.

All of this is a long way of saying that in the Hebrew Bible, there is no distinction between referring to Israel's God as either Elohim or Jehovah/Yahweh. When Joshua says that "the Israelites blessed God (*'elohim*)" (Josh. 22:33), he could have just as correctly said that the Israelites blessed Yahweh. This is why the Old Testament so often refers to God as "the LORD God" (*yhwh 'elohim*) or "the God Yahweh"; the name Yahweh is what distinguishes Israel's god from the god Chemosh or the god Baal. The LDS distinction, therefore, between Jehovah and Elohim as different people does not arise from the Old Testament itself. This is not to say that LDS theology is wrong; it simply arises from an external distinction that the Old Testament itself does not make.

What, then, do we make of the fact that Yahweh was originally thought of as a son of El? Here the evidence becomes murkier. El is the proper name of the Canaanite high god, but in many Semitic languages the word אל, *'el*, also became a general term referring to any god. There is a difference, therefore, between the Canaanite god El and the general term *'elohim*, even though both words came to be used in similar fashion. Again, the similarity between the relationship of El/*'elohim*/Yahweh in ancient Israel and the relationship between Elohim and Jehovah in LDS theology is tantalizing, but the differences are significant enough that we should be wary of claims that align them too closely.

Genesis as Legend

In our tour through the Ugaritic myths, we have seen how the patriarchal stories of Genesis draw from common characters, ideas, and tropes in ancient Canaan. We have further seen how the Canaanite pantheon influenced Israel's conception of Yahweh as a member of

El's council and as a storm god similar to Baal. We also used the Greek ancestral myths to help us understand the function the patriarchal stories played in ancient Israel. Do these parallels and connections mean that the stories in Genesis are completely made up?

Before answering that question, I should point out that, in a certain sense, the answer should not matter. Since I grew up in an LDS tradition, particularly a tradition in which the "truthfulness" of the Book of Mormon was often treated as being synonymous with its historicity, I have to constantly stop myself from judging a narrative by whether it is factually accurate or not. If we insist on historicity being the most important measure for evaluating the worth of scripture, we will effectively blind ourselves to the myriad other ways scripture creates meaning for those who engage with it. Jesus' parable of the prodigal son is not historically accurate—there was no actual son or father behind the story—but the fact that the story is a parable does not mean we should not value it along with, say, the story of Jesus healing the blind man. We are much better off judging the scriptures by whether they are helpful or harmful, whether they inspire or mire, whether they teach true or false principles. For those of us who approach the scriptures as believers, our faith needs to be flexible enough to accommodate stories that do not meet modern standards of historical accuracy; otherwise, we will miss most of what the scriptures have to offer.

Despite the evidence presented in this chapter that Genesis best fits in the genre of myth, we would be wrong to dismiss all its stories as complete fiction. There are numerous indications, particularly within the patriarchal narratives, that the stories do preserve some authentic memories of Israel's past. We can tell because these early stories are replete with behavior that was later forbidden, such as setting up shrines outside of Jerusalem, offering sacrifices without priests, marrying sisters from the same family, setting up cultic pillars, and planting sacred trees—to say nothing of the fact that the patriarchs are all depicted as worshiping the Canaanite god El. For many scholars, the core of these stories strikes an ancient and authentic tone, even as we recognize that they were shaped by the various literary forces we have discussed so far.

Perhaps we would do better, then, to consider the patriarchal stories as legends rather than myths. If we could strip back the way later tribal relationships influenced the stories, if we could remove the patterning that arose from the Ugaritic myths, we may well be able to find a person named Abraham or Jacob, much as there may have been a historical King Arthur buried beneath the later legendary accretions. The interesting question then becomes not, "What did Abraham actually do," but rather, "How can we use his stories to understand the issues that animated later Israelite authors?" We will begin to answer that question in the next chapter, but first let us examine the story of the exodus.

Exodus

The exodus story maintains the pattern we have been discussing, being a narrative that, though possibly based in historical fact, has been extensively expanded and reshaped over time. Among the few authentic aspects of the story seem to be the fact that the names of Moses, Aaron, and Phineas are indeed Egyptian in origin, but evidence for the historicity of the narrative beyond these few indications is decidedly sparse. Consider, for example, the claim in Exodus 12:37–38 that the Israelites numbered "about six hundred thousand men on foot, besides children. A mixed crowd also went up with them, and livestock in great numbers, both flocks and herds." If we assume (conservatively) that on average each man had only one wife and two children, then the Israelites would have numbered at least 2.4 million people. This number is impossibly large. It rivals estimates for the entire population of Egypt at that time. If you lined all those people up in a column eight people wide with seven feet between rows (not even counting the room needed for livestock and other possessions), the people at the front of the column would have arrived at Jerusalem before even half of the Israelites had finished crossing the Red Sea.

Even more problematic is the lack of Egyptian influence in Israel's culture. Archeologists can tell a lot about a people from their material culture, which includes everything a group might leave behind in the archeological record: the kinds of pots they make, the shapes they build their homes in, the kinds of altars they build, the kind of clothing they wear, the kinds of animal bones they leave behind, and so on. When the evidence of Israelite settlements starts appearing in Canaan, their material culture shows no Egyptian influence whatsoever. It does, however, show extensive influence from Israel's Canaanite neighbors. Similarly, Hebrew language and religion show no sign of Egyptian influence beyond what we would expect from two countries living as far apart as they did. Consider how improbable the claim is that a group of Israelites lived among the Egyptians for *400 years* without any discernible impact on their language and culture. This is equivalent to saying that a group of Mongolians settled in New York in the year 1600 and intermingled with other Americans, but by the year 2000 knew no English and made no use of American clothing, cooking, architecture, etc.

What we do see when we look at the Exodus narrative is the same kind of mythic concerns that permeate the book of Genesis. The story of the baby Moses being placed in a basket of reeds and released onto the river to be found by the royal household and raised as royalty mimics perfectly the legend of the Akkadian king Sargon. Even the escape from Egypt and the crossing of the Red Sea is patterned after Marduk's splitting the sea with his wind in *Enuma Elish*.[12]

The function of the Exodus story is to give the Israelites a narrative of their origins. For the rest of its history, Israel will remember itself as having been redeemed by God from Egypt, and its relationship with God will be defined by the covenant established at Sinai. God tells the Israelites throughout the Old Testament, "When Israel was a child, I loved him, and out of Egypt I called my son" (Hosea 11:1), and the prophets continually call the Israelites to repentance for having forsaken God's law, revealed at Sinai.

Our best analogy for understanding the Exodus narrative may still be America's founding story of the *Mayflower* and the pilgrims seeking religious freedom. Only a tiny fraction of Americans are descended from the people on the *Mayflower*, yet we have come to adopt the story as a kind of national myth, much as likely happened with the Israelites and whatever group may have been in Egypt.

---

12. Although modern depictions usually show Moses striking the sea with his staff, Exodus 14:21 states that Yahweh "drove the sea back by a strong east wind all night." Both stories also culminate with Marduk and Yahweh building their temples (Ex. 15:17) and being declared king (Ex. 15:18).

For our purposes, what matters is the significance the story gathers within the Hebrew Bible and beyond, particularly as this story is the setting in which the law of Moses is given. The law will be our focus in chapter four, but before we turn to the law, there is one more aspect of the Genesis–Exodus narratives that needs to be addressed, namely: if these stories are so influenced by the surrounding culture, did Moses produce them? If not, who did, and when did they do it?

3

THE
OLD TESTAMENT
AS STORY

(Genesis–Deuteronomy)

Most English speakers are familiar with the story of the three little pigs. Three pigs build houses of straw, sticks, and bricks; then along comes a wolf who blows the first two down but cannot make the third budge. Beyond these basics, however, there are endless variations. In some versions, the pigs are siblings, while in others they are not; some versions have the wolf eating the first two pigs, while others have the pigs running away to join the third pig in the house of bricks. In some versions, the wolf is killed at the end when he falls into a pot of boiling water (or a fire), while in others he runs away after being smoked out of the chimney. There is no one official version of the story; rather, there are many ways of telling this childhood classic.

The creation of competing versions of a story happens frequently when stories are told over and over again, and it is particularly common with legends and myths—i.e., stories whose value lies in their function rather than their factuality. Ask a specialist on Greek culture to tell you the story of Herakles, for example, and you will be barraged with a stream of variations, some sources saying one thing and some another. The stories of Genesis and Exodus are much the same: multiple sources confirm the broad story arc but diverge on details. What makes the Old Testament unique, however, is that these many versions do not exist in separate places; rather, they are all found in Genesis and Exodus.

For millennia, readers of the Old Testament assumed that Moses wrote the first five books of the Bible: Genesis, Exodus, Leviticus, Numbers, and Deuteronomy, which together are referred to as the Pentateuch (a Greek word that literally means "five books"). After all, Moses is a key figure in the narrative, and the bulk of the material from Exodus to Deuteronomy describes the law of Moses, so it is easy to assume that Moses wrote it.

But around the time of the European Enlightenment, careful readers began to notice oddities in the Pentateuch that cast doubt on whether Moses—or any single author—could have written the text. While the narrative often flows smoothly, glaring inconsistencies occasionally pop up. Isaac, for example, is on his deathbed when Jacob tricks him and steals Esau's blessing (Gen. 27), but Isaac does not actually die until Genesis 35, more than twenty years later. When Hagar is sent into the wilderness, the story seems to present Ishmael as a newborn: Abraham places Ishmael on her shoulder, and when her water supply runs out, Hagar places the child under a bush so that she may not hear his cry as he dies (Gen. 21:14–16). But according to Genesis 16:16 and 21:5, Ishmael would have been at least fourteen years old when Hagar was banished. Joseph dreams that his father, mother, and eleven brothers will bow down to him (Gen. 37:9–10), but according to Genesis 35:19, Joseph's mother had died earlier while giving birth to Benjamin. Some parts of the story say that Joseph was sold to the Ishmaelites, but others say it was the Midianites (Gen. 37:28). In the wilderness, the Israelites repeatedly complain that they have no meat (Ex. 16; Num. 11), yet we are continually told of the "very great multitude" of livestock they have with them (Ex. 12:38; Num. 32:1). The examples go on.

Some readers also noticed that many of the Pentateuch's stories happen twice. God gives Jacob the name Israel twice (Gen. 32 and 35); the city of Beersheba is named twice, and for different reasons (Gen. 21:31 and 26:33); Jacob names Bethel twice (Gen. 28:19 and 35:15); and Moses brings forth water from a rock at Meribah twice (Ex. 17 and Num. 20). Some stories happen multiple times but with small variations, such as the two announcements of Isaac's birth (Gen. 17 and 18), the expulsion of Hagar into the wilderness where she finds a well and is saved by God (Gen. 16 and 21), the giving of the Abrahamic covenant (Gen. 15 and 17), and a patriarch passing his wife off as his sister—which actually happens three times (Gen. 12, 20, and 26).

Then readers noticed that not only do the stories happen twice, but they seem to be told in two distinct voices. Take, for example, the renaming of Jacob as Israel. In the A version of the story, God is called Yahweh (or "the LORD" in English translations, Gen. 32:9), and Yahweh is portrayed with human qualities, wrestling with Jacob at night. Jacob's new name is presented as a pun on the fact that Jacob won the wrestling match (Gen. 32:28), and the story ends with an etiology, or an explanation of modern practice, saying, "Therefore to this day the Israelites do not eat the thigh muscle that is on the hip socket, because he struck Jacob on the hip socket at the thigh muscle" (Gen. 32:32). Though Jacob receives a new name, he does not receive any other blessings from Yahweh.

Three chapters later, the B version of this story shows no awareness that Jacob has already been renamed. In this version, God is only referred to as Elohim (or "God" in English), and God is portrayed as more of a cosmic being; he does not wrestle with Jacob but simply appears and pronounces blessings upon him. There is no wordplay involving the name Israel, nor is the story presented as an etiology. Instead, Jacob's renaming is the occasion for God to command him to "be fruitful and multiply," promising that his posterity will include nations and kings (Gen. 35:11).

This difference of style in and of itself would be unremarkable, but careful readers soon found that while each episode of these doublets differed in style, the style *across* doublets was consistent. The announcement of Isaac's birth also has an A version and a B version, and its A version looks stylistically identical with the A version of Jacob's renaming, while the B version matches the B version of Jacob's renaming. For Isaac's birth, the A version (Gen. 18) refers to God as Yahweh and portrays Yahweh as sitting down and eating a meal with Abraham, much as a human might do. Similarly, a humanlike Yahweh wrestles with Jacob in the A version of Jacob's story. The B version of Isaac's birth announcement only refers to God as "God," and God simply speaks with Abraham rather than sharing a meal with him. Further, the B version uses the occasion of Isaac's birth to reiterate that he will be the ancestor of nations and kings, along with a be-fruitful-and-multiply command. All of these characteristics match the B version of Jacob's renaming.

Doublets are not the only place where we find stories that resemble the A and B style. Many stories—even those that appear only once—are told in one of these styles. The story of Eden is clearly told in the A style: God is referred to as Yahweh, Yahweh acts much as humans do (e.g., he "walk[s] in the garden at the time of the evening breeze," Gen. 3:8), and the story is full of puns and etiologies. On the other hand, the seven-day creation in Genesis 1 is clearly presented in the B style. God is portrayed as less humanlike and more cosmic; rather than forming man from dust and breathing into him (as happens in the A-type Eden story), God simply speaks to bring objects into being. Humans are commanded to "be fruitful, and multiply" (Gen. 1:28)—the same command seen in the two B stories above— and God is exclusively referred to as "God," never Yahweh.

The similarities among A-style stories go well beyond shared themes. Their vocabulary is internally consistent and markedly different from B-style stories. God is portrayed as humanlike: he walks in Eden, he wrestles with Jacob, he barters with Abraham over the number of righteous people in Sodom, he repents, he shows mercy, and he occasionally worries that humans will become like gods (e.g., Gen. 3:22 and 11:6). Most importantly, A-style stories all make a consistent set of historical claims about Israel's past. For example, A-style stories maintain that humans have always known God by the name Yahweh; as Genesis 4:26 explains: "At that time people began to invoke the name of Yahweh." As a result, A stories overwhelmingly prefer the name Yahweh rather than "God," beginning with the creation. Similarly, A-style stories take for granted that sacrifice has always been part of human culture, which is why A-style texts frequently depict characters offering sacrifice—even before the sacrificial commandments were given to Moses on Mount Sinai.

B-style stories have their own internally consistent vocabulary, and their conception of God is uniform, with God portrayed as a cosmic being concerned with order and justice.[1] The B stories also

---

1. As Richard Elliott Friedman points out, the words mercy, grace, and repentance never occur in any B-style story. *Who Wrote the Bible?* (New York: Harper Collins, 1997), 238–39.

share a set of internally consistent historical claims—but different claims than we see in the A stories. According to B-style stories, no one offered sacrifice before God revealed the sacrificial system on Mount Sinai, so in the B version of the Abrahamic covenant, the renaming of Jacob, and the flood, no sacrifices are mentioned. Even the name of Yahweh is presented as being unknown until God reveals it to Moses in Exodus 6. God tells Moses, "I am Yahweh. I appeared to Abraham, Isaac, and Jacob as God Almighty, but by my name Yahweh I did not make myself known to them" (Ex. 6:2–3). Thus, in the B stories that occur before Exodus 6, God is always referred to as "God" or "God Almighty," never as Yahweh.

"A" Stories	"B" Stories
• God is humanlike (wrestling with Jacob, eating a meal with Abraham).	• God is cosmic.
• God is merciful. He can change his mind and even repent.	• God is concerned with order and justice. He does not change.
• Humans have known the name Yahweh from the beginning.	• Humans do not know the name Yahweh until God reveals it to Moses.
• Humans have always offered sacrifice to God.	• No one offers sacrifices before Sinai.
• Stories often contain wordplay and etiologies.	

Once scholars were able to identify and separate out the A and B sources, they were left with a number of stories in the Pentateuch that were unlike both the A and B stories. When taken together, these leftover passages show the same kinds of internal similarities we see in both A and B texts, including their own unique writing style, theology, and historical claims. In these C stories, God is portrayed much like a human, but he often communicates with human beings through intermediaries, such as dreams, visions, and prophets. The C texts agree that Moses met with God on a mountain, but they say this mountain was called Horeb, not Sinai. As with the B stories, the C stories claim that the name Yahweh was not known until God revealed it to Moses on the mountain—and it has its own version of that moment: "Thus you shall say to the Israelites, 'Yahweh, the God of your ancestors, the God of Abraham, the God of Isaac, and the God of Jacob, has sent me to you': This is my name forever" (Ex. 3:15). Accordingly, the C stories always refer to God as "God" until this point, never as Yahweh.

Based on literary style and historical claims, scholars assigned every verse in Genesis through Numbers to an A, B, or C text. Then they saw something remarkable. Once every story was classified and separated out, they were left with three independent, self-contained narratives. In other words, if you ignore all the A and C texts and read only the B texts, you see an independent narrative that does not depend on anything in A or C. The same holds true if you read either A or C on its own. In fact, each of these three sources does not seem to know that the other two sources even exist, for no source ever refers to anything outside of its own stories. For example, according to A, Jacob goes to his uncle Laban (who lives in Haran) because Jacob had tricked Esau out of his birthright and fears that Esau will kill him in revenge (Gen. 27:42–45). But according to B, Jacob receives the blessing without any trickery (Gen. 28:1), and Jacob goes to Laban (who now lives in Padan-Aram) because Isaac did not want him to marry a Canaanite woman (Gen. 28:1–3). Both sources say that Jacob went to live with Laban, but neither shows any awareness of the events recounted in the other.

When the three sources are separated into three separate narratives, all of the contradictions noted at the beginning of this chapter—and many, many more—disappear. The reason that Joseph refers to his mother bowing down to him is because, according to this source (A), Rachel had not died yet; Rachel only dies in childbirth in the C source. The oddity of a teenage Ishmael being described as if he were a baby disappears, for the story of the infant Ishmael belongs to the C source, while the verses describing a teenage Ishmael belong to the B source. The confusion over who brought Joseph to Egypt is resolved when we realize that according to the A source, the Ishmaelites bought Joseph from his brothers, while the C source says that the Midianites pulled Joseph out of the pit without his brothers' knowledge.

Each source has its own unique style. Each source has a different conception of who God is and how he interacts with humans. No source refers to stories or events in the other sources. When the sources are separated, the contradictions in the text disappear.

And each source has its own narrative with details that often conflict with the narrative of the other sources. These observations led scholars over a century ago to conclude that the A, B, and C sources were not merely different styles, they were three separate documents spliced together to form our modern Pentateuch. This theory—that the Pentateuch is composed of separate documents—is known as the Documentary Hypothesis, and its proposal has led to a profound paradigm shift in how both scholars and believers understand the Old Testament.

Since the initial proposal of the Documentary Hypothesis, scholars have questioned its details in numerous ways. For example, was the Pentateuch compiled from written documents or from various oral traditions? Does the C text collection comprise a complete, coherent narrative or a loose collection of traditions? Was the Pentateuch formed through a process of scribal expansion or through the combination of complete sources? The debates over these details are ongoing, but the evidence supporting multiple authors in the Pentateuch is so wide-ranging and so persuasive that it is accepted in some form by virtually every Bible scholar from almost every religious tradition. Academics will undoubtedly continue to argue over the number or nature of the sources, but there is near-unanimous agreement that the Pentateuch as we know it is a composite text.

The Classical Documentary Hypothesis

In brief, the classical Documentary Hypothesis runs as follows: what we have been calling "source B" focuses primarily on matters of priestly concern, such as sacrifice, circumcision, and proper worship. This priestly and ritual legislation is quite extensive, constituting the vast majority of the book of Leviticus. Thus, this document is known by scholars as the Priestly source, or P for short. The Priestly source is the most well-ordered of the sources, and P provides almost every date and chronological notice in the Pentateuch.

The Priestly source has only a few stories in Genesis, including the seven-day creation account (Gen. 1), the flood (Gen. 6–9), God's covenant with Abraham (Gen. 17), Jacob's sojourn with Laban (Gen. 28), Jacob's name change to Israel (Gen. 35), and a brief account of Joseph in Egypt, all of which are tied together by genealogies. P's primary interest is in the Sinai and wilderness stories, so after its Exodus account of Moses delivering the Israelites, the Priestly source focuses mainly on the construction of the tabernacle and the ritual ordinances associated with it, followed by the wilderness wanderings and arrival at the promised land.

The Yahwistic Source (="A" Source)	The Priestly Source (="B" Source)	The Elohistic Source (="C" Source)	The Deuteronomic Source
• Refers to God as Yahweh from the beginning • God is portrayed anthropomorphically • People offer sacrifice from the beginning • Uses wordplay and etiologies	• Refers to God as "God" or "God Almighty" until Sinai • God is portrayed cosmically • No one offers sacrifice before Sinai • Focuses on matters of priestly concern: circumcision, purity, dietary laws, etc. • Strictly ordered: emphasis on dates, ages, and chronology • Portrays Aaron and the priests in a positive light	• Refers to God as "God" until Sinai • God is portrayed anthropomorphically, with a greater emphasis on mediators • Emphasis on prophets and prophetic authority • Tends to reflect poorly on Aaron and the priesthood	• Occurs only in Deuteronomy • Seems to be aware of both the Yahwistic and Elohistic sources, but not the Priestly source • Centers on a law code (Deut. 12–26) that differs in many regards from both Elohistic (Ex. 20–23) and Priestly laws (Leviticus)

The other sources are inserted within the chronological framework of the Priestly source. What we have been referring to as "source A" is known as the Yahwistic source, due to its frequent use of the divine name Yahweh/Jehovah. For short, it is often called the "J source" (for Jehovah). The Yahwistic (J) source begins with the creation and Garden of Eden stories (Gen. 2–3), followed by Cain and Abel (Gen. 4), the flood (Gen. 6–9), the Tower of Babel (Gen. 11), and then a whole series of stories revolving around Abraham, Isaac, Jacob, and Joseph. The J source's account of Moses and the plagues runs parallel with P's account, though in the J source God does not reveal the name Yahweh to Moses, since it assumes that the Israelites had known the name Yahweh since the time of Adam. The

J source has its own account of the revelation at Sinai, but it focuses exclusively on God's appearance to Moses, who receives no laws. J continues with stories of wilderness wanderings and ends with the Israelites on the edge of the promised land.

What we have been calling "source C" is known by scholars as the Elohistic source—or E for short—because it refers to God as Elohim until the name Yahweh is revealed to Moses at Mount Horeb (Ex. 3). This term is unfortunate, since the Priestly source also refers to God as Elohim until the name Yahweh is revealed to Moses. But luckily the Elohistic source and the Priestly source are distinct in both style and theological outlook, so the two sources are easy to distinguish.

The beginning of the E source seems to have been lost, as it does not appear in the Pentateuch. The first time we see an Elohistic text is when Abraham passes his wife off as his sister (Gen. 20, as opposed to the J version of this story in Gen. 12). E recounts a smattering of stories in the lives of the patriarchs and contributes to the Joseph story in Genesis. E alone tells the story of the golden calf forged by the Israelites while Moses is on Mount Sinai. Just as with J and P, the narrative arc of E concludes at the edge of the promised land.

Scholars have also isolated a fourth source known as the Deuteronomic source, or D for short. As the name implies, the Deuteronomic source is found exclusively in, and comprises the majority of, the book of Deuteronomy. As the Pentateuch is currently organized, Genesis, Exodus, Leviticus, and Numbers all tell the story of Israel from the creation of the world until the Israelites arrive at the promised land. This account is composed from the J, E, and P sources. At the end of the book of Numbers, the Israelites have arrived at the river Jordan and are ready to enter Canaan and conquer the land. But Moses stops and delivers a massive speech where we hear almost the entire story of the Pentateuch yet again. This speech bears all the hallmarks of a separate source: it is internally consistent, it has its own style, and it contradicts the other sources on numerous points. This has led scholars to conclude that Moses's speech must come from a separate source.

Since modern readers tend to be most familiar with the narrative portions of the Pentateuch and less familiar with the laws, the discussion in this chapter has centered on the narrative arguments for the Documentary Hypothesis. But evidence for the various sources may also be found in the law codes. For example, the Elohistic source states that enslaved Hebrew males must be released after six years, while enslaved females must serve for life (Ex. 21:2–11); meanwhile, the Deuteronomic source claims that both enslaved males and females must be released after six years (Deut. 15:12–18). The Priestly source, on the other hand, says that Hebrew men and women cannot be enslaved to begin with (Lev. 25:39), but if a Hebrew becomes an indentured servant, he or she must be released after forty-nine years, not six (Lev. 25:40).

That some narratives in the Old Testament occur twice, that some refer to God by different names, that some use different writing styles, that different stories embrace contradictory historical claims, that different stories have different names for Moses's father-in-law or Mount Sinai, that contradictions appear throughout the text—all of this is interesting, but none would be conclusive in its own right. It is the confluence of all this evidence that is nothing short of astounding. That the themes, styles, claims, and names all align within the same texts over and over again attests to the power of the Documentary Hypothesis to explain the Pentateuch as we know it.

The Documentary Hypothesis in Action

We have focused so far on generalities regarding the first five books of the Old Testament, but let us take a moment to see the Documentary Hypothesis in action.

Genesis opens with the Priestly creation account, comprising Genesis 1:1 through the first half of Genesis 2:4. This story is easily recognizable as belonging to P. The account uses only the name "God," and as we saw in chapter one, it centers on separation and division in the natural world—an important concern for the priestly system of dietary and other laws. Its conception of God is cosmic, not humanlike, and the story is highly structured: its formulaic repetition for each day is almost ritualistic, and the scheme of days has a parallel arrangement, where the first three days represent the creation of an environment and the last three represent the creation of each environment's inhabitants, culminating in the Sabbath. God creates both male and female humans (Gen. 1:27), and he commands them,

"Be fruitful and multiply, and fill the earth" (Gen. 1:28). The story then ends with a repetition of the story's opening verse: "These are the generations of the heavens and the earth when they were created" (Gen. 2:4).

Beginning in the second half of Genesis 2:4, it is suddenly as if nothing has been created. There are no plants, no animals, and no humans. But instead of the watery chaos of Genesis 1, the earth is a dry wasteland, "for the God Yahweh had not caused it to rain upon the earth" (Gen. 2:5). Instead of calling God "God," the story switches to "the God Yahweh," or, as most Old Testament translations render it, "the LORD God." Along with this switch in names comes a totally different conception of God, who is now humanlike. Even the order of creation is different. Whereas Genesis 1 presents the order of creation as starting with animals and ending with humans, Genesis 2 presents the order as man, then animals, then woman. This second creation account, attributed to the J source, tells how man and woman aspire to become like gods but get cast out of Eden by Yahweh to a ground that is cursed because of their actions (Gen. 3:17). This story has all the attributes we would expect of J: the name of God is Yahweh, God is portrayed as humanlike, the story is full of wordplay,[2] and a great deal of attention is given to etiologies such as marriage (Gen. 2:24), childbirth (3:16), clothing (3:7), agriculture (3:17), and why snakes do not have legs (3:14).

Immediately after the J version of Eden comes another J story dealing with Cain and Abel. Once again, God is only referred to as Yahweh, and the story is full of wordplay[3] and etiologies, such as the origin of cattle herders (Gen. 4:20) and musicians (Gen. 4:21). The respective offerings of Cain and Abel imply that humans offered sacrifices before Sinai (unlike P's view), and the story refers to J's account of the ground being cursed.[4]

2. E.g., the man and woman are naked (*'arumim*) while the serpent is clever (*'arum*), humans (*'adam*) are taken from the dust (*'adamah*), woman (*'ishah*) is taken out of man (*'ish*), and Eve (*hawwah*) is the mother of all living (*hay*).

3. Eve "bore Cain [*qayin*], saying, 'I have produced [*qaniti*] a man with the help of Yahweh." Cain becomes a wanderer (*nad*) in the land of Nod, and Abel's name means "nothingness" or "transitory." Unsurprisingly, he does not last long in the story.

4. Gen. 4:11. The NRSV reads, "Now you are cursed from the ground," but the Hebrew can also be understood to mean, "You are more cursed than the ground" (*'arur attah min-ha'adamah*). The allusions to Eden within the Cain and Abel story are extensive:

As soon as J finishes Cain's genealogy, the P source picks up as if the entire Cain and Abel story never happened: "This is the list of the descendants of Adam. When God created humankind, he made them in the likeness of God. Male and female he created them, and he blessed them and named them 'Humankind' when they were created. When Adam had lived one hundred thirty years, he became the father of a son in his likeness, according to his image, and named him Seth" (Gen. 5:1–3). Notice how P opens with its standard formula about "the list of the descendants of [name]" (Gen. 5:1; cf. 2:4, 6:9, 10:1, etc.), how God is once again referred to as "God," and how the language draws exclusively from P's creation account: man is created in the likeness of God, "Male and female he created them," and Adam's son Seth is "in his likeness, according to his image" (compare Gen. 1:26–27).

P then lists Adam's descendants through Seth, but this genealogy looks practically identical to the list that the Yahwistic source gives for Cain's descendants. According to J (Gen. 4), Cain's descendants were Enoch, Irad, Mehujael, Methushael, and Lamech. According to P (Gen. 5), Seth's descendants were Enoch, Jared, Mahalalel, Methuselah, and Lamech. It seems that both J and P knew the same genealogy, but each incorporated it into their story differently. And, just as we would expect, J's genealogy is full of wordplay,[5] etiologies, and the name Yahweh, while P's genealogy uses only the name "God" and shows a near obsession with dates, as does the rest of P's stories.

After these two genealogies comes the story of the flood. The flood story differs from much of the rest of the Pentateuch in that the separate sources are not presented side by side but interwoven as

---

immediately after eating of the fruit of the Tree of Knowledge, Adam knew his wife; Adam is driven out "to till the ground" (Gen. 3:23), and Cain is "a tiller of the ground" (Gen. 4:2); God "drove out" Adam and Eve (Gen. 3:24), and Cain complains to God, "You have driven me away" (Gen. 4:14); Adam and Eve "hid themselves from the presence [literally, "the face"] of Yahweh" (Gen. 3:8), and Cain says to God, "I shall be hidden from your face" (Gen. 4:14); Adam and Eve are driven out "at the east of the garden of Eden" (Gen. 3:24), and Cain likewise is driven out "east of Eden" (Gen. 4:16). See Michael Fishbane, *Biblical Text and Texture: A Literary Reading of Selected Texts* (Oxford: Oneworld Publications, 1998), 17–27.

5. For example, Enoch builds a city (*'ir*) then bears a son named *'irad*; and Seth (*sheth*) is given (*shath*) as a replacement for Abel.

one continuous story. You can see this in Genesis 7:16–24, quoted below, where the regular text comes from J and the bold text from P:

> And Yahweh shut him in. [17]The flood continued forty days on the earth; and the waters increased, and bore up the ark, and it rose high above the earth. [18]**The waters swelled and increased greatly on the earth; and the ark floated on the face of the waters.** [19]The waters swelled so mightily on the earth that all the high mountains under the whole heaven were covered; [20]**the waters swelled above the mountains, covering them fifteen cubits deep.** [21]**And all flesh died that moved on the earth, birds, domestic animals, wild animals, all swarming creatures that swarm on the earth, and all human beings;** [22]**everything on dry land in whose nostrils was the breath of life died.** [23]He blotted out every living thing that was on the face of the ground, human beings and animals and creeping things and birds of the air; they were blotted out from the earth. Only Noah was left, and those that were with him in the ark. [24]**And the waters swelled on the earth for one hundred fifty days.**

Since the flood story is composed of two separate texts, everything happens twice: God commands Noah to build an ark twice, he brings in the animals twice, the door is closed twice, the rain begins twice, and so on.

The J version begins with the birth of Noah, who will bring relief "out of the ground that Yahweh has cursed" (Gen. 5:29), and ends with another reference to the ground curse: "Yahweh said in his heart, 'I will never again curse the ground'" (Gen. 8:21). God is called Yahweh, and he even repents of his previous actions, just as a human might do (Gen. 6:6). Noah makes a distinction between clean and unclean animals, and he offers sacrifice to God, both of which are anachronistic from P's perspective.[6] The story serves as an explanation for the seasons, and we see the author using wordplay, just as in the other J accounts.[7]

The P version of the flood begins with the standard P formula ("These are the descendants ..."), and only uses the name "God." Just as the J version of the flood refers back to J's creation account, so the

---

6. According to the Priestly source, the Hebrews did not distinguish between clean and unclean animals until the law of Moses was revealed on Mt. Sinai.

7. Noah's name is punned on twice, both at his naming, where Noah "comforts" (*yenaḥamenu*, Gen. 5:29) the people, and in Gen. 6:8, where נח finds חן.

P version refers back to its own creation story. For P, the flood is an undoing and then reenactment of God's initial creation: the fountains of the deep and the windows of heaven break open (Gen. 7:11; cf. 1:6–8), God sends his wind over the waters and dry land appears (Gen. 8:1, 13; cf. 1:2, 9), the initial command to be fruitful and multiply is repeated (Gen. 9:1; cf. 1:28), and humans are permitted to eat meat in words directly parallel to God's initial command to eat only vegetables (Gen. 9:3; cf. 1:29–30).

After the flood, J and P give separate genealogies for Noah's descendants, and each genealogy shows the characteristics we would expect of J and P respectively. J's genealogy in Genesis 10 is peppered with wordplay,[8] explanations for human phenomena like hunters, and references to Yahweh. P's genealogy, on the other hand, begins with P's standard formula, "These are the descendants of Shem" (Gen. 11:10). P's genealogy does not contain any wordplay or explanations for modern phenomena, but instead focuses almost exclusively on dates: how many years after the flood Shem had his first son, how long each character lived, each father's age when his sons were born, and so on.

Following J's genealogy, we come across the story of Babel, which follows the J pattern. Humankind spreads out "from the east" (Gen. 11:2), which is the direction of Eden according to the J source. God is referred to exclusively as Yahweh, and he worries that humans are becoming too powerful, just as he had worried in the Garden of Eden that humans had become "like one of us" (Gen. 3:22). The story is based on the wordplay between Babel/Babylon (*babel*) and "to confound" (*balal*), and it seems to serve as an explanation for the temple-towers frequently found in places like Babylon.

The styles of the Yahwistic and Priestly sources are so distinct and so internally consistent that if we analyzed every story in the Pentateuch this way, you would quickly get bored ("*yet again* J uses the name Yahweh; *yet again* P alludes only to his own creation account and not to J's, etc."). In fact, even if this chapter is the only exposure you have had to the Documentary Hypothesis, you could probably already start separating J from P on your own. For example, there

---

8. E.g., Gen. 10:25, in the days of Peleg the earth was divided (*palag*).

are two versions of the Abrahamic covenant, one in which Abraham offers sacrifice and makes a covenant with Yahweh (Gen. 15:7–21), and one in which Abraham makes a covenant with "God," without any sacrifice and with multiple allusions to the command to be fruitful found in Genesis 1 (Gen. 17:1–22). It is not too difficult to see that the first belongs to J, while the second belongs to P.

Who Wrote These Sources? And When?

What I have laid out above is the classical Documentary Hypothesis as first proposed in the late 1800s. Since that time, scholars have debated the relationship between the various sources in the Pentateuch, and while there is near-unanimous agreement about the fragmentary nature of the text, there is no consensus on how to understand the fragments themselves. This disagreement makes the task of describing the date and provenance of the sources especially fraught.

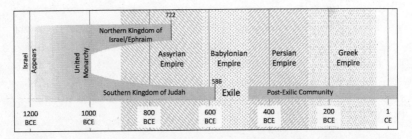

What scholars do know is that most of the Old Testament was written around the time of the exile, in 586 BCE, which can be seen in the form of Hebrew used throughout. Just as English has changed drastically in the 400 years between Shakespeare's day and ours—to the point that many modern readers have a hard time understanding his plays—so did Hebrew change over the course of its early history. Despite the centuries it covers, the majority of the Old Testament is written in a fairly consistent dialect, which scholars refer to as "standard Biblical Hebrew." It is the dialect used to write the history of 1 Samuel through 2 Kings, which ends at the exile. It is also the dialect used in Jeremiah and Ezekiel, who were active when Israel went into exile. However, it morphs into "late Biblical Hebrew" a few decades later, as seen in the post-exilic books of Chronicles, Ezra, and Nehemiah. There are a few sections of the Old Testament, such as Genesis

51

49 and Judges 5 (mentioned earlier), that are linguistically archaic and date centuries before standard biblical Hebrew, but the dialect of the vast majority of the Old Testament is clearly identifiable as standard biblical Hebrew.

What this means is that from a linguistic standpoint, the Pentateuch undoubtedly comes from around the period of exile. Moses lived at least 600 years before the exile, so, linguistically, Moses or his contemporaries could not have written the Pentateuch any more than Shakespeare could have written *Harry Potter*.

The exile also constitutes the milieu in which the Priestly source of the Pentateuch makes the most sense. We saw in chapter one that Genesis 1 (a P story) assumes that its audience is intimately familiar with the Babylonian creation myth *Enuma Elish*; otherwise, the listeners would not have been able to make sense of the ways in which *Enuma Elish* was deliberately inverted to show God's power. The educated elite may have been familiar with international myths and traditions, but where would the average Israelite have been exposed to Babylonian myths other than in Babylon? Genesis 1 also ends not with the creation of a temple, as we might expect from the *Enuma Elish* story, but with the setting apart of the Sabbath—a sacred day that could be observed even without the temple, which had been destroyed just as the Israelites were carried into exile. The Priestly source overwhelmingly focuses on how to keep a distinct religious identity, a concern that makes no sense in a pre-exilic setting where Israelite religion, national borders, and ethnicity were inextricable. (This is why the possibility of religious conversion is never even addressed in pre-exilic sources; one could not convert to the Israelite religion any more than one could convert to being a different ethnicity.) The Priestly laws even conclude with a threat that is a clear reference to exile, that if the Israelites do not follow the laws, then "you I will scatter among the nations ... your land shall be a desolation, and your cities a waste" (Lev. 26:33). In short, the Priestly source is written in the temporal dialect of exile, assumes its audience is familiar with Babylonian stories, contains laws specifically designed to help the Israelites understand themselves in light of the destruction of their temple, and explicitly mentions exile as a punishment for disobeying God's commands.

Even if we ignore the Priestly source's focus, the entire shape of the Pentateuch is centered on the promise of inheriting land and the idea of exile. Adam and Eve are driven out of their garden due to transgression; Cain is banished from the land; Abraham is promised to inherit the land but then must flee to Egypt; Jacob inherits the same promise but has to flee to Aram to save his life from Esau; Joseph is sold from his homeland; and a famine drives all the Israelites down to Egypt. Even the stories of the wilderness wanderings center on the question of when the Israelites will be able to return to their homeland.

Other biblical writings help reinforce the conclusion that the Pentateuch was compiled during or after exile. The prophets before the exile are constantly calling Israel to repentance for violating God's laws, yet in well over a hundred chapters, not a single prophet mentions the Pentateuch. Contrast this with the first prophets after exile, Ezra and Nehemiah, who speak at length about "the book of Moses" (Ezra 6:18) and "the book of the law of Moses" (Neh. 8:1). Though the law had been known for centuries, only with exile did there emerge a book of this law to which the prophets started referring.

While the texts themselves date from around the period of exile, many of the oral traditions that lie behind the stories in the Pentateuch are quite old. As we saw in the previous chapter, the stories/legends of the patriarchs must have been passed down for a considerable time before being written down, particularly given how many of them refer to practices that later Israelites viewed as unacceptable, such as building pillars and planting sacred trees. This extensive oral history helps explain why the characters in Genesis–Deuteronomy are some of the only ones in the entire Old Testament to be recorded with two different names (often with a narrative explaining why): Israel is also known as Jacob; Esau is known as Edom; Abraham is known as Abram; Sarah is known as Sarai; Jethro is known as Reul and as Hobab; Sinai is known as Horeb, etc. Separate traditions most likely circulated with variations on the names of the protagonists, much as the protagonists in the fairy tale "Hansel and Gretel" were elsewhere known as "Jan and Janette."

Thus we know that the Priestly source and final form of the Pentateuch both come from the period of exile or later. Another piece of evidence comes from the book of Deuteronomy, which was most likely written toward the end of the seventh century during the reign of Josiah. We know this because of an odd story in 2 Kings where a priest claims to have "found the book of the law" in the temple (22:8). When King Josiah hears the contents of the book, he realizes that even though the people have been trying to follow God's commandments, they have not been following the rules in this particular book of law, so he enacts a sweeping set of religious reforms, all of which line up with the commands found only in the book of Deuteronomy (2 Kgs. 23). The story in 2 Kings 22 serves to explain how this alternative source of law came about, even though people already knew some version of Mosaic law. A combination of linguistics and content suggests that the other non-priestly writings in the Pentateuch come from shortly before the reign of Josiah.

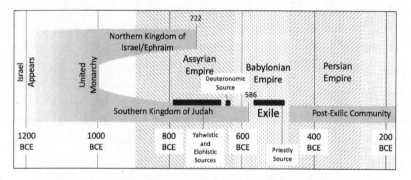

The Documentary Hypothesis and LDS Scripture

It might seem that dating the sources of the Pentateuch would be unimportant to the average layperson. But for LDS readers this debate is central to one of the thorniest implications of the Documentary Hypothesis, namely, that if we accept the academic consensus, we are forced to reevaluate prevailing orthodox assumptions about the origin and historicity of Restoration scripture. Regardless of whether you accept the classical Documentary Hypothesis or any of its alternatives, the composite nature of the Pentateuch runs contrary to how the Pentateuch is treated in other LDS scripture.

For example, the Book of Mormon narrative of Nephi and his brothers retrieving the brass plates in 1 Nephi 3–5 presupposes the existence of a well-developed corpus of scripture around 600 BCE, over a decade before the exile even began. In 1 Nephi 5:11, Nephi says of the brass plates that "they did contain the five books of Moses, which gave an account of the creation of the world, and also of Adam and Eve, who were our first parents." The phrase "five books of Moses" implies that the brass plates contained Genesis through Deuteronomy, or possibly an earlier version of these books, but as we have seen, for the Pentateuch to have been compiled before the exile is extremely unlikely. Nephi even mentions two different creation stories: "the creation of the world," which is presumably the Priestly account in Genesis 1, "and also of Adam and Eve," which would be the Yahwistic account of Genesis 2–3. Again, it is highly unlikely that the Priestly source had been written by Nephi's day, much less for it to have already been combined with the Yahwistic source into one continuous narrative.

A more serious issue arises in the books of Moses and Abraham. The book of Moses is the Joseph Smith Translation of the King James Bible (JST) of the first few chapters of Genesis, but since the changes are both lengthy and theologically important, they have been placed separately in the Pearl of Great Price rather than in the footnotes, as most JST verses are. While the Bible itself never directly claims that Moses wrote the Pentateuch, the JST does. Just before Genesis 1:1, the book of Moses has God commanding Moses to write down what he sees (1:40; 2:1), after which the narrative flows directly into the first creation story, a transition that makes an explicit claim to Mosaic authorship.

The book of Moses goes on to recount both the Priestly (Gen. 1) and Yahwistic (Gen. 2–3) creation stories, and it ties the two even more closely together than the Old Testament does. As we saw above, the transition between the two stories is fairly jarring in the Old Testament, where the fully created world in Genesis 2:3 disappears in Genesis 2:4 and Yahweh starts all over again. In the book of Moses, however, right in the transition between the two stories the text reads: "For I, the Lord God, created all things, of which I have spoken, spiritually, before they were naturally upon the face of the earth" (Moses 3:5). This addition effectively reimagines the Priestly account as a purely spiritual creation, and while it does make the text read more smoothly, it highlights the problem of what are clearly different sources from different authors being presented as if both came from Moses.

The book of Abraham faces a similar challenge. Abraham 4 gives a rewritten version of the Priestly account in Genesis 1 while Abraham 5 gives the Yahwistic account from Genesis 2. Only now the problem is compounded because the two stories are presented together in one continuous text supposedly written by Abraham, more than a thousand years before the sources of the Pentateuch were likely composed and brought together.

My focus here is on the Old Testament, so I do not want to spend too much time on how LDS authors have responded to the problems the Documentary Hypothesis presents to Restoration scripture. There are, however, certain regular patterns in how LDS authors tend to respond, and the patterns hold true across a broad range of potentially troubling issues, such as the historicity of the patriarchal narratives, the Documentary Hypothesis, Second Isaiah (see chapter eight), the historical Jesus, the disputed Pauline letters, and so on.

The first category of response is either to dismiss biblical scholarship altogether or to accept biblical scholarship only on points that do not contradict orthodox LDS thought. I personally find this type of apologia to be unsatisfactory, as it pre-determines the conclusion and then goes out hunting for only those facts that support what the author already believes. Such an approach runs contrary to the spirit of honest inquiry, and it assumes that the way we currently understand the gospel will never need revision—an assumption that is repeatedly debunked by even a superficial tour through church history.

The second category of response accepts the basic tenets of biblical scholarship but carves out space for LDS orthodoxy on the fringe of that scholarship. For example, some authors accept the validity of the Documentary Hypothesis but latch onto the fact that a pre-exilic compilation of the Pentateuch is possible, even if it is extremely unlikely. In this view, the fact that Nephi refers to the five books of Moses simply means that the compilation of the Pentateuch's various sources must have happened before 600 BCE—a view that is technically not impossible but that few biblical scholars support. These types of approaches are similar to claiming that

THE OLD TESTAMENT AS STORY

scientists have shown that Earth's atmosphere is not warming or that archeologists have uncovered evidence of extraterrestrial influences on ancient Egyptian civilization. There will probably always be scientists, archeologists, and others on the fringe of their professions who make such claims, but to represent these claims as constituting a substantive debate within the profession is incorrect.

A third category seeks to preserve the historicity of Restoration scripture by shifting the paradigms through which we understand it. A common approach within this category is to give Joseph Smith a much broader role in the translation process. So, instead of presenting him as reading the English text of the Book of Mormon text word-for-word from the seer stone, he is presented as encountering an ancient text and trying to find via inspiration as well as his own intellectual processes the English words to express its ideas. In this view, Nephi would have read something on the brass plates that dealt with the creation of the world and the law of Moses, which led Joseph to assume that Nephi was reading the five books of Moses. Versions of this approach have Joseph taking the core of the Book of Mormon and expanding it with modern ideas, so that while much of the recounted fact of the Book of Mormon may be accurate, most of the ideas, images, theology, etc., were produced by Joseph as "translator."

Finally, some LDS authors resolve the tension between Restoration scripture historicity and biblical scholarship by abandoning the claim of historicity altogether. In this view, works such as the Book of Mormon, book of Abraham, and book of Moses may be inspired by God, but that inspiration does not imply that there were actual Nephites living in the Americas or that Abraham actually wrote the book of Abraham. To bring back a comparison I used earlier, in this view, Restoration scripture would be like the parable of the Prodigal Son—inspired by God, true in the sense of conveying eternal truths, but not true in the sense of recounting events that actually happened. This approach does not question Joseph's role as a prophet, but it does reimagine what that role entails.

Debates among these various camps are ongoing, and only time will tell which approaches gain dominance in the broader community and for how long. Regardless of the outcome, reading the Old

Testament as a story provides an interesting lens through which the text can be interpreted. Just as the different versions of "Goldilocks" or "The Three Little Pigs" add variety to their narratives, so the different stories of the Pentateuch give us a richer, more complex view of early Israel and its sacred traditions.

4

THE
OLD TESTAMENT
AS LAW

(Exodus–Deuteronomy)

Many readers see the Old Testament primarily as a rulebook—as God's instructions about what believers should and should not do. In one sense, this characterization is unfair. The past few chapters have shown the many ways the Old Testament is much more than a collection of commandments. But there are certainly portions of the Old Testament, particularly in Exodus through Deuteronomy, that explicitly present themselves as laws. This chapter explores the ways in which these chapters can be read as law, both by the Old Testament's ancient and modern adherents. However, there are also ways these Old Testament chapters break with traditional stereotypes of what a law is. We look at the laws themselves first and then examine three biblical notions important to understanding those laws: covenant, temple, and priesthood.

Societal Law

What exactly is a law? The question may seem straightforward, but the term "law" encompasses many different concepts.

Laws today are usually thought of as rules that carry penalties enforceable by the state. For example, your parents may forbid you from speeding, and they may punish you if you disobey, but what actually makes speeding against the law is the fact that if you speed, a police officer can pull you over and put you in jail. By this definition, the Pentateuch contains many laws. For example, in Deuteronomy

22:28–29: "If a man meets a virgin who is not engaged, and seizes her and lies with her, and they are caught in the act, the man who lay with her shall give fifty shekels of silver to the young woman's father, and she shall become his wife." The form of this law matches our modern sense of a secular legal code: an offense is laid out with an affixed punishment. The text assumes that someone will actually enforce the penalty, whether that enforcer be a judge or the community.

If we focus only on regulations enforced by the state, we find within the Pentateuch a fairly comprehensive legal framework for running an ancient society. It contains laws dealing with injury, homicide, theft, marriage, rape, inheritance, family relations, divorce, slavery, lending, borrowing, debt, and adoption—all the major categories of dispute that a person might encounter in the ancient world. But while each of these categories is indeed covered, the coverage tends to be fairly minimal. That is because most of these laws were not meant to act as sweeping generalizations designating what was and was not permissible. Rather, they were meant to act as case studies from which interpreters were to derive general principles.

Consider the law on goring oxen in Exodus 21:28–32. The text reads:

> When an ox gores a man or a woman to death, the ox shall be stoned, and its flesh shall not be eaten; but the owner of the ox shall not be liable. If the ox has been accustomed to gore in the past, and its owner has been warned but has not restrained it, and it kills a man or a woman, the ox shall be stoned, and its owner also shall be put to death. If a ransom is imposed on the owner, then the owner shall pay whatever is imposed for the redemption of the victim's life. If it gores a boy or a girl, the owner shall be dealt with according to this same rule. If the ox gores a male or female slave, the owner shall pay to the slaveowner thirty shekels of silver, and the ox shall be stoned.

To an ancient reader, this law was not just about ox gorings. The ox was a stand-in for any of the various means of involuntary manslaughter, such as donkeys, camels, human-made fires that got out of control, and boating accidents. The Pentateuch does not cover these other types of deaths because the case of the ox serves to establish the law governing all forms of involuntary manslaughter. Notice how the text lays out principles for determining liability: a man is not liable for a fatality his property causes unless that property had been involved in a previous incident ("the ox has been accustomed to gore in the past") and he had not taken reasonable action after being warned. Once liability has been determined, the text lays out possible means of redress (death of the owner or ransom for the victim). Then it states that children's lives are as valuable as adults' but that the death of a slave could be remedied simply by paying a fee to the slave's owner.

Seeing the way these texts operate will not suddenly transform the legal sections of the Pentateuch into enjoyable reading—after all, they are essentially the equivalent of state or federal legislation—but it can help us better understand the purpose of the text and its intended audience. Modern legal codes are designed to be read by judges and lawyers, not average citizens. Similarly, the laws in the Pentateuch seem to be aimed primarily at those who interpret and enforce the law. However, knowing the text's purpose can help us see how statements such as "eye for eye, tooth for tooth" (Ex. 21:24) do not mean that biblical law endorsed barbaric punishments (indeed, the earliest evidence we have suggests that such punishments never actually took place); rather, such sayings can be seen as laying out general principles, in this case that punishments should be commensurate with the crime committed.

We saw in the previous chapter that the laws of the Pentateuch come from different sources and that these sources were not written down until close to the time of exile in 586 BCE. If Moses did not receive these laws on Sinai, where did they come from? Much as we saw with the mythic material of Genesis, the material in the legal sections of the Pentateuch seems to be borrowed directly from other ancient Near Eastern societies.

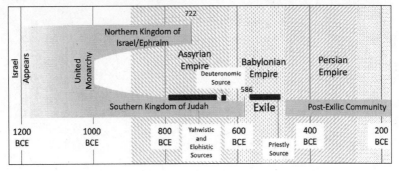

For example, the Laws of Eshnunna and the Code of Hammurabi both refer to ox goring, and both were written at least 500 years
before Moses would have lived. The Code of Hammurabi states:

> If an ox gores to death a man while it is passing through the streets, the
> case has no basis for a claim. If a man's ox is a known gorer, and the au-
> thorities of his city quarter notify him that it is a known gorer but he does
> not blunt its horns or control his ox, and that ox gores to death a member
> of the [upper] class, he (the owner) shall give 30 shekels of silver. If it is a
> man's slave (who is fatally gored), he shall give 20 shekels of silver.[1]

The parallels to Exodus could not be more apparent. Both laws
describe involuntary manslaughter through the case of the goring
ox; both qualify that the owner is liable only if the ox is known to
have gored in the past, if he was told of this goring, and if he did not
take reasonable action to stop it; and both prescribe a lesser penalty
if the victim is a slave. Hammurabi says that a liable man is to be
fined, while Exodus gives the option of a fine or the death penalty,
but the overall structure of the legislation is identical.

The same analysis could be carried out on practically every law
in the Pentateuch, no matter how odd or obscure. Exodus 21:22–25,
for example, describes what happens if two men are fighting and
they happen to injure a nearby pregnant woman who then miscar-
ries—a scenario that, while possible, surely cannot have occurred
with any regularity. Yet this obscure law appears in substantially the
same form in cultures all over the ancient Near East: the Middle
Assyrian Laws, the Code of Hammurabi, the Laws of Lipit-Ishtar,
and the Hittite Laws. All these laws were written before the Old
Testament, and some were written almost a full millennium before
Moses would have lived.

We will most likely never know what the earliest laws governing
Israel were. But we do know that it had developed a monarchy, a
royal bureaucracy, and an international class of scribes before the
Pentateuch was written. Rather than reinvent the wheel (or the law,
as it were), these scribes used the material available to them and in-
tentionally patterned Israel's legal code after other legal codes in the

---

1. Martha Roth, *Law Collections from Mesopotamia and Asia Minor*, 2nd ed. (Atlanta,
GA: Scholars Press, 1995), 128.

ancient Near East, much as they adapted the Ugaritic myths of Baal, the Babylonian creation myth, and *The Epic of Gilgamesh* to their mythology. And just as the Code of Hammurabi was ascribed to a famous king who claimed to have been commissioned by Marduk, so the Israelite laws would be ascribed to Moses, who claimed to have been called by Yahweh.[2]

Cultic Regulations

While much of the Pentateuch deals with secular or societal law, there are also many "cultic regulations." While the term "cult" might seem to imply shadowy figures chanting rituals in a dark room, in an academic context the word is simply used in its original sense: "care." Thus, agriculture is literally care (*cult*) of the field (*agri*). Similarly, in the ancient Near East, deities were cared for by their followers. In the Babylonian creation myth, humans were created for the express purpose of caring for the gods and doing their labor. Priests throughout the Near East dressed the statue of the god each morning and prepared multiple meals each day for the god to consume. These ritual preparations—or sacrifices—were simply part of what the gods required in exchange for their protection.

Israel, as part of the Near East, conceptualized its sacrificial system in the same way. The altar was called "Yahweh's table" (Mal. 1:12), and upon it the priests offered all the components of a traditional meal, such as meat, grain, and "cakes mixed with oil" (Lev. 2:4), which needed to be seasoned with salt (Lev. 2:13). Whenever meat

---

2. The same source divisions noted in the previous chapter apply to the law codes as well. The oldest collection of laws, usually ascribed to E, occurs in Exodus 20–23 and is known as the Covenant Code. In this code, the head of household seems to be the main locus of authority, and any case that could not be solved locally was left for God to sort out (e.g., Ex. 22:8–9). The code assumes a fairly complex society, including slaves and foreigners, and most scholars place it in the eighth or seventh century BCE. Chronologically, the next code would be the Deuteronomic Code of Deuteronomy 12–26, where authority has been centralized. In this code, elders and judges are called to arbitrate unsolved cases, and the code generally assumes a more complex bureaucracy than the Covenant Code does. These laws all fit well with the centralization and bureaucratic strengthening undertaken during Josiah's reforms of the seventh century BCE, which is the most likely origin point of the book of Deuteronomy as a whole. The final collection of law would be those of the Priestly source, the so-called Holiness Code in Leviticus 17–26. These laws reimagine Israel first and foremost as a religious community, and their primary focus is on separating Israelites from the other nations. The Holiness Code fits best in an exilic or post-exilic context when separation from other nations had become a major issue.

or bread was offered, wine needed to accompany it—the amount being determined by the kind of meat being sacrificed (Num. 15:2–5). Israelites were commanded to give these offerings "as food to your God" (Lev. 22:25), and Yahweh is often described as particularly enjoying the smell of a good meal. In the Babylonian version of the flood story, Ut-napishtim offers sacrifice immediately after the flood, and it is the cooking meat's aroma that causes the gods to remember how much they need humans to feed them. Similarly, after the biblical flood, Noah offers sacrifice, and "when Yahweh smelled the pleasing odor" (Gen. 8:21), he vows never to destroy humankind.[3]

By this point, you will probably not be surprised to learn that much of Israel's cultic system was borrowed and adapted from its neighbors. For example, the Old Testament describes a category of sacrifice known as "burnt offerings," where the entire animal is burnt upon the altar and neither the offeror nor the priest eats any of the meat. A second category is the peace offering, or offering of well-being, which is given in the temple courtyard and then eaten by those offering the sacrifice (Lev. 3). Ugaritic texts describe the same system, with whole burnt offerings given at the temple and peace offerings given in the temple's courtyard. Other cultures likewise divided animals into categories of "clean" and "unclean," as seen in the eighteenth-century texts from Mari, a city just north of Israel in modern-day Syria.

Though these cultic regulations tend to make boring reading, they open an interesting view into how the ancient Israelites conceptualized the world. For example, for them, the transition between life and death was sacred. They felt that the earthly and eternal realms briefly came together at the moment an animal was killed, so the sacrificial meal was a moment of communion with God. If anyone killed an animal without consecrating the moment through sacrifice, they were considered "guilty of bloodshed" and "cut off from the people" (Lev. 17:3–4). The meal thus shared was thought to include God as he partook of the parts of the animal burnt on the altar.

---

3. Biblical authors occasionally push back against this notion that sacrifices were meant to feed the gods. In Psalm 50:12–13 God is presented as saying, "If I were hungry, I would not tell you, for the world and all that is in it is mine. Do I eat the flesh of bulls, or drink the blood of goats?" The fact that the author has to make this argument shows how widely such a view of sacrifice was circulating among the Israelites.

Indeed, in the moments that God reveals himself in the Old Testament, it is often while the participants are sharing a meal. When making a solemn oath before God, Jacob climbs a mountain, offers sacrifice, and shares a meal with those entering the oath with him (Gen. 31:51–54). In Exodus, Moses and the leaders of Israel climb Mount Sinai, and there "they beheld God, and they ate and drank" (Ex. 24:11).

These insights may not make wading through the cultic regulations a more pleasant experience, but they do make it more meaningful. Indeed, if you are going to brave this section of the Pentateuch, three concepts will help you better understand what you read: purity, holiness, and the temple.

Purity

Modern conceptions of purity tend to focus on perfection (as in pure gold) or moral uprightness (as in keeping your thoughts pure), but in an ancient Israelite context, the term we translate as "pure" would be better rendered as "proper" or "socially acceptable." So, in American society, pure actions would include such behaviors as submitting an RSVP before attending a party, washing your hands after using the restroom, not wearing a top and bottom with different patterns, or eating beef but not cats. For Americans, violating these social norms is not sinful, nor does following them mark a person as particularly holy, but people who transgress these rules mark themselves as "other," or "not like us." The proper or "pure" place for a cat is on the couch, not the dinner plate.

Though social norms are rarely morally right or wrong, societies do tend to attach moral significance to them. Showing up to a party without notifying the host beforehand is considered rude in American society, and thus, to some degree, a moral failing. Objectively, eating a cat is no more morally wrong than eating a cow, but if you found your neighbor whipping up kitty soufflé, you would most likely feel some degree of moral repugnance.

There is also some overlap between social norms and perceived cleanliness. I would be loath to shake hands with someone who did not wash his hands after using the restroom, even though the odds of catching an illness from him are objectively quite low. In many East

Asian societies, lower parts of the body are considered dirtier than higher parts, so to touch someone's head with your feet—even if you had just finished showering—would be a grave social violation.

The peoples in ancient Canaan did not raise pigs for food. The sole exception was the Philistines. So the eating of pigs, along with many other animals, was seen as "other"—or, in the Old Testament's terms, "impure" or "unclean." Such categorizations most likely lie behind the prohibition against wearing clothing made from two types of fabric or sowing two types of seed in a field (Deut. 22:9–11).

As I noted before, for the Israelites, the transition between life and death was a sacred event, therefore, it needed to be set apart from quotidian affairs. Since semen and menstrual blood were connected with the transition to life, and corpses and diseases were connected with the transition to death, these were seen as "impure"—not because they were morally wrong or dirty, but because their proper place was separate. So labeling a menstruating woman as "impure" was not a moral judgment against her. In fact, though modern interpreters often imagine Israelites as being obsessed with legal minutiae, guarding their every waking moment against impurity, purity was not an overarching concern for them. Just ask yourself how much time you spend every day wondering if beef is socially acceptable or if you should wash your hands after using the restroom. That is probably about how much energy the ancient Israelites spent on it.

Holiness

The regulations in Leviticus 17–26 are collectively known as the Holiness Code, so called because while the first half of Leviticus focuses on purity, the overarching concern of these later chapters is on the holiness of the people. Scattered throughout the cultic regulations is the constant refrain: "You shall be holy, for I, Yahweh your God, am holy" (Lev. 19:2; cf. 20:7, 20:26, 21:8, etc.). Over and over again, Yahweh entreats the people to approach him through sacrifice, pilgrimage festivals, and moral living in order that they might share in his holiness.

The concept of holiness in the Old Testament is similar to that of purity: both describe how something relates to its surroundings. Pure items were pure not because of any intrinsic property, but rather because they remained in their proper sphere. Similarly, holy items were so designated not because they had any supernatural powers, but simply because they were close to God.

Holiness also manifests itself in people, places, and even times. People could be separated into three degrees of holiness according to their literal proximity to God. Priests were the most holy, due to their work serving Yahweh in the temple. Run-of-the-mill Israelites were less holy but could become more holy through righteous living and ritual observance. Foreign nations, being the most removed from Yahweh's presence, were the least holy. Time was likewise divided into three degrees of holiness, with festival days being the times most proximate to God, Sabbath days next, and regular non-Sabbath days furthest. For space, the first degree of holiness was occupied by the temple, the second by the land of Israel, and the third by the land outside of Israel. Similarly, within the temple, the inner sanctum, closest to God, was called the "holy of holies"; the main vestibule, a little further, was called "the holy place"; and the outer courtyard was the farthest from God's presence.

From a modern standpoint, proximity to God seems like it would be more desirable than distance, but although the Old Testament generally enjoins the people to holiness, it also recognizes the danger proximity to Yahweh brings. The ancient Israelites did not share our conception of God as a benevolent, cosmic, grandfatherly figure. To them, Yahweh was a storm god. While storms are certainly powerful and life-giving, they are also liable to strike out and kill you if you get too close. Accordingly, the Old Testament is full of examples of the danger of approaching a god who, like the storm, may seem capricious in whom he strikes down. For example, Moses meets Yahweh at the burning bush and is called to deliver the Israelites, but on his way back to Egypt, the text tells us that "at a place where they spent the night, Yahweh met him and tried to kill him" (Ex. 4:24).

The Israelites shook with fear when God appeared at Mount Sinai, and for good reason—God told Moses that if the people came too close, he "will break out against them" (Ex. 19:24). Indeed, when the Israelites fell short of God's expectations by worshiping the golden calf, Yahweh told Moses to "let me alone, so that my wrath may burn hot against them and I may consume them" (Ex. 32:10). Moses successfully intervenes on behalf of the people, but he still slaughters 3,000 of them for having turned away from God (Ex. 32:28). When the Ark of the Covenant almost falls over, Uzzah reaches out to keep it upright, and "the anger of Yahweh was kindled against Uzzah; and God struck him there because he reached out his hand to the ark; and he died there beside the ark of God" (2 Sam. 6:7).

Holiness—proximity to God—was dangerous. Levites were commanded not to touch holy objects "or they will die" (Num. 4:15). Nadab and Abihu, two sons of Aaron, experienced this punishment when they performed a ritual incorrectly. When they went to the altar, "fire came out from the presence of Yahweh and consumed them, and they died before Yahweh" (Lev. 10:2). When Moses sees what happened, he explains the danger of holiness to Aaron, saying, "This is what Yahweh meant when he said, 'Through those who are near me I will show myself holy'" (Lev. 10:3). When the Israelites take back the Ark of the Covenant from the Philistines, Yahweh kills seventy men in one particular town because they "did not rejoice … when they greeted the ark of Yahweh," and the Israelites exclaim, "Who is able to stand before Yahweh, this holy God? To whom shall he go so that we may be rid of him?" (1 Sam. 6:19–20).

In this context, holiness was not something the average Israelite strove for. The closest modern analogue to holiness would probably be what Rudolf Otto called the numinous, or the *mysterium tremendum*—the feeling of being in the presence of something unknown, powerful, dangerous, awe-inspiring. While Yahweh's presence was important for the blessings he showered on Israel, that numinous presence also needed to be contained, appeased, and kept at a safe distance. Hence the need for a temple to house Yahweh's presence and priests who were specially trained in how to safely interact with this power. The covenant Yahweh made with the average Israelite was a similar safety device. It conceptualized the relationship between God and his people in understandable, manageable terms.

Temple and Priesthood

The temple in Israel did not serve the same purpose that modern LDS temples do. While LDS temples are built primarily for the benefit of the worshiper, the ancient Israelite temple was primarily built for Yahweh. It was meant to serve as a physical place where the divine and earthly realms could meet, and from which Yahweh could watch over the people. Latter-day Saints today tend to think of the "house of the Lord" in metaphorical terms, but in ancient Israel, the temple was literally built as Yahweh's house. In fact, it had the same building pattern as regular houses in Canaan, including a basin where Yahweh could wash, a table for bread, a sacrificial altar where his meals could be served, a throne and footstool for him to sit on, and an altar for incense to clear the air.

Indeed, house-like temples were widespread in the ancient Near East, as was the tripartite design of the Jerusalem temple. The court-yard, vestibule, inner sanctum design, along with the placement of its altars and accoutrements, follows the same pattern we see in other Canaanite temples.[4] With the exception of the statue of the god in the inner sanctum, Canaanite temples were essentially indistin-guishable from the temple of Yahweh: they shared the same designs, sacrificial systems, priestly functions, and even founding myths. Just as Baal, who originally resided on Mount Zaphon, needed a place to live among his people after he defeated Yamm (the sea), so Yahweh, who originally resided on Mount Sinai, needed a place to live among his people after his splitting of the Red Sea. As Moses declares im-mediately after their crossing: "You brought them in and planted them on the mountain of your own possession, the place, O Yahweh, that you made your abode, the sanctuary, O Yahweh, that your hands have established" (Ex. 15:17).[5]

In the inner sanctum, or the holy of holies, sat two massive cherubs that formed Yahweh's throne, which was fifteen feet tall and fifteen feet wide (1 Kgs. 6:23–28; a cubit is roughly 1.5 feet). Although the Old Testament never describes what cherubs look like, archeologi-cal discoveries of carvings from Israel and its surrounding cultures

4. 1 Kings 5 even admits that when Solomon wanted to build a temple, he hired his builders from Phoenicia.

5. The wash basin in the temple is referred to as םי (*Yam*), "the sea" (1 Kgs. 7:23), possibly as a memorial to Yahweh's victory over it. Note, by the way, how incongruous Moses's statement is from a historical perspective: the Israelites would not build a tem-ple on Mount Zion for a few more centuries, so it seems odd for Moses to mention it after having just crossed the sea. The mention of the temple makes perfect sense, how-ever, from a mythic perspective, as seen in the myths of Baal and Marduk where temples are established after the gods' victory over water.

depict winged lions with human heads. Such a creature would help make sense of verses such as Psalm 18:10, which describes Yahweh riding on a cherub as he flies through the wind. Other Near Eastern cultures also used winged creatures to form thrones or to guard temples, as seen in Phoenicia, Assyria, Babylonia, and even Egypt with its half-human sphinx guarding the pyramids.

At the base of Yahweh's cherub throne lay the Ark of the Covenant, which was referred to as Yahweh's footstool (1 Chr. 28:2). This fifteen-foot throne, with the Ark as a footstool, means that the Israelites thought of Yahweh as a giant. Isaiah, for example, sees Yahweh in the temple and describes a figure so large that "the hem of his robe filled the temple" (Isa. 6:1). On Mount Sinai, Yahweh completely covers Moses with his hand as Yahweh passes him (Ex. 33:17–23). Interestingly, the temple at Ain Dara was practically identical to Solomon's temple, including carved cherubs guarding the sanctuary, but in its floor were carved massive footprints, about three feet long, proceeding towards the inner sanctuary where the god resided. The size of the footprints and the length between them suggests that the builders envisioned their god as being sixty to seventy feet tall—just the size we would expect Yahweh to be if he sat on a fifteen-foot throne.

Many aspects of the temple seem to have been crafted to represent a garden scene. The walls of the sanctuary were carved with "engravings of cherubim, palm trees, and open flowers" (1 Kgs. 6:29); the two pillars leading into the temple were topped with lilies and pomegranates (1 Kgs. 7:19–20); the lampstands were made with "branches," "petals," and "cups shaped like almond blossoms" (Ex. 25:33). The psalmist describes the righteous as being "like the palm tree ... they are planted in the house of Yahweh" (Ps. 92:12–13). Extending the garden metaphor, when we compare the cherubs guarding the inner sanctuary to the cherubs placed in the Garden of Eden to guard the tree of life, we can say that, in addition to being God's house, the temple represented the paradise where humans once walked with God.

The priests' primary role was to perform the rituals associated with the temple and festival days. As a general rule, the priests could trace their ancestry back to Aaron, and they were given the more important temple duties. The Levites were a kind of second-class helper charged with more menial tasks. Note that these two types of temple workers did not hold two different priesthoods. In ancient Israel, there was only one group identified with the priesthood—the priests themselves. While different priestly families did vie for control of the temple throughout the Old Testament, their battles were not debates over types or gradations of priesthood.[6]

We should note that the distinction between priests and Levites is not totally consistent throughout the Old Testament. This is because the Old Testament covers roughly 1,000 years of history, and things can change drastically in timeframes that large. (Just compare LDS Church practice from 1850 to 1950—only 100 years.) In Numbers 16 (a fairly early source) the Levites decide they want the priesthood and stage a rebellion. But by the period of Josiah, when Deuteronomy was written, the priests and Levites seem to have merged to some degree; the text even speaks of "the Levitical priests" (Deut. 17:9). Chronicles, one of the latest books in the Old Testament, gives Levites an elevated status, caring for the Ark and playing a large role in the temple (1 Chr. 15–16, 23–26). But by the time Jesus was born, the Levites had disappeared entirely.

Law as Instruction

So far, we have covered two types of legislation in the Pentateuch: societal law and cultic regulations. But there is a third category. Exodus 20:17 commands, "You shall not covet your neighbor's house." This is not a societal law, for the statute is unenforceable; you could

---

6. We see, for example, the families of Abiathar and Zadock in 1 Samuel 22:20–23 and 2 Samuel 15:24–29, both of whom end up supporting different parties in the succession battle after the death of King David (see 1 Kgs. 1:7–2:22). There was a significant faction who opposed the family of Aaron's claim to the priesthood, as seen in the numerous stories in the E source of the Pentateuch that denigrate Aaron (e.g., the golden calf in Ex. 32 and Aaron's complaint in Num. 12). But these were not different orders of priests. There is also no evidence of a separate Melchizedek priesthood at this time. Melchizedek is presented in Genesis 14:18 as a priest of "El Most High" (*'El 'Elyon*), not a priest of Yahweh, and he then disappears from the Old Testament entirely, except for a cryptic verse in Psalm 110:4. The KJV renders this verse as, "Thou art a priest for ever after the order of Melchizedek," most likely because the Christian translators were connecting it to the discussion of Melchizedek in the book of Hebrews, but the underlying Hebrew is highly ambiguous. One could just as easily render this verse, "You are a priest forever on account of Melchizedek," or even, "You are a priest forever; upon my word, a righteous king."

not take your neighbor to court if she wished she had your house. Even if you could, there is no penalty specified. Nor is the law given any cultic significance beyond the fact that it is spoken by God. No ritual will be rejected if the command is not followed, nor is the command tied to the purity or holiness of the people. Rather, this type of command is God's will for how his people should act, both in the secular and religious sphere. This definition is what the Hebrew word תורה (torah) means. The Pentateuch contains the torah of Moses, which modern translations usually render as "the law of Moses," but the phrase could equally as well be translated as "the instruction" or "the advice of Moses." Thus, in Proverbs we see a father tell his child, "Do not forsake my teaching (torah)" (Prov. 4:2), while God tells Moses in Exodus 16:28, "How long will you refuse to keep my commandments and instructions (torah)?" So the Old Testament was law to the ancient Israelites in much the same way that the Book of Mormon or Doctrine and Covenants is law to modern Latter-day Saints: it was a record of God's desires for how they should act in all spheres of life.

This definition of law reinforces what we see throughout this chapter: ancient Israelite religion was not legalistic. Israelites were not obsessed with the law any more than later Christians were; nor did they think that they could earn their way to heaven by following these rules. Thinking of law as instruction is especially useful in helping us see how the concept of covenant plays out within the Hebrew Bible.

Covenant

While the LDS Church is becoming more global, many of its teachings have been influenced by its being founded in the United States. The traditional LDS conception of covenant is a particularly striking example of this influence. Growing up in the church, I almost invariably heard covenants described as contracts: two-way promises where we fulfill our end of the bargain and, in return, God grants us certain blessings. The Doctrine and Covenants lends itself to a contractual view of obedience, particularly in the popular verses, "There is a law, irrevocably decreed in heaven before the foundations of this world, upon which all blessings are predicated—And when we obtain any blessing from God, it is by obedience to that law upon which it is predicated" (130:20–21). Covenants are presented as simply being a more formal arrangement of these commandments and blessings. When we go through a ritual to enter covenants, we see it as analogous to signing a contract that makes the obligations of each party official.

This contractual view of covenants has much to commend it, but it has a decidedly American emphasis. Contracts existed in the ancient Near East, certainly, but *covenants* were first and foremost about establishing a relationship, not entering into a legal agreement. Just as purity is determined by an item's relationship to its surroundings, and just as holiness is a question of proximity to God, so a covenant is the creation of a relationship between two people, along with attendant duties and obligations. Once two people enter a covenant, they become family.

Consider political treaties in the ancient Near East. Whenever two nations joined an alliance, they became kin. In letters, covenant-bound kings would address each other as "my brother," and each was expected to defend the other as if they were family. Amos refers to such a treaty as a "covenant of kinship" (Amos 1:9), and he expects Israel's allies to act like kin. When Edom attacks Israel in violation of its treaty, Amos calls Edom to account "because he pursued *his brother* with the sword" (Amos 1:11, emphasis mine).

The idea of a covenant creating a type of family unit lay at the base of the various Israelite tribes' relationships with each other. Though the tribes that made up Israel came from different regions and even spoke different dialects (see Judg. 12), they covenanted that they would behave toward each other as family. When they chose David as their king, the representatives of all the tribes came together and told him, "We are your bone and your flesh" (2 Sam. 5:1)—the same wording used by Adam in the Garden of Eden to describe how a man and woman would come together to create a family: "This at last is bone of my bones and flesh of my flesh. ... Therefore a man leaves his father and his mother and clings to his wife, and they become one flesh" (Gen. 2:23–24).

When the Israelite tribes covenanted to come to each other's aid in times of need, they became "one flesh," and the stories of Jacob's sons in Genesis frequently touch on how brothers are supposed to act within this covenant relationship. When Dinah is raped, Simeon and Levi put their lives at risk to defend the family honor (Gen. 34). When Joseph puts Benjamin in prison, Judah begs him to relent because of the pain it will cause their father, who happens to be named Israel (Gen. 44:18–34). When the brothers plot to kill Joseph, Judah intercedes, saying, "He is our brother, our own flesh" (Gen. 37:27). The tribal ancestors are portrayed as brothers in Genesis because the tribes had entered a "covenant of kinship" (Amos 1:9).

When equals join a covenant, they become brothers, but what about when one country conquers another? Assyria made the kingdom of Judah into a vassal state in the eighth century BCE, but Judah was a tiny speck on the map when compared to the Assyrian empire, so we would hardly expect Assyria to consider Judah its "brother." Instead, when one party to a covenant is superior to another, the superior party becomes the father, the inferior becomes the son. Assyria, in assuming the role of father to Israel, agreed to protect it from other invaders, and in return asked for tribute, loyalty, and love. While love may seem an odd request to make of a conquered people, the request is less bizarre in the context of filial duties to a father. In one typical Assyrian treaty, Esarhaddon commands the conquered people: "You shall love [the Assyrian king] as yourselves."[7]

Similarly, when God enters into covenants with people, he always does so as the superior party, and so, through the covenant, becomes the father. In his covenant with David, God says, "I will be a father to him, and he shall be a son to me" (2 Sam. 7:14), and in Psalm 2:7, a psalm most likely recited at the coronation of a new king, God says, "You are my son; today I have begotten you."

The covenant on Mount Sinai between God and Israel is presented as precisely this kind of relationship. Israel becomes God's son, and God is adopted as Israel's father. God tells the Israelites, "When Israel was a child, I loved him, and out of Egypt I called my son" (Hosea 11:1). God promises to protect the Israelites, and in return he asks for tribute (i.e., sacrifice), loyalty, and love: "You shall love Yahweh your God with all your heart, and with all your soul, and

---

7. Frank Moore Cross, *From Epic to Canon: History and Literature in Ancient Israel* (Baltimore: Johns Hopkins University Press, 1998), 10.

with all your might" (Deut. 6:5). The similarity here to the Assyrian vassal treaties is not accidental; in fact, the entire book of Deuteronomy is patterned after the Assyrian vassal treaties. Deuteronomy and the Assyrian treaties both begin with a prologue describing the history of the parties (Deut. 1–3) then present a number of stipulations that are practically identical (Deut. 4–26).[8] Both contain a series of curses that will be called down on anyone who violates the treaty. Many of the curses—and even the order they appear in—are identical (Deut. 28). Both call a series of witnesses, including "heaven and earth" (Deut. 31:28), to testify that the treaty has been ratified (Deut. 31:19–28).

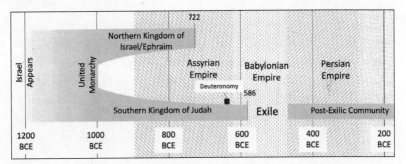

In the seventh century, Israel was a vassal to Assyria, so when Deuteronomy was written (also in the seventh century), Israel patterned its covenant with God on the covenant it had already entered into with Assyria. The message of Deuteronomy is thus that while Israel may be vassals to an earthly "father," its true father and protector would always be Yahweh. Indeed, Deuteronomy seems to have been written right as Josiah was trying to break free from Assyrian vassalage and establish Judah as an independent kingdom again.

Latter-day Saints tend to speak of Judaism as a legalistic religion obsessed with the minutiae of the law, but the parallels between the Assyrian treaties and Deuteronomy show us that ancient Israelites did not believe that following the law saved them. As vassals to Assyria, the protection Assyria offered was contingent not upon the Israelites' strict obedience to every stipulation of the treaty; rather, it

---

8. See particularly the command to love the superior party and the command that nothing be added or removed from the document (Deut. 13:1).

was contingent upon their being part of the covenant relationship. They were expected to follow the stipulations of the treaty, but obedience to these stipulations only mattered insofar as it demonstrated the people's loyalty to Assyria. The same concept held true for the law of Moses; the covenant that came to be associated with Moses and Sinai did not make Israel's salvation contingent upon how strictly the laws were observed. Rather, Israel was saved because of its relationship to Yahweh. The stipulations of the covenant were simply ways for Israel to demonstrate its loyalty. Ancient Israelites did not fret over the minutiae of the law; such fretting would have made no sense in the context of the father-son/suzerain-vassal bond envisioned in Mosaic law.

Finally, the parallels with the Assyrian treaties illuminate an important difference between modern conceptions of individualism and ancient ideas of community. Modern Western societies are individualistic, and this individualism has come to be inscribed even in the way we envision salvation: we are saved or damned as individuals—or in the words of Joseph Smith, "men will be punished for their own sins" (A of F 2). But such individualism makes no sense in the context of Assyrian vassalage. One person's choices would hardly have caused Assyria to revoke its protection of Israel. The covenant would only be nullified if the people as a whole rose up in rebellion or refused to recognize the Assyrian king as father.

Accordingly, in the Old Testament we often see individuals punished or rewarded for their actions, but individuals never gain or lose salvation.[9] Instead, Israel as a whole is either saved or cast off depending on its loyalty to Yahweh. The nature of the Mosaic covenant was communal, not individual. As a general rule, when Old Testament prophets preach, they do not call individuals to repentance for breaking individual commandments; instead, their primary concern is the community's fidelity to Yahweh. Joshua tells the people to "choose this day whom you will serve" (Josh. 24:15). Elijah, challenging the priests of Baal on Mount Carmel, demands, "If Yahweh

---

9. What exactly constituted "salvation" for biblical authors is a tricky question and is dealt with in more detail in chapter nine. The confusion is partly a function of when each text was written, for while the earliest biblical authors did not envision salvation in terms of an afterlife, the latest biblical authors did. For the original authors of Deuteronomy, salvation was predominantly defined as having Yahweh's protection in this life.

is God, follow him; but if Baal, then follow him" (1 Kgs. 18:21). The book of Isaiah opens with an invocation of the heavens and earth, the original witnesses to the covenant in Deuteronomy 31:28, where God complains, "Hear, O heavens, and listen, O earth; for Yahweh has spoken: I reared children and brought them up, but they have rebelled against me" (Isa. 1:2). In Jeremiah, God's primary complaint of Israel is that "they have forsaken me" (Jer. 2:13).

These past few chapters have shown the Old Testament to be immensely complex. The law of Moses, for example, seems in places to be a collection of societal law drawn from the ancient Near Eastern legal tradition, giving directions that a judge would need to resolve civil and criminal cases. In other places, it lays out a religious system of sacrifice and purity. In others, it seems to offer general advice for good living. Each of these laws comes from separate biblical sources written in different historical circumstances. The laws of the J or E source come from the early period of the monarchy and assume a society whose main locus of authority is the father or the town elders. The laws of Deuteronomy come from shortly before the exile, when religious and secular authority were being centralized in Jerusalem. The laws of the Priestly source come from the exile or later and deal with the creation of a religious community after the trauma of Jerusalem's destruction. Later sources rework the laws that appear in earlier sources. For example, the laws around slavery in Exodus 21 are reworked by the laws in Deuteronomy 15, which are in turn countermanded in the Priestly slavery laws of Leviticus 25. These different strands are brought together and presented as if they were given back in the time of Moses, roughly half a millennium before the sources were actually written.

All these observations hold for the narrative portions of the Pentateuch as well. And we have not even touched on some of the thornier interpretive problems. For example, to what extent does the Old Testament reflect only the literary elites' view of Israelite religion as opposed to the way Israelite religion was practiced by the average person?[10]

---

10. To give just a few examples, Exodus 20:24–26 assumes that the Israelites could offer sacrifice to God anywhere, but in Deuteronomy 12:13–25, sacrifice is only allowed to take place at the temple in Jerusalem. Did Israelites actually stop offering sacrifices

Yet I find that a complex Old Testament is much more interesting than a simple one. For religious readers, the Old Testament offers a fascinating glimpse into how the process of revelation unfolds—into how culture is intertwined with inspiration and how later generations update and expand on that initial moment of divine revelation. It brings up important questions, such as whether a law or story has to actually come from Moses to be considered binding, or whether later traditions are better or more refined than earlier ones. Are the changes in LDS Church practice from 1900 to 2000—such as the inclusion of Black members of African descent in priesthood and temple ordinances—a reflection of better understanding God's will, or are they different adaptations for different times, each iteration of church practice being as inspired as the other? For non-religious readers, a complicated Old Testament helps explain the process by which Christianity and Judaism came to be.

When the various strands of the Pentateuch were brought together, the redactor/writer tasked with creating one coherent document had some choices to make. Should he create a document that matched his own point of view? Should he choose only those stories and laws that were relevant to the people of his time? Should he change those traditions that contradicted or were no longer relevant to the way he saw Israelite religion? The fact that he did none of these—that he instead included whole sources and law codes from earlier writers—speaks to the value Israel placed on its history. Preservation was more important than creating a unified, univocal text. After seeing the emphasis Israel placed on preserving its history, we are now ready to explore another way of approaching the Old Testament: as history.

---

in other locations? Or does the law in Deuteronomy reflect more of an ideal—one that the average person never actually followed? When God commands that no images be made or worshiped, we know that the priests in the temple followed this commandment strictly, as the throne of God in the inner sanctum was left empty, but the archeological record attests that people possessed thousands of figurines and pictures of Yahweh during that time.

5

THE
OLD TESTAMENT
AS HISTORY

(Joshua-2 Kings)

Beginning with the book of Joshua, the Old Testament begins to leave the realm of myth and move closer to what we might call history. No longer is the focus on Israel's origin as a people or God's miraculous interventions on their behalf; in fact, God slowly disappears from the story altogether. In the Pentateuch we see God walking with Adam, talking with Abraham, and using Moses to send plagues down on Egypt, but when the time to conquer Canaan arrives, God's help is mostly passive, with the exception of his destruction of Jericho's walls. For the most part, God simply chooses the leaders and lets them lead. By the end of 2 Kings, the most we hear about God is that various kings either "held fast to Yahweh" (2 Kgs. 18:6) or "did not obey the voice of Yahweh" (2 Kgs. 18:12), both meant as explanations for why Israel prospers or struggles. This shift in God's portrayal, from active interventionist to behind-the-scenes worker, reflects not a decline of belief, but rather a shift in genre from myth to history.

As we saw in the previous chapters, communities do not preserve stories merely to document history; rather, the stories are meant to convey an important message. The history found in Joshua through 2 Kings was written and passed on because it helped the people to understand the most traumatic event in Israelite history: the destruction of Jerusalem and the exile in Babylon.

The Deuteronomistic History

Scholars have long recognized the books from Joshua to 2 Kings as a continuous literary unit, referring to them together as the Deuteronomistic History.[1] The history starts at around 1200 BCE and continues through the Babylonian exile in 586 BCE. This means, of course, that the final product cannot have been written before the exile actually happened (much as we see with the Pentateuch). The author of this history drew upon many sources, as he (and it most likely was a he, given the culture of the time) freely admits. Again and again, the reader is told to consult the book of Jashar (Josh. 10:13), the Book of the Acts of Solomon (1 Kgs. 11:41), the Book of the Annals of the Kings of Israel (1 Kgs. 15:31), and so on. Sometimes these sources were mined for information; other times they were incorporated wholesale into the text.

Just as we saw with the composition of the Pentateuch, the Deuteronomistic historian rarely took pains to smooth over the patchwork narrative. For example, the story about David and Goliath does not fit with its surrounding context at all. Though David is introduced in the previous chapter as a main character, he is introduced again in the Goliath story as if the reader has never heard of him (1 Sam. 17:12; cf. 16:11–13). Further, Saul shows no recollection that David is already part of his court, even though David had been inducted only a few verses before (1 Sam. 17:55; cf. 16:19). In the chapter immediately following the David and Goliath story, Saul offers to let David marry his daughter if he performs a difficult feat of war. No one seems to remember that Saul had already promised David could marry his daughter for slaying Goliath (1 Sam. 17:25; cf. 18:17). Equally problematic is how David brings Goliath's head back to Jerusalem even though Jerusalem had not yet been captured by the Israelites (1 Sam. 17:54; cf. 2 Sam. 5:6–7). Most problematic of all, the Old Testament says that Elhanan, son of Jaare-oregim, slew Goliath of Gath, "the shaft of whose spear was like a weaver's

---

1. Ruth is not included in this group; even though Ruth follows Judges in Christian Old Testaments, the book of Ruth does not fit with the surrounding narrative either in terms of style or content, and numerous indications show it to be written by a different author and in a different context than the other books of the Deuteronomistic History. Jewish Bibles accordingly place the book of Ruth toward the end of the Old Testament, not between Judges and 1 Samuel.

beam" (2 Sam. 21:19). The parallel description leaves no doubt that this is the same Goliath that David killed a few chapters earlier. Apparently, for the Deuteronomistic historian, preservation of the sources was more important than narrative consistency.

The author's penchant for leaving his source material intact also explains why the different stories within the Deuteronomistic History embrace wildly different ideas about God. The Deuteronomistic historian unquestionably sees human sacrifice as evil (2 Kgs. 16:3; 23:10), yet the book of Judges has the story of Jephthah, a leader chosen by God, who vows that if God will grant him military victory, he will sacrifice as a burnt offering the first thing that comes through his door to greet him upon his return. He is upset when his daughter comes out first, but "I have opened my mouth to Yahweh, and I cannot take back my vow" (Judg. 11:35). He performs the sacrifice with no hint of condemnation from the text.

Equally perplexing is an account in 2 Kings of Mesha, king of Moab, who is waging war against Israel. The text tells us that "when the king of Moab saw that the battle was going against him … he took his firstborn son who was to succeed him, and offered him as a burnt offering" to his god (2 Kgs. 3:26–27). The sacrifice works, and the text recounts that "great wrath came upon Israel," forcing its army to retreat (2 Kgs. 3:28). The text assumes both the efficacy of human sacrifice and the existence of another god whose assistance could be summoned by such a sacrifice, but the Deuteronomistic historian includes the story without changing it to bring it in line with his own theology.

While the individual sources and stories within the Deuteronomistic History show a broad range of literary styles and theological outlooks, the narrative surrounding them is remarkably consistent. The language is all in the same temporal dialect of Hebrew, and it uses the same vocabulary and themes when it frames the individual sources. The history focuses on key moments in Israelite history: when Joshua becomes the leader of Israel (Josh. 1), when the conquest of the land is complete and Israel formally accepts Yahweh as its god (Josh. 24), when kingship is instituted (1 Sam. 12), and when Solomon completes the temple (1 Kgs. 8). At each of these points, the main character gives a lengthy speech that contextualizes the moment—and the content and style of these speeches are identical.[2]

The term "Deuteronomistic" comes from the fact that in the places where outside sources are stitched together—where we hear the editor's voice come through—the outlook and theology overwhelmingly line up with the book of Deuteronomy. If you recall from chapter three, the book of Deuteronomy was written at a time when Israel was undergoing political and religious centralization. Sacrifices and shrines outside of Jerusalem, which had been permitted up until that point, were banned (see Ex. 20:24–26 and Deut. 12:13–25), and Israel's legal system was placed more directly under Jerusalem's control. Accordingly, the editor evaluates the kings of Israel and Judah primarily by the degree to which they follow Deuteronomic law. For example, those who permit sacrifice and the continued operation of the "high places" are condemned, while those who forbid such sacrifice are commended for doing "what was right in the sight of Yahweh" (2 Kgs. 22:2). Hardly a king passes without the author giving some remark as to what the king did regarding worship outside of Jerusalem.[3]

The narrative arc of the Deuteronomistic History culminates with the destruction of the temple and the carrying away of captive Israelites into Babylon. Thus, this history seems to be the Israelites' attempt to make sense of the trauma they had just experienced. The text asks its readers to consider how much of the blame should be given to kings, to idolatry, to political miscalculations. And it does not provide a simple answer, leaving the decision to the reader.

Joshua and the Conquest

The Deuteronomistic History begins where Deuteronomy leaves off. Moses has just died at the edge of Canaan and Joshua has been appointed to lead the Israelites in conquering the land. As the Old

---

2. The same pattern can be seen in the New Testament book of Acts, where the narrative is interrupted by speeches from Paul, Peter, Stephen, and James, all of which share a similar vocabulary and theological outlook.

3. The discovery of the "book of the law," which is usually identified with the book of Deuteronomy, is treated as a central event in the Deuteronomistic History. After the book is discovered and brought to Josiah, he completely reforms Israelite worship in line with Deuteronomic law, and the text holds nothing back in its praise: "Before him there was no king like him, who turned to Yahweh with all his heart, with all his soul, and with all his might, according to all the law of Moses; nor did any like him arise after him" (2 Kgs. 23:25).

Testament presents it, the Israelites begin with Jericho and then proceed to the other cities with a command to wipe the Canaanites out completely—"You must not let anything that breathes remain alive" (Deut. 20:16). After much bloodshed, "Joshua took the whole land, according to all that Yahweh had spoken to Moses; and Joshua gave it for an inheritance to Israel according to their tribal allotments" (Josh. 11:23).

Modern readers understandably struggle with the moral implications of this wholesale genocide. If we take the text at face value, God not only endorses enslavement and genocide, but actively commands it. Attempts to defend God in this case—such as claiming that, since God takes an eternal view, death is not as serious a punishment as we might think, or that God has a different view of morality than we do—leave me more uncomfortable than I was before the explanation. In my opinion, any belief system that justifies genocide needs a serious re-examination.

Ancient readers, however, seem not to have been bothered by it. In a cutthroat world where a people's options were usually to kill or be killed, wiping out the Canaanites might have seemed the best method for inhabiting the land. To say that ancient readers had a different moral matrix than we does not make the story any less reprehensible to a modern sensibility, but it does help us understand that the story was written in a different *zeitgeist* than our own.

Modern scholarship has added an interesting twist to the story, however. As near as we can tell, the genocide never actually happened. First, the Old Testament itself contains contradictory accounts. The book of Joshua presents an efficient conquest, with Joshua taking "the whole land" (Josh. 11:23); but only a few dozen verses later, God tells Joshua that "very much of the land still remains to be possessed" (Josh. 13:1). Indeed, the Israelites continue interacting with Canaanite cities in Israel up through the book of 2 Samuel. Similarly, Joshua 6 depicts the fall of Jericho as occurring without a fight—the walls tumbling down and the Israelites putting its citizens to the sword, but Joshua 24:11—most likely from a different source—speaks of how Jericho's leaders fought against Israel.[4]

---

4. The NRSV follows the Greek translation, rendering Joshua 24:11 as "the citizens of Jericho," but the Hebrew text reads, "the lords of Jericho fought against you."

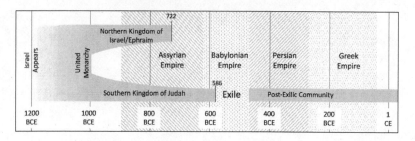

The real problem with the historicity of the conquest, however, comes not from the Old Testament, but from archaeology. The most likely date for the conquest of Jericho would be around the year 1200 BCE. The problem is, the archeological evidence is unmistakable: Jericho was uninhabited in 1200 BCE—and had been for hundreds of years.

The next stop in Joshua's conquest is the city of Ai. The Old Testament tells us that the Israelites trick the city's army into leaving the city and then run in, burn it to the ground, and slaughter the inhabitants. The archeological evidence for this conquest is even more problematic than Jericho's. Ai had been destroyed and left uninhabited in the third millennium BCE—a full thousand years before Joshua got there. In fact, the Hebrew name for the city, עי (*'ai*), literally means "ruins." Appropriate, since the city of Ai had lain in ruins long before the Israelites arrived.

The story is the same for practically every city listed in the book of Joshua. Some of the cities do show signs of having been destroyed at some point, but these destructions are separated by centuries, and they usually occur well before or well after Joshua would have lived. Others, such as Tirzah (Josh. 12:24), were continuously occupied and show no evidence of ever being destroyed. The Old Testament claims that Joshua destroyed thirty-one cities in Israel, but of these, only two or three could plausibly be attributed to an Israelite conquest—and even in these cases the attribution is tenuous.

What the archeological record does show is a marked increase in settlements around the year 1200 BCE, so there does seem to have been a population influx around this time. But most of these settlements were small villages, and, as noted in chapter two, their material culture is thoroughly Canaanite. At the end of the thirteenth century

BCE, the Egyptian Pharaoh Merneptah set up a monument at Thebes to commemorate his battles in Canaan, and his mention of Israel as one of the defeated people is our first attestation outside the Old Testament for the existence of a separate people going by this name.

So how did Israel actually end up in Canaan? Up until around 1200 BCE, Canaan was under Egyptian control. But then, during the thirteenth to tenth centuries BCE, all the major empires of the Near East fell into a steep decline, including Egypt, Assyria, Ugarit, the Hittites, and Babylonia. All these empires struggled to even stay afloat, and cities across the Near East show evidence of destruction and abandonment during this period. With the Egyptian dominance over Canaan gone, a group of small pastoral tribes from the surrounding highlands began to move into the area we now know as Israel. The migration brought the pastoralists into conflict with the farmers and city-dwellers who were already there (remember the Cain and Abel story?), and occasionally they conquered some cities and resettled them. Eventually, as the books of Judges and 1 Samuel attest, the return of powerful external forces, such as the Egyptians and Philistines, caused these tribes to band together into one cohesive political entity: Israel.[5] But by 500 BCE, as Assyria, Egypt, and Babylonia regained their empires, the entirety of Canaan was brought back under foreign control.

The book of Joshua is thus best understood as a kind of extended etiology: an exaggerated and glorified story of how Israel conquered the land and created a new nation. We can see a kernel of historical truth behind the narrative in that the Israelites did in fact migrate to the land and that there was some conflict, but the story is not primarily history. Rather, it is structured to culminate when Israel comes together in Joshua 24 and pledges to follow Yahweh. The people unite and recite as one:

> It is Yahweh our God who brought us and our ancestors up from the land of Egypt, out of the house of slavery, and who did those great signs in our sight. He protected us along all the way that we went, and among all the peoples through whom we passed; and Yahweh drove out before

---

5. Other small kingdoms had also coalesced around Israel during this same period, such as Moab and Ammon. But they would be short-lived.

us all the peoples, the Amorites who lived in the land. Therefore we also will serve Yahweh, for he is our God (Josh. 24:17–18).

In other words, Joshua blends myth and history to construct a story about how the people of Israel came to be.

Judges

The Book of Mormon presents Nephite government as going through two stages: a monarchy and a reign of judges that are democratically elected. Israelite government also goes through two stages, one ruled by judges and the other by a monarchy, but the similarity ends there. The Old Testament description of judges bears little resemblance to the Nephite model.

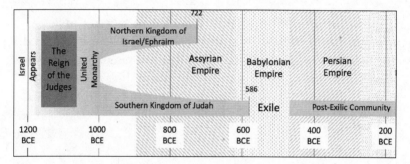

In pre-monarchic Israel, when the tribes were still a loose confederation, there was no overarching government body to which all the tribes were beholden; nor did the people, living mostly in remote villages, have a developed legal system.[6] In this early environment, when the concept of "Israel" or "Israelite" was first forming, the individual tribes would have found it difficult to fend off incursions from their more powerful neighbors, such as the Moabites or the Philistines. So whenever such an external threat arose, a charismatic leader would often take command, rally the tribes, and try to defend the people. Ehud, the first leader depicted in Judges, delivers Israel from Moab by killing the Moabite king, after which he cries out to

---

6. As we saw in the previous chapter, the earliest law code in the Old Testament, known as the Covenant Code from the J or E source, was not written until centuries later. It presupposes the existence of slaves, courts, foreigners living among the people, etc.—in other words, the kind of complicated society that would not exist until well after the monarchy was formed.

the tribes, "Follow after me; for Yahweh has given your enemies the Moabites into your hand" (Judg. 3:28). Another threat comes from a Canaanite king at Hazor (even though Joshua had supposedly burned Hazor to the ground back in Joshua 11:11–13), but Deborah delivers the Israelites by calling them to battle: "Up! For this is the day on which Yahweh has given Sisera into your hand" (Judg. 4:14). Another threat then arises from Midian, which is countered by Gideon. "He sounded the trumpet, and the Abiezrites were called out to follow him. He sent messengers throughout all Manasseh, and they too were called out to follow him. He also sent messengers to Asher, Zebulun, and Naphtali, and they went up to meet them" (Judg. 6:34–35). This pattern continues through the entire book.

These wartime leaders are called judges, and the Hebrew word "judge" (שֹׁפֵט, *shofet*) simply means "leader." Judges were not voted in; rather, they were ad hoc leaders who had risen to a particular occasion. The other tribes appear to have followed them only loosely. Notice, for example, in the verses cited above, that Gideon does not call on all the tribes. He only calls on Abiezer, Manasseh, Asher, Zebulun, and Naphtali. Deborah seems to have called most of the tribes, but only Ephraim, Benjamin, Machir, Naphtali, Zebulun, and Issachar respond, while Reuben, Gilead, Asher, and Dan ignore the summons (Judg. 5:14–23). These lists speak to the fluidity of the tribes' relationships during this period. Some groups, such as Abiezer, Gilead, and Machir, later disappear or are subsumed into the larger tribes around them. Other tribes that we later hear are part of Israel are not mentioned at all.

If the stories in Judges had been wholly invented by the Deuteronomistic historian, we would expect them to align much more closely with later traditions—at a minimum, we would expect the author to get the names and number of the twelve tribes right. That the stories portray Israel as a loose confederation of tribes is largely in line with what was happening during that period. These, and other marks of presumed authenticity, suggest that many of these traditions are quite ancient. Of course, "ancient" is not the same as "completely historically accurate," but there are grounds for supposing that the Israelite tribes indeed functioned this way before the monarchy arose.

What kinds of ancient traditions did the Deuteronomistic historian incorporate into the book of Judges? Some of them are etiological, explaining the origin of various places and traditions. For example, after rescuing Israel from a foreign enemy, Jephthah gives his daughter as a burnt offering to God, which explains part of Israelite culture. "So there arose an Israelite custom that for four days every year the daughters of Israel would go out to lament the daughter of Jephthah the Gileadite" (Judg. 11:39–40).

Other stories present the judges almost as superheroes, as we see with Samson. Samson's case is interesting, for although he is called a judge, he is never depicted filling any kind of leadership role. In fact, other Israelites seem to view him as more of a nuisance than a leader. Nor is Samson distinguished by any high virtues. If anything, he is depicted as a trickster with little regard for God's commandments. What seems to set Samson apart as a "judge" is simply the fact that he kills several thousand Philistines.

Other stories show clear marks of the Deuteronomistic historian fitting them to a particular narrative pattern: Israel sins, a foreign invader gains power, a leader rises up and calls Israel to battle, and the tribes respond to drive the threat out. But there are still swaths of original material, such as the so-called Song of Deborah in Judges 5, which, as we saw in chapter two, is likely the oldest piece of writing in the Old Testament.

The wide array of material in Judges was included because the Deuteronomistic historian wanted to tell a particular story: How Israel went from Sinai to Babylon, from standing in God's presence to becoming exiles in a foreign land. A major part of this history hinges on the political debates that later tore Israel apart: what kind of government should we have, and who should run it?

Just as the modern United States exists in the tension between federal power and states' rights, so Israel struggled with the tension between tribal and national identities. The book of Joshua shows the tribes swearing to work together as a national unit, but as the book of Judges shows, when threats arise and the tribes are called to defend Israel, they repeatedly fail to show up. Deborah laments the laxity of the tribes that did not heed her call: "Among the clans of Reuben there were great searchings of heart. Gilead stayed beyond the Jordan; and Dan, why did he abide with the ships? Asher sat still at the coast of the sea, settling down by his landings" (Judg. 5:16–17). She outright curses the city of Meroz: "Curse Meroz ... because they did not come to the help of Yahweh, to the help of Yahweh against the mighty" (Judg. 5:23). (Interestingly, the American revolutionaries sometimes invoked the curse of Meroz against those who refused to join the fight against Britain.)

When leaders do arise and temporarily unite the tribes, the people are portrayed as briefly obtaining peace, but soon slipping into moral decay until another leader calls them together to defend the land again. The depravity of Israel's situation builds until the story of Sodom is replayed, but this time men from Benjamin are the antagonists who demand that a visitor be handed over to be raped. They eventually settle on the man's concubine, whom they rape through the night, leaving her at the point of death. The narrator mocks the concept of calling the tribes to aid in a fight by showing the husband taking "a knife, and grasping his concubine he cut her into twelve pieces, limb by limb, and sent her throughout all the territory of Israel." He is summoning the people to battle, but this time against fellow Israelites (Judg. 19:29).

If Israel was to function as a national unit, it needed a system that could unite the tribes more effectively. And for the Deuteronomistic historian, that system was the monarchy. Only a king could convince the tribes to give up their autonomy and work together. The book of Judges is designed to show how life without a king could not work from a political perspective—or even a moral one. As Israel reaches its various low points, the editor repeatedly notes, "In those days there was no king in Israel; all the people did what was right in their own eyes" (Judg. 17:6; see also 18:1, 19:1, 19:25, 21:25).

Not just any king would work for Israel, however. For the Deuteronomist, that king needed to be from the Davidic dynasty. Shortly after the monarchy was formed, tribalism reared its head again, and the northern ten tribes broke away to form their own separate kingdom, asking, "What share do we have in David?" (1 Kgs. 12:16). The Deuteronomistic historian saw this split as a critical moment that moved Israel much closer to Babylonian exile. This is why Judges glorifies David and his tribe, Judah, and denigrates other potential monarchs. Saul, for instance, is implicitly criticized in the final story of Judges where his tribe, the tribe of Benjamin, rapes the man's concubine in the city of Gibeah, the city where Saul was based (1 Sam. 15:34). In the ensuing civil war, the city of Jabesh-Gilead, a city that later aligned itself with Saul, refuses to avenge the concubine's death (2 Sam. 2:4). Saul, according to the author, was not the kind of person you wanted to have as your king.

Northern kings are also criticized, as seen in the story of Gideon and Abimelech (Judg. 6–9). Gideon is from Manasseh, one of the northernmost tribes, and although he frees the Israelites from the foreigners' oppression, he creates a golden idol that the Israelites subsequently worship—just as the northern kings would eventually create two golden calves to keep the northern tribes from worshiping at Jerusalem. His son Abimelech kills seventy (!) of his brothers in order to establish himself as king, and he is soon killed by his own people as they vie for the throne. Such intrigue and assassination were a near-constant feature of the northern kingdom; almost half of all northern kings died at the hands of their successors. The northern throne passed through almost a dozen different families in only two centuries. Compare this chaos with the constancy of the tribe of Judah—David's tribe. Judges tells us, "Yahweh was with Judah" (Judg. 1:19), so that when Israel is called upon to avenge the raped concubine, God chooses Judah to take the lead (Judg. 20:18).

Samuel and Kings

The books of 1–2 Samuel and 1–2 Kings are the closest the Old Testament comes to qualifying as history (at least, our modern conception of it). In these books, the author continues to draw from numerous sources, but the sources are much more reliable. God mostly retreats to the background, and the Deuteronomist turns his

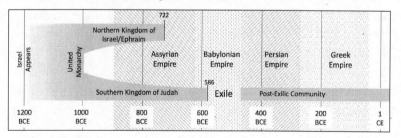

attention to four pivotal moments in Israelite history: the establishment of a king, the splitting of the kingdom between North and South, the destruction of the Northern Kingdom at the hands of Assyria, and the destruction of the Southern Kingdom at the hands of Babylonia. We explore each of these events in turn.

The Establishment of a King

After its appearance in Canaan around 1200 BCE, Israel existed as a loose confederation of tribes for roughly two centuries before finally uniting under a king. 1 Samuel details the establishment of Saul's kingship, tracks his brief moment of favor with God, and then shows his downfall. 2 Samuel deals almost exclusively with David, the founder of the Davidic dynasty and, in the eyes of the Deuteronomist, the true and rightful king of Israel.

Saul likely did exist, but since our only records of him come from the Old Testament itself, we know little of him as a historical personage. However, we know a great deal about Saul the literary character. In 1 Samuel, Saul serves as a foil to David—a cautionary tale about the potential pitfalls of kingship. Saul is the hook upon which the Deuteronomistic editor hangs all the negative traditions about kingship.[7]

Despite Saul's failure as a king, kingship becomes deeply ingrained in Israel's history and religion. Kings take it upon themselves to offer sacrifices, apparently with no objection from the priests (2 Sam. 6:13). Kings both design and build the temple (1 Kgs. 5–8), the central focus of Israelite worship. According to Chronicles, David even organizes the duties of the Levites and temple musicians. And when the northern tribes secede, it is King Jeroboam who sets up the northern system of worship at Bethel and Dan. Kings become such central figures that the Old Testament records David's sons as being priests even though David is not a descendant of Levi (2 Sam. 8:18).

Israelite religion soon begins to orient itself around the king. Solomon constructs the temple in the capital city of Jerusalem with

---

7. See, for example, Saul's performance of unauthorized sacrifice (1 Sam. 13) or his tendency to issue poorly conceived decrees (1 Sam. 14:24–30). Saul's coronation is also the occasion on which the author portrays kingship as a rejection of God (1 Sam. 8:7) and an invitation to oppression (1 Sam. 8:11–18). While the prophets overwhelmingly see kingship as positive, these negative traditions do occasionally find expression in prophetic writings, such as in Hosea 13:11, where God declares, "I gave you a king in my anger."

the palace lying between the temple and the rest of the city. From that point on, no one accesses God's house without literally going through the king's house. The king is presented as God's son: chosen and protected by him. Much as happened in other ancient Near Eastern cultures, the king begins to be seen as semi-divine. This merging of the human and divine can be seen in verses such as Isaiah 9:6–7: "For a child has been born for us, a son given to us; authority rests upon his shoulders; and he is named Wonderful Counselor, Mighty God, Everlasting Father, Prince of Peace. His authority shall grow continually, and there shall be endless peace for the throne of David and his kingdom." Such a description, where the king is referred to as "Mighty God," would not be out of place in any major Egyptian, Assyrian, or Babylonian record from this period.

If those verses sound familiar, it is because Israel foresaw its temporal salvation in terms of a future king—a Messiah. Once again, we see the merging of human and divine traits. It is no coincidence that many of the Old Testament passages later applied to Jesus were originally written in reference to an Israelite monarch.

The advent of kingship also caused Israel to conceptualize the divine in royal terms. As we saw in the previous chapter, the covenant at Mount Sinai created a family relationship between God and Israel, with God as father and Israel as son. But with the establishment of kingship, that covenantal relationship faded to the background. God became primarily a king, and Israel became part of God's kingdom. If you read through the Old Testament from beginning to end, you find that references to God as king far outnumber references to God as father.

In fact, beginning at the establishment of kingship, the concept of "Zion" practically takes over the Old Testament. Zion in the Old Testament was not a loose concept dealing with "the pure in heart" or God's special people; rather, Zion was the mountain upon which Jerusalem was built. While the covenant with Moses took place on Mount Sinai, the covenant with David took place on Mount Zion, and these two mountains and covenants comprise the two main ways that Israelites came to think about God.

Starting with King David, God's covenant on Mount Zion in many ways comes to eclipse the covenant made with the people on Mount

Sinai. When David is first established as king, God's promises to David's offspring are both extensive and unconditional: "I will establish the throne of his kingdom forever. I will be a father to him, and he shall be a son to me" (2 Sam. 7:13–14). Here it is the king, not Israel as a whole, who takes his place as God's son. Like any son, that king may occasionally need correction, but God makes clear that any punishment will be limited: "I will not take my steadfast love from him. ... Your house and your kingdom shall be made sure forever before me; your throne shall be established forever" (2 Sam. 7:15–16). God promises that no matter what happens, and no matter how a king might stray from the right path, God will always preserve the monarchy.

Accordingly, when Israel is threatened with annihilation, the people overwhelmingly turn to the Davidic covenant and God's promises regarding Zion for comfort, not to the covenantal promises of Sinai. According to Isaiah, God says that he will "defend this city to save it," not because of anything promised through the law of Moses, but "for the sake of my servant David" (Isa. 37:35). Since God explicitly promised that Zion would never fall, the mountain and temple came to be seen as physical manifestations of God's covenantal loyalty. As the psalmist says, "Those who trust in Yahweh are like Mount Zion, *which cannot be moved*, but abides forever. As the mountains surround Jerusalem, so Yahweh surrounds his people, from this time on and forevermore" (Ps. 125:1–2). Zion is invoked constantly throughout the Old Testament: Yahweh builds it up (Ps. 102:16), he secures the kings' rule from it (Ps. 110:2), he blesses the people from it (Ps. 134:3), he redeems it (Isa. 1:27), he issues the law from it (Isa. 2:3, Micah 4:2), his glory protects it (Isa. 4:5), and it is a refuge (Jer. 4:6, Joel 3:16). The list goes on. Sinai, on the other hand, is only mentioned nine times outside of the Pentateuch.

The Deuteronomistic historian was deeply influenced by the covenant at Sinai (indeed, it is why modern scholars refer to him as "Deuteronomistic") and he judges every king based on the degree to which he follows the laws of Deuteronomy. Yet he also gives pride of place to the Davidic covenant, and the Davidic monarch is always the most important character in his history. The books of Judges through 2 Kings thus provide an interesting window into the tension between these two covenants.

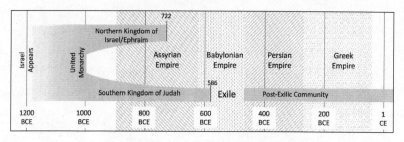

The Divided Kingdom and the
Destruction of North and South

David's son Solomon was the last king to rule over a united kingdom. Upon Solomon's death, Jeroboam led the northern ten tribes as they broke away to form a separate kingdom, referred to as either the Kingdom of Israel or Ephraim. The southern kingdom continued to be ruled by a Davidic monarch from Zion/Jerusalem; it was called the Kingdom of Judah. The names are confusing; the term "Israelite" can refer either to both the northern and southern kingdoms or to only the northern Kingdom of Israel. In this book, I use the terms "Israel" and "Israelite" to indicate both kingdoms, but I specify when I refer only to the northern kingdom. The Old Testament is much looser in its usage.

For the Deuteronomistic historian, the split between Judah and northern Israel was one of the moments that sealed the two nations' fate. The northern tribes' secession weakened both kingdoms and left them open to conquest. It also represented a rejection of God's promised protection to David (see 1 Kgs. 12:19). The northern tribes are thus portrayed as apostates in every major respect. The two golden calves set up by Jeroboam, most likely intended as thrones for Yahweh (just as the half-animal cherubs in the temple made up Yahweh's throne) are described simply as idols. Northern kings are portrayed as killing the prophets and leading the people after Baal, even though, as we have seen, Baal and Yahweh had mostly merged by this point.

The northern Kingdom of Israel only lasted for about two centuries before it was swallowed up by the rising Assyrian empire in 722 BCE—a fate that Judah only narrowly escaped by submitting itself as an Assyrian vassal state. (If you recall, the book of Deuteronomy is patterned after the Assyrian vassal treaties, which Judah experienced firsthand.) The Assyrians kept their conquered territories in line by deporting many locals and importing many foreigners—the general idea being that if the people had less in common, they would be less likely to revolt. Thus, many people from the northern ten tribes were scattered throughout the Assyrian empire, a fate that gave rise to the idea of the "lost ten tribes."

But shortly after the northern kingdom fell, Assyria started losing ground to its southern opponents, the Babylonians, and within the next century Babylonia rose to dominate the Near East. The Kingdom of Judah managed to hold out for a century and a half longer than the northern kingdom had, but in 586 BCE Babylonia conquered Jerusalem and destroyed the temple.

The Babylonians took a different approach to running an empire. Rather than scattering its conquered peoples, they took much of the population and resettled it in a single spot elsewhere in Babylonia. The idea was that you were much less likely to revolt if your family (1) was still alive, (2) was living happily in Babylonia, and (3) might be killed if you tried to fight for independence.

This tactic shaped the Old Testament profoundly. History may be written by the victors, but in the Old Testament's case, religion was written by the survivors, because at this point, the Old Testament becomes a southern book. The northern Kingdom of Israel had its own traditions, its own prophets, and its own emphases, but when the Assyrians scattered those tribes, their traditions mostly died out. Of the dozen or so prophets included in the Old Testament, only Hosea comes from the north. You can tell because in Hosea, Moses and Sinai are central to God's relationship with his people, but the covenant at Zion goes unmentioned. Israel—not the king—is God's son (Hosea 11:1), and kingship itself is seen as a curse (see Hosea 13:11). Only in Hosea do we see that people referred to Yahweh as "My Baal" (Hosea 2:16).

When the northern kingdom was destroyed, refugees flooded into Judah, bringing many of their writings with them. Some of these writings were incorporated into the Old Testament, such as the Elijah and Elisha narratives in the Deuteronomistic History, and many scholars believe that the E source of the Pentateuch derived from the north. For the most part, however, these northern traditions are lost; we see them only through the eyes of their southern neighbors. It was the Judeans, not the northern tribes, that ultimately compiled the Old Testament we have today. Hence, the religion that emerged after exile is known as Judah-ism, or Judaism, while scholars refer to pre-exilic religion as simply "Israelite religion."

For the Deuteronomistic historian, the secession of the northern tribes marked a breach in God's covenant with David, and their conquest naturally followed. The Davidic monarchy now stood alone in its fight against the giants of the Assyrian and Babylonian empires, giving new meaning to the David and Goliath story.

Two covenants governed the Kingdom of Judah's fate: the conditional Mosaic covenant at Sinai that decreed destruction if it were violated, and the unconditional Davidic covenant at Zion that promised the monarchy would never fall. The Deuteronomistic historian resolves these competing covenants by first painting the destruction of Jerusalem as being a direct result of the Israelites violating the covenant at Sinai and then urging the reader to imagine what it might mean for God to keep his promises to David. This approach plays out in the history's odd final scene. Jerusalem has been destroyed and its people carried off captive to Babylonia. But a small ray of hope is held out for the Davidic monarch: Jehoiachin is released from prison and brought to the Babylonian emperor's table, "above the other seats of the kings who were with him in Babylon" (2 Kgs. 25:28). Was this God's way of honoring the Davidic covenant? Is the editor implying that the Davidic monarchy will one day be restored? The question is ultimately left for readers to answer as they look back on the sweep of Israelite history. It is this thought-provoking ending to an epic story that makes the Deuteronomistic History such a work of art.

6

THE
OLD TESTAMENT
AS REVISIONIST HISTORY

(1–2 Chronicles)

In my high school history classes, I learned a history that seemed set in stone. I was taught a series of facts that combined to paint a broad picture of where society had been. It seemed to me that while learning more facts might let me see the picture in greater detail, the picture itself would not change. Imagine my surprise the first time I sat down to read a book whose picture of history did not match my own. My picture of history, as it turned out, had been shaped by the fact that I learned it at the end of the twentieth century. So my teachers and books focused on the Civil Rights movement but not the LGBTQ movement. We talked about states' rights and the American Revolution but not women's rights and Abigail Adams. As time has passed and the world has changed, so has the focus of those who write our history books, making our current picture of history look decidedly different from before. If you want to see this change firsthand, just go to your local library, check out a history book written in the 1950s, and notice how it treats, say, Jim Crow segregation.

The changes I have seen in the teaching of American history have happened in only a few decades, but the Old Testament was written over the course of roughly a thousand years. The passage of time changes the way people see their own history. Their concerns shift, their sensibilities change, and the broad picture they create takes on new meaning in light of recent events. As we saw in the last chapter, the Deuteronomistic History was written during or shortly after the exile, when Israel was wondering how something so traumatic could have happened. But eventually exile came to an end and the Israelites returned to Jerusalem. Israelite religion changed drastically, the temple was rebuilt, and instead of a reinstatement of the Davidic monarchy, the Persian empire took over as the Israelites' rulers. In this new situation, the most pressing question was, "What happens now?" The books of 1 and 2 Chronicles helped answer that question.

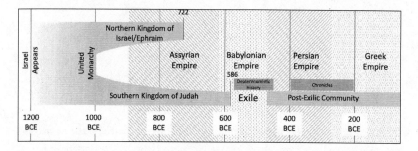

Chronicles was most likely written in the fifth or fourth century BCE, well after exile had ended.[1] By this period, the Deuteronomistic History had become less relevant, so someone decided to update it. The Chronicler, as he is called, created his new history as any good historian does: by stealing from the work of others. He took the Deuteronomistic History as his base and rewrote the story, often copying entire stretches of the text verbatim and changing anything that he felt needed it.

The Devil's in the Details

After reading Samuel and Kings, Chronicles can feel a bit repetitive. But the differences between the two stories tell us a great deal about how Israelite beliefs and concerns had changed. For example, up until this point, Satan is practically nowhere to be found. In the Garden of Eden, Genesis recounts that Adam and Eve were tempted by a serpent, not Satan or the devil. Satan does not need to lead

---

1. The late date for Chronicles is based on (1) its temporal dialect, which is much later than the Deuteronomistic History, (2) its familiarity with an almost fully formed Old Testament (see below), and (3) the inclusion of Cyrus's decree in 2 Chronicles 36, which means the book cannot have been written earlier than the Persian period (from the late sixth to the late fourth century).

humankind to sin; people sin all on their own, "for the inclination of the human heart is evil from youth" (Gen. 8:21).

In fact, nowhere is sin or evil ascribed to the influence of the devil. They always come either from humans themselves or from God. God is the one who hardens Pharaoh's heart (Ex. 9:12), and he is the one who sends an evil spirit upon Saul (1 Sam. 16:14). In Isaiah 45:7 God admits to creating both peace and evil. Amos asks rhetorically, "Does disaster [literally "evil"] befall a city, unless Yahweh has done it?" (Amos 3:6). As with every other question in this chapter of Amos, the implied answer is "no." The only comfort the Israelites can take is in the next verse where it is said that God will give warning before doing something evil: "Surely the Lord Yahweh does nothing, without revealing his secret to his servants the prophets" (Amos 3:7).

After the exile and the fall of Babylon, however, Israel came under the control of the Persians, who believed in Zoroastrianism. In Zoroastrianism, the divine world is divided between two forces: one fully good and one fully evil. Soon, the Israelites began to reconsider their own beliefs, and the idea of a devil began to emerge. Since God was often envisioned as judging in a divine courtroom, this evil influence was first conceptualized as a plaintiff bringing an accusation against someone. The Hebrew word for a plaintiff, שׂטן (satan), stuck, and to this day the devil is often referred to as Satan.

We see this theological development at work in Chronicles—one of the few books written during the Persian period. Take, for example, the story of David counting the people. In 2 Samuel God provokes David to take a census, then punishes him for it: "Again the anger of Yahweh was kindled against Israel, and he incited David against them, saying, 'Go, count the people of Israel and Judah'" (2 Sam. 24:1). The idea of evil coming from God fit perfectly within the Deuteronomistic historian's worldview, but for the Chronicler, a divine being tempting humans to sin sounded more like the devil than God. So Chronicles renders this verse quite differently: "Satan stood up against Israel, and incited David to count the people of Israel" (1 Chr. 21:1).

Satan appears in other Persian-era books as well, such as Zechariah where the idea of Satan as a plaintiff/accuser comes to the fore. Zechariah writes that he saw in a vision "the high priest Joshua standing before the angel of Yahweh, and Satan standing at his right hand to accuse him. And Yahweh said to Satan, 'Yahweh rebuke you, O Satan!'" (Zech. 3:1–2). Daniel, which is the latest book written in the Old Testament, shows angels fighting against "the prince of the kingdom of Persia" (Dan. 10:13), in other words, Satan.

People of the Book: Judaism as a Biblical Religion

As we saw in previous chapters, written traditions had long existed in ancient Israel. The J and E sources were most likely written during the early centuries of the monarchy, and the Deuteronomistic historian drew on a wide array of sources in compiling his history. But it is not until after the exile that we begin to see these traditions come together into an authoritative collection. Only with Ezra and Nehemiah—the first leaders to bring the Israelites back from exile—do we hear of "the book of Moses" (Ezra 6:18) or "the book of the law of Moses" (Neh. 8:1). In other words, this is the period where we watch the transition from Israelite religion to Judaism occur.

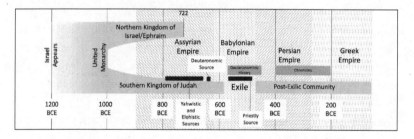

Chronicles clearly had access to biblical sources the Deuteronomistic historian did not. When the exile occurs, for example, it is "to fulfill the word of Yahweh by the mouth of Jeremiah" (2 Chr. 36:21). When Jehoshaphat encourages the people to listen to the prophets, he uses language borrowed from Isaiah 7:9 (2 Chr. 20:20). References appear to Psalms, Ruth, Ezekiel, and the newly combined sources of the Pentateuch. Indeed, the combination of these sources produced problems that the Chronicler had to solve. Every year, for example, families had to cook the Passover lamb, but the Pentateuch gives two contradictory commandments about how to cook it. Exodus 12:9 states that the Passover lamb must be roasted with fire, not boiled in water. Deuteronomy 16:7, however, says that the Passover lamb must be boiled. These two injunctions come from different time periods, so when the sources of the Pentateuch were combined, readers were faced with a dilemma: should the lamb be boiled or roasted? The Chronicler found a way to harmonize the two commands: in his description of the Passover celebrated by Josiah, he says that the people "boiled the Passover lamb with fire" (2 Chr. 35:13, my translation), combining elements from both verses.

Bringing a collection of authoritative writings together during the exilic or post-exilic period helped move Judaism toward becoming a biblical religion. In other words, answers to difficult questions were no longer found in the latest decree from the Davidic monarch, but rather from the sacred writings—the groups of texts that would eventually turn into scripture. Chronicles gives us a front-row seat to how this process played out. Over and over again we see the Chronicler changing the Deuteronomistic history in an effort to harmonize it with other scriptures.

For example, we saw earlier that, according to Amos, "Surely the Lord Yahweh does nothing, without revealing his secret to his servants the prophets" (Amos 3:7). If this is true, then why, in the Deuteronomistic History, did so few prophets foretell the impending exile? To fix this problem, the Chronicler inserts a half-dozen prophets throughout his version of the story, where God "sent persistently to [the people] by his messengers ... but they kept mocking the messengers of God, despising his words, and scoffing at his prophets" (2 Chr. 36:15–16).

Another major problem Chronicles addresses is the idea, pervasive in earlier biblical literature, that God could punish someone for the sins of their fathers (see Ex. 20:5). In the Deuteronomistic History, the fall of Jerusalem is attributed not to the sins of the final king, but to the sins of Manasseh, a king who had died a half-century before exile took place. According to 2 Kings, the later monarchs tried to do right but could not avert God's anger "because of all the provocations with which Manasseh had provoked him" (2 Kgs. 23:26). But Ezekiel, one of the prophets active during the exile, had gone out of his way to debunk the idea that God punished people for the sins of others. "The person who sins shall die," Ezekiel says.

"A child shall not suffer for the iniquity of a parent, nor a parent suffer for the iniquity of a child; the righteousness of the righteous shall be his own, and the wickedness of the wicked shall be his own" (Ezek. 18:20).

To fix this problem, the Chronicler does not include the passages that attribute the fall of Jerusalem to Manasseh. In fact, he shies away from blaming any king at all. If the people were killed, then—according to Ezekiel—the people must have been sinful, so the Chronicler inserts widespread sin into the places where the Deuteronomistic historian had only blamed the king. In 2 Chronicles 36:14, for example, just before the fall of Jerusalem, the Chronicler inserts a verse claiming that "all the leading priests and the people also were exceedingly unfaithful." Thus, God's judgment against Judah and Jerusalem was justified.

In fact, the Chronicler takes the idea of individual punishment one step farther. In Samuel and Kings, individuals can be—and often are—sinful but prosperous. Such is the case with Manasseh, whose sins take up all of 2 Kings 21 but who yet reigns a total of fifty-five years (2 Kgs. 21:1). How could someone so wicked be blessed with a long and prosperous reign? To solve this problem, Chronicles invents a story about Manasseh repenting. The king of Assyria "took Manasseh captive in manacles, bound him with fetters, and brought him to Babylon," where Manasseh repents of all his evil and is eventually restored to his throne (2 Chr. 33:11). Assyria and Babylonia were warring empires, so the odds of an Assyrian king having actually taken a prisoner to Babylon are pretty slim, but the story does neatly solve the problem of God blessing the sinful Manasseh.

Similarly, if anything bad happens to a king, Chronicles needs to insert a sin into the story to preserve God's justice. In 2 Kings, Uzziah "did what was right in the sight of Yahweh," yet God "struck the king, so that he was leprous to the day of his death" (2 Kgs. 15:3–5). Why would God have struck a righteous king? The Chronicler tidies things up by telling a story about how Uzziah grew proud and tried to make an offering in the temple despite not being a priest. His violation of the temple caused his leprosy (2 Chr. 26:16–21).

This revisionist tendency in Chronicles finds its fullest expression with David. David receives some of the greatest blessings recorded in scripture, yet, according to the account in Samuel, he was also guilty of serious sin. To ameliorate this situation, Chronicles simply takes out the sins. David's affair with Bathsheba and his murder of Uriah are never even mentioned. The prophet Nathan no longer condemns David's actions; David does not spend time fighting for the Philistines; and he does not lose his temper and threaten to kill Nabal. The Chronicler deletes every questionable action from David's life.

Making the Text Relevant

The Chronicler's primary goal with these revisions was to make the text more relevant to the people of his time. While the Deuteronomistic History explained how the people had arrived in exile, the Chronicler was writing to people who had never lived in exile. The Persian empire that currently ruled over them had been largely benign, even allowing them to rebuild the temple and worship as they pleased.

Early in the Persian period, numerous authors had held out hope that the Davidic monarchy would be reestablished. Zerubbabel, a descendant of David, is promised in Haggai that God would "overthrow the throne of kingdoms" and "take you, O Zerubbabel ... and make you like a signet ring" (Hag. 2:22–23)—a promise that never came to fruition. Zechariah likewise envisions a government led by a Davidic king (Zech. 4). But by the time Chronicles was written, that hope had largely faded. Life under the Persians was not that bad, and the people knew that a war for independence would be a losing gamble.

This is the setting in which the Chronicler reimagined the significance of the Davidic covenant. In 2 Samuel, God promises that a Davidic monarch would always sit upon the throne in Jerusalem, saying that "your house and your kingdom shall be made sure forever" (2 Sam. 7:16). In Chronicles, however, God's promise centers not on a monarch, but on the temple. No longer is it "your house and your kingdom" that God establishes; instead, God confirms the monarch "in *my* house and in *my* kingdom forever" (1 Chr. 17:14). God still has a unique covenant with David, but this covenant is no longer one of unconditional protection for the city. Now, David's favored position is a mere accessory to the establishment of God's house, i.e., the temple.

103

The temple becomes an almost obsessive focus for the Chronicler, for in a post-exilic, Persian context, the temple was Israel's physical reminder of the ultimate kingship of God. Thus the Chronicler cleans up David's life to make him worthy of this temple-centered covenant. He also devotes significant space to describing how David organizes the priests, Levites, singers, and even the materials for building the future temple. The Chronicler's message is that even though Israel is subject to the Persian empire, God is their true king, and the temple—not the monarch—is what really matters. The final verse of the Deuteronomistic History leaves open the possibility that the Davidic monarch will be restored. But the final verse of 2 Chronicles ends with Persian emperor's command: "Yahweh, the God of heaven, has given me all the kingdoms of the earth, and he has charged me to build him a house at Jerusalem, which is in Judah. Whoever is among you of all his people, may Yahweh his God be with him! Let him go up" (2 Chr. 36:23). The Chronicler portrays Persia's dominance over Israel as ordained by God, and God accompanies the people who return to build up the temple.

David is likewise portrayed as recognizing the people's precarious position. As he finishes preparing the temple materials, Chronicles has David praying, "We are aliens and transients before you, as were all our ancestors; our days on the earth are like a shadow, and there is no hope"—a statement that seems primarily intended to describe post-exilic Israel (1 Chr. 29:15). Yet the temple is this people's anchor. They offer sacrifices "freely and joyously." And so that the reader does not miss the point, David goes on to implore: "keep forever such purposes and thoughts in the hearts of your people, and direct their hearts toward you" (1 Chr. 29:17–18). Chronicles uses David to focus the people's attention on the temple at Jerusalem.

Rewriting History

As we have seen over and over again in this book, the authors in the Old Testament did not care about history for its own sake. The author of J did not include the stories of Jacob and his sons because they were historically accurate; he included them because they conveyed the later relationships between the tribes. The Priestly source attributed its laws to Moses not because Moses actually promulgated those laws, but because Moses was seen as a foundational figure in Israel and attributing the Priestly laws to him conveyed how integral these laws were to the functioning of Israelite society. We know that the conquest of Canaan never happened, but the stories about Joshua gave the Israelites a sense of common origin and destiny. As we move farther into the Deuteronomistic History, more and more of the events it describes are historically verifiable, but the Deuteronomistic historian did not include them because they actually happened; he included them because they contributed to the story he was trying to tell.

If accuracy was not these authors' primary aim, it makes little sense to judge the "truthfulness" of the Old Testament by its historicity. The writers of the Old Testament used myth, legend, stories, law, *and* history to tell a particular story. Since we have access to the traditions the Chronicler used, we can watch him change them to create a narrative relevant to his own day. His editing was so pervasive that it would be more accurate to say that he wrote a revisionist history; reexamining the old stories to develop a new grand narrative.

If the Chronicler were a modern historian, he would doubtlessly be skewered by the academic community. He changes the facts he disagrees with; he deletes entire episodes once central to the story; he makes up entire narratives to fix perceived problems in the text. Yet despite what appears to us to be a lack of regard for factual accuracy, the Old Testament nevertheless bears witness to a surprising urge on the part of the Israelites to preserve and maintain their history. Between Chronicles and the Deuteronomistic History, the Old Testament preserves not one, but two extensive histories of its people, even though Chronicles seems designed to replace the Deuteronomistic History. Similarly, when the Pentateuch was compiled, the editor did not throw out the earlier versions of the story; instead, all the separate sources were combined into one flowing narrative. Contradictory laws were placed side by side, and narrative inconsistencies were left to stand because the preservation of tradition was more important than only having the "right" version of the story. We see the same process at work in the Deuteronomistic History. When that historian used other sources, he often incorporated those sources wholesale, even when they presented problems for the narrative flow or contradicted his own worldview. The New Testament books of Matthew, Mark, Luke, and John work in much the same way, where four separate histories are preserved rather than presenting only one official version of Jesus' life. In all these cases, both the revision of later authors and the preservation of older sources greatly enrich our understanding not only of the events in question but also of how the Israelites changed as they made meaning of these events.

7

THE
OLD TESTAMENT
AS PROPHECY

(Isaiah–Malachi)

For many people today, the Old Testament no longer functions as law. Its myths, stories, and histories are increasingly irrelevant as modern cultural touchstones. Gone are the days when characters such as David or Solomon were central characters in Western art and literature. For many believers, however, the Old Testament continues to be relevant as a source of prophecy, predicting such things as the coming of Jesus Christ, the Book of Mormon, the latter-day Restoration, and the end of the world. These readers use the Old Testament to interpret events that have already happened and predict how the future will unfold. But despite their central position in Christian theology, the prophetic works, such as Isaiah, Jeremiah, and Amos, are among the most difficult to interpret in the Old Testament. It is no accident that most modern LDS attempts to read the Book of Mormon flounder in 2 Nephi when Nephi begins to quote Isaiah at length. In this chapter, we try to make these books more comprehensible by focusing on the context, purpose, and conventions of prophetic writing.

Prophecy in the Old Testament

Before we begin, we need to understand that Israelite prophecy was not a unique phenomenon. Israel was deeply enmeshed in the culture of ancient Near Eastern divination. The Old Testament bears ample witness to the prevalence of dream interpretation (Gen. 40), necromancy (1 Sam. 28:7), casting lots to determine God's will (Lev.

THE OLD TESTAMENT FOR LATTER-DAY SAINTS

16:8), enchantments (2 Kgs. 21:6), and wizards (Deut. 18:10–11). Prophecy was one branch of divination. It differed from the others in that a prophet would predict the future not by observing signs, but by receiving a direct message from the gods. Essentially every ancient Near Eastern culture had such prophets.

Members of the LDS Church tend to assume that biblical prophets functioned much like modern LDS prophets—leading an ecclesiastical organization and giving talks that reach a wide audience. But in ancient Israel there was no organized church, and prophets tended to embrace the exact opposite of the social conservatism implied by modern apostles' business suits. Dozens, or even hundreds, of prophets were active simultaneously, and most looked and acted more like the prophets of Baal and Marduk than modern LDS prophets.

Biblical prophecy bears all the hallmarks of ancient Near Eastern divination. For example, prophets would often fall into trance-like states as they communicated with the gods. Their contact with the divine realm would often lead them to ecstatic crazes. When Saul was moved upon to prophesy, he "fell into a prophetic frenzy ... stripped off his clothes, and ... lay naked all that day and all that night" (1 Sam. 19:23–24)—an action reminiscent of Isaiah's walking around Jerusalem naked for three years (Isa. 20:3). In 2 Kings 9:11–12, the prophet is called a "madman," and the king dismisses him: "You know the sort and how they babble." When they wanted to communicate with the divine, Israelite prophets would often use music to fall into their trances (2 Kgs. 34:14–15). After receiving a message, they would sometimes use symbolic sign-acts such as carrying baggage while blindfolded (Ezek. 12:3–6), burying a loincloth (Jer. 13:1–7), or marrying a prostitute (Hosea 1:2). The reputation of prophets as madmen was so pervasive that Amos even rejected the title, claiming, "I am no prophet" (Amos 7:14).

Some prophets in the Old Testament, such as Elijah and Elisha, are described primarily as miracle workers, causing axes to float, rain to cease, and the dead to revive. These miracle-working prophets left no written collection of oracles; all we have are secondhand accounts of their deeds. Other prophets, such as Isaiah and Jeremiah, have no recorded miracles at all. Their legacies are the books they wrote about Israel and its neighbors. Some prophets, like Samuel, seem like local fortune-tellers, the kind of people who, for a fee, could tell you where to find your lost donkeys (1 Sam. 9:1–7). Others, such as Nathan, are more analogous to royal counselors (2 Sam. 7).

Prophecy addressed a wide range of subjects, but one of its unifying characteristics throughout the entire ancient Near East was that prophecy was always thoroughly political. The prophets' involvement in political affairs is often surprising to modern readers, but it pervades the text. Elisha's counsel pushes Hazael to murder the king of Aram and take his throne (2 Kgs. 8:7–15); Ahijah convinces Jeroboam to take the northern ten tribes and break away from the Davidic monarch (1 Kgs. 11:29–39); Isaiah pushes Ahaz to ignore the alliance between Damascus and Samaria (Isa. 7); and Hosea berates the northern kingdom for seeking help from Assyria (Hosea 5:13). Kings controlled the state religion, so prophets invariably found themselves either supporting or attacking them. It is no accident, then, that prophecy in the Old Testament rises and falls with kingship. Prophets enter the scene around the time of the first king, Saul, and essentially disappear with Babylonian captivity and the abolition of an independent monarchy. The prophetic portions of the Old Testament are usually divided according to the prophets acting in early Israel, those active during the Assyrian crisis, those active during Babylonia's rise to power, and those operating during and after the exile.

So, if we want to understand the prophetic books, we must understand the political movements around Judah and the northern kingdom of Israel. A book such as Ezekiel, for example, is incomprehensible without understanding both the conventions that governed prophecy in the ancient Near East and the Babylonian conquest of Jerusalem.

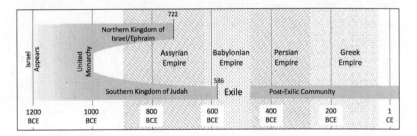

Israel emerged in the thirteenth and twelfth centuries BCE during a time known as the Bronze Age collapse, when all the major Near

Eastern empires went into a period of decline. By the eleventh century these empires had regained some of their power, and their increasing encroachment into Israel pushed the tribes to unite under a monarchy. It is in this context that we see the earliest of Israel's prophets, such as Elijah and Elisha.

By the eighth century BCE Assyria had risen as the dominant empire, and the small, divided kingdoms of Israel and Judah were essentially powerless against it. By 722 BCE the northern kingdom of Israel had fallen to Assyria, and by 701 BCE the southern kingdom of Judah had survived only because it submitted as an Assyrian vassal state, paying tribute and homage to the emperor. This is the context in which prophets such as Isaiah, Micah, Hosea, and Amos operated. Their books are suffused with the threat of Assyrian conquest, "See, you have heard what the kings of Assyria have done to all lands, destroying them utterly. Shall you be delivered?" (Isa. 37:11).

As the seventh century wore on, Babylonia came to power. Within a few short years it would destroy the Assyrians and establish an empire stretching from modern-day Iran to Egypt. Accordingly, Israelite prophets changed their focus to the new Babylonian threat. It is in this context that Jeremiah, Ezekiel, and Nahum were active, and it is here that the Book of Mormon places Lehi. The prophets of the Babylonian period focused on the temple, on God's promises at Sinai and to David, and on what a life in exile would mean. In 586, King Nebuchadnezzar laid siege to Jerusalem, captured it, and carried the people off to Babylon, thus ending ancient Israel's brief period of political autonomy.

The Persian King Cyrus captured Babylon in 539 BCE and allowed the Jews to return to the land of Israel and rebuild the temple. This return was initially met with euphoria. Prophets such as Haggai and Zechariah prophesied a return of the Davidic monarchy and the reestablishment of an independent Jewish state. But, as we saw in Chronicles, within a few decades that hope had largely died. Soon apocalyptic prophecy arose, the book of Daniel being one of its most popular examples.

Prophecy, Then and Now

With all this in mind, how should we approach these books of prophecy?

Should we treat prophetic oracles like the words of a fortune-teller—interesting, but not inspired? Did prophets see the future clearly, or did they only get impressions? Did the prophets predict the coming of Christ? Did they foretell the Book of Mormon? Do their words reveal hidden meanings to those who plumb their depths?

To answer these questions, let us consider a prophecy from Isaiah that is often interpreted to refer to Christ:

> Therefore the Lord himself will give you a sign. Look, the young woman[1] is with child and shall bear a son, and shall name him Immanuel. He shall eat curds and honey by the time he knows how to refuse the evil and choose the good. For before the child knows how to refuse the evil and choose the good, the land before whose two kings you are in dread will be deserted. (Isa 7:14–16)

The connection to Christ seems fairly straightforward. The young woman in question is Mary, and the name Immanuel means "God is with us." So Jesus' birth as the Son of God would be the literal fulfillment of the idea of God being with the people.

While this interpretation is uplifting to Christians, there is good reason to believe that if you were to ask Isaiah about it, he would not understand these words as referring to Jesus. This is simply because prophecy as a genre was not meant to be clear.

Regardless of if you believe Israelite prophets could see the future, there were plenty of diviners from Egypt to Babylonia who most certainly could not. How, then, did diviners stay in business? They made sure that their predictions were vague enough that they could be considered true no matter what happened.

For example, one Mesopotamian divination text reads, "If there is an eclipse of the moon in Nisannu and it is red—prosperity for the people."[2] This sounds straightforward enough, but how can you tell whether the people are prospering, and thus whether the prediction has come true? Short of a major catastrophe, such as a famine or having your city burn to the ground, almost any circumstance could

---

1. The King James Version translates this as "virgin," but it does so primarily due to the influence of Christian tradition. The Hebrew word here, עלמה ('almah), simply means "young woman."

2. William W. Hallo and K. Lawson Younger, *The Context of Scripture* (Leiden: Brill, 1997), 1:423–24.

be seen as prosperous. Another text tells us, "A prophet of Marduk stood at the gate of the palace, proclaiming incessantly, 'Išme-Dagan [the king] will not escape the hand of Marduk. That hand will tie together a sheaf and he will be caught in it.'"[3] Again, this prediction is fairly safe. Everyone dies eventually, and in a time when kings rarely had long and prosperous reigns, it was only a matter of time before war, rebellion, palace intrigue, or sickness would bring this particular king down. These kinds of predictions are impossible to disprove, and if one believes that the diviner can actually see the future, one tends to look for evidence that confirms the prediction while ignoring any evidence to the contrary.

Like their non-Israelite counterparts, Old Testament prophets also tended to utter vague predictions that were difficult to falsify. For example, in the Isaiah passage above, is he describing a young woman who will one day give birth, or one who is currently pregnant? The Hebrew verb is ambiguous, hence the reason the NRSV translates it as "the young woman is with child" while the King James Version translates it as "a virgin shall conceive." Immanuel means "God is with us," but in this context is that a good thing or a bad thing? We are inclined to read it positively, but you do not want an angry or judgmental god to be with you, as seen a few verses later, when Yahweh brings the king of Assyria in judgment upon the people. What does it mean that the child will "eat curds and honey"? In verses 21–22 we read that "one will keep alive a young cow and two sheep, and will eat curds because of the abundance of milk that they give; for everyone that is left in the land shall eat curds and honey." This seems to be an oracle of salvation, but the very next verse describes a deserted land that "will become briers and thorns." So maybe the curds and honey are signs of how desolate the land will become after the Assyrian invasion. We do not even know the identity of the woman who stands at the center of this prophecy. Regardless of whether the Assyrian invasion goes well or poorly, Isaiah could claim that this prophecy was fulfilled.

Isaiah is not trying to pull a fast one on us. He is simply following Near Eastern prophetic conventions. Almost every prophecy in

3. Marti Nissinen, *Prophets and Prophecy in the Ancient Near East*, ed. Peter Machinist (Atlanta, GA: Society of Biblical Literature, 2003), 73.

the Old Testament was designed to be ambiguous enough that even their immediate meaning would not always be clear, much less any secondary or tertiary meanings. Whether it be the famine of the word of the Lord (Amos 8:11), the star that arises from Jacob (Num. 24:17), or the gathering of Israel (Isa. 66:20), these prophecies were meant to be vague. If a reader had only the Old Testament and no knowledge of subsequent history, they would not be able to identify the famine as referring to the Great Apostasy, the star as a Davidic Messiah, or the gathering of Israel as LDS missionary work. These prophecies were designed to resist such concrete interpretations.

There is a second reason why Isaiah is almost certainly not referring to Jesus in the passage quoted above. Archeologists have uncovered thousands of prophecies from the ancient Near East, and across the board, these prophets did not foretell events in the far future. The whole purpose of a prophet was to provide a glimpse into what would shortly happen. If a prophet said the gods were about to unleash catastrophe, the people rushed to repent and offer sacrifice. If a king was about to wage war, he needed to know whether he would win. And if a merchant was beginning a venture, the prophet could tell him how to prepare.

This prophetic role is seen throughout the Old Testament. Before going to war, Ahab "gathered the prophets together, about four hundred of them, and said to them, 'Shall I go to battle against Ramoth-gilead, or shall I refrain?' They said, 'Go up; for Yahweh will give it into the hand of the king'" (1 Kgs. 22:6). When Saul searches for his father's lost donkeys, his servant says, "There is a man of God in this town; he is a man held in honor. Whatever he says always comes true. Let us go there now; perhaps he will tell us about the journey" (1 Sam. 9:6). When Jeremiah writes to the captives at Babylon, he says that "only when Babylon's seventy years are completed will [God] visit you" (Jer. 29:10).

In all these examples, and in practically every other prophecy in the Old Testament, the timeframe is either implicitly or explicitly short. Prophets foretell what will happen today, tomorrow, or at most within the span of a lifetime, but not what will happen thousands of years from now. Long-term predictions were not part of the prophets' job.

In the case of Isaiah and the Immanuel prophecy, we can actually see the context and immediate time frame clearly. At the beginning of the chapter, we learn that Judah is being attacked by both Aram and the northern kingdom of Israel (which was also known as Ephraim). Isaiah 7:1 reads, "King Rezin of Aram and King Pekah son of Remaliah of Israel went up to attack Jerusalem." When Ahaz, king of Judah, hears about Israel's alliance with Aram, he is terrified (Isa. 7:2), so Isaiah comforts him, saying, "Do not let your heart be faint because of these two smoldering stumps of firebrands, because of the fierce anger of Rezin and Aram and the son of Remaliah … thus says the Lord Yahweh: It shall not stand, and it shall not come to pass" (Isa. 7:4, 7).

Kingdom	King
Judah	Ahaz
Israel (also known as Ephraim)	Pekah, son of Remaliah
Aram	Rezin

Isaiah exhorts King Ahaz to be faithful and to trust in the Lord. He even predicts that "within sixty-five years Ephraim will be shattered" (Isa. 7:8). That is to say, Ahaz does not need to fear being attacked by these two kings, for their attack will not be successful; and the Northern Kingdom of Israel/Ephraim will be destroyed within sixty-five years. Ahaz is skeptical of Isaiah's prophecy (Isa. 7:11–12), so Isaiah offers him a sign that what he has prophesied is true: "Therefore the Lord himself will give you a sign. Look, the young woman is with child and shall bear a son, and shall name him Immanuel. … For before the child knows how to refuse the evil and choose the good, the land before whose two kings you are in dread will be deserted" (Isa. 7:14–16).

Notice the immediate time frame of this prophecy. The child Immanuel is not going to be born 700 years in the future; Immanuel is going to be born shortly after Isaiah gives the prophecy; and before the child is even old enough to know right from wrong ("before the child knows how to refuse the evil and choose the good"), both Israel and Aram will be defeated ("the land before whose two kings you are in dread will be deserted"). The child Immanuel is meant as a sign

114

to Ahaz that the Lord will protect him from this foreign invasion, though as we saw above, Isaiah is vague about whether this child also signifies the destruction of Judah at the hands of the Assyrians.

So did Isaiah foretell the coming of Jesus? His words *can* be applied to Jesus—a young woman giving birth to a child whose name signifies that "God is with us"—but the prophecy does not apply equally well to both Ahaz and Jesus. If we want to say that this prophecy is about Jesus, we have to deliberately ignore the references to the king of Assyria, to the eating of curds and honey due to the desolation of the land, to the fall of Israel and Aram, and to the whole purpose of the sign in shoring up Ahaz's resolve. But that is precisely what we do in Sunday school, quoting only the verse about Immanuel and never touching the rest. Saying that this is a prophecy about Jesus also goes against everything we know about how prophecy worked in Israel and the Near East.

Everything we know about the Immanuel prophecy suggests that if we look to the Old Testament prophets for proof of Jesus or the latter-day Restoration, we do so at our own peril. To take just one more example, consider Ezekiel's prophecy of joining together two sticks. The prophecy reads: "The word of Yahweh came to me: Mortal, take a stick and write on it, 'For Judah, and the Israelites associated with it'; then take another stick and write on it, 'For Joseph (the stick of Ephraim) and all the house of Israel associated with it'; and join them together into one stick, so that they may become one in your hand" (Ezek. 37:15–17). Latter-day Saints have long held that these verses predict the coming forth of the Book of Mormon: the stick of Judah is the Bible and the stick of Ephraim is the Book of Mormon. Both come together to establish the whole gospel.

This interpretation, however, fits the prophecy poorly for two reasons. First, according to the Book of Mormon, Lehi and his family were descendants of Manasseh, not Ephraim (Alma 10:3), so they would not have written a "stick of Ephraim." The second and more serious problem is that this prophecy is clearly about the unified tribes of Israel, not their writings. "Stick" here most likely refers to a scepter, and Ezekiel is clearly talking about the reunification of Israel and Judah under a single monarch, as shown in the text itself. Ezekiel continues,

115

And when your people say to you, "Will you not show us what you mean by these?" say to them.... I will take the people of Israel from the nations among which they have gone, and will gather them from every quarter, and bring them to their own land. I will make them one nation in the land, on the mountains of Israel; and one king shall be king over them all. Never again shall they be two nations, and never again shall they be divided into two kingdoms.... My servant David shall be king over them; and they shall all have one shepherd. (Ezek. 37:18–24)

The political meaning of this text could hardly be more explicit. Ezekiel is participating in a long tradition of prophets foretelling such a unification (see Hosea 1:11, Jer. 3:18).

Readers may object that a prophecy can have multiple meanings. But if we want to interpret this passage as prophesying the Book of Mormon, we would have to deliberately misread the text, ignoring the mention of David, the misalignment between Ephraim and Manasseh, and the broader context of Israelite prophets foretelling the reunification of Israel and Judah.

The Prophetic Call to Repentance

One of the most striking characteristics of biblical prophecy is how frequently the prophets lambast the Israelites for their sins. They are constantly proclaiming, "Repent and turn away from your idols; and turn away your faces from all your abominations" (Ezek. 14:6), which leaves modern readers with the impression that Israel was particularly depraved. Such an impression is false.

We have to keep in mind that in ancient Israel there were two dominant ways of conceptualizing the relationship between Yahweh and his people: the covenant with Moses on Mount Sinai and the covenant with David on Mount Zion. These covenants were not mutually exclusive, but individual prophets tended to use only one in their preaching. Hosea, for example, was a northern prophet, and thus did not adhere to the promises attached to Zion and the Davidic monarch of the southern kingdom. Rather, his preaching draws from the exodus—for example, when he describes God's judgment on Israel as resembling the east wind drying up the Red Sea (Hosea 13:15). He also subscribes to the Sinaitic notion that no mediator stands between God and Israel. In line with this theology, Hosea speaks of God's relationship with his people as familial. "When Israel was a child, I loved him," God says, "and out of Egypt I called my son" (Hosea 11:1). Hosea also envisions Israel as God's wife. So, when Israel seeks alliances to protect itself against Assyria, Hosea interprets it as adultery. When Israel approaches Assyria in an attempt to placate it, Hosea responds, "The spirit of whoredom is within them. ... Ephraim went to Assyria, and sent to the great king. But he is not able to cure you" (Hosea 5:4, 13). Thus, Hosea's sign-act, and the overriding metaphor throughout the book, is that of a righteous man marrying a prostitute (Hosea 1:2)—an inversion of the familial relationship established at Sinai between God and Israel.

Jeremiah likewise adheres to the covenant at Sinai, which makes sense given that he lived through the religious reform of Josiah. Previous kings had paid tribute to Assyria, but Josiah reigned during the brief period of calm when Assyrian power was declining but Babylonia had not yet arrived. Josiah therefore embraced a kind of religious and political nationalism. While Josiah's predecessors were vassals to Assyria, the book of Deuteronomy reworked the vassal treaty to give Israel's sole allegiance to Yahweh.

For Jeremiah, the promises of the Sinai covenant were more than sufficient to help Judah survive the Babylonian onslaught. As we saw in chapter four, covenant promises were contingent not upon individual righteousness, but upon the nation as a whole maintaining its covenantal relationship. In Sinai's conception, God was Israel's family ("I have become a father to Israel" [Jer. 31:9], he says), thus the expectation was that the people would seek God when they needed a father's protection. But rather than trusting in God to protect them, the Israelites broke the relationship, both politically and religiously. Politically, the Judean kings sought alliances with foreign powers, and religiously, the people failed to embrace Josiah's centralizing reforms. Jeremiah called both these breaches idolatry.

Isaiah, on the other hand, embraces what we might call a Zion theology, which is based on the promises God made to the Davidic monarch. In a Zion theology, what mattered was not individual sin, but rather the faithfulness the *king* showed to this covenantal relationship. When Assyria threatens Jerusalem, God tells the king, "I will defend this city to save it, for my own sake and for the sake of my servant David" (Isa. 37:35). God himself dwelt in the temple in Jerusalem, a physical symbol of God's special relationship to the king, and accordingly the city was a refuge. With his focus on Zion theology, Isaiah spends his time with kings, going "to meet Ahaz" (Isa. 7:3), to "the gates of the nobles" (Isa. 13:2), or "to Hezekiah" (Isa. 37:21) where he lambasts them for not trusting God (Isa. 7) and seeking alliances with other powers (Isa. 30:1–3; 39:1–7).

The theology of both kinds of prophets show what we already saw in chapter four: individual sins did not matter to the Israelites. They did not share our modern Western sense of individualism. Regardless of which covenant they used to explain God's relationship with his people, these prophets cared much more about the relationship than about the actions of the individual. This is why idolatry and foreign alliances mattered—not because they were sinful, but because they indicated a lack of faith in the covenant.

Our modern emphasis on individuality often colors the way we interpret the Old Testament. Take, for example, our interpretation of the prophetic criticism of ritual. Prophets were often critical of the cult, or the rituals carried out at the temple. Amos presents God as saying, "I hate, I despise your festivals, and I take no delight in your solemn assemblies" (Amos 5:21). Isaiah likewise writes, "What to me is the multitude of your sacrifices? says Yahweh; I have had enough of burnt offerings of rams and the fat of fed beasts; I do not delight in the blood of bulls, or of lambs, or of goats" (Isa. 1:11). We often assume from these verses that the Israelites were observing the cultic rites while ignoring the moral injunctions of the law. But this assumption misunderstands both the role of prophets and the development of Israelite religion. As we saw in chapter three, the Pentateuch as we know it did not exist before the exile. The tradition of a covenant between Israel and God at Mount Sinai existed, but its story had not yet been written. Though Amos knew the tradition of the Israelites wandering in the wilderness, in his understanding, the sacrificial system did not exist at that point. That is why he asks, rhetorically, "Did you bring to me sacrifices and offerings the forty years in the wilderness, O house of Israel?" (Amos 5:25). We might be tempted to dismiss Amos as an oddity, but Jeremiah makes the same point when he has God outright deny that the sacrificial system was revealed on Sinai: "In the day I brought your ancestors out, I did not speak to them or command them concerning burnt offerings and sacrifices" (Jer. 7:22). Here we have two prophets explicitly stating that the sacrificial system was not revealed by God after the exodus, in direct contradiction to the Pentateuch. They did this because the Pentateuch had not been written yet, so the Israelites did not think that the cultic rituals had been revealed by God on Sinai.[4]

If the cultic rituals did not originate on Sinai, where did these prophets think they came from? Remember, kings were some of the primary movers behind Israelite religion. It was David and Solomon who built the temple and moved the ark of the covenant to Jerusalem. It was Josiah who forbade all sacrifice outside the temple and centralized worship at the capital city. It was Jeroboam who created the cultic rites of the northern kingdom. In Amos we learn that the sanctuary at Bethel was not the people's but "the king's sanctuary" (Amos 7:13). When they criticized the cult, prophets such as Amos and Isaiah were criticizing the king, not the people. In their view, these sacrifices were an addition to the covenant, not part of it.

It was also at the beginning of the monarchy that Israelite society diverged into clear social classes. We can see this divergence both in the Old Testament's descriptions of the burgeoning bureaucracy and in the archeological record. The institution of prophecy arose as a kind of counterbalance, protesting the rising inequality and the changes brought about by the kings. If you look through the prophetic books and catalog the sins they list, you see that the prophets overwhelmingly care about social injustice and the actions of the king. Only rarely do we read mention of "moral" issues such as sexuality, honesty, theft, etc. The prophets' harshest judgments are against "you that trample on the needy" (Amos 8:4), "rob the poor of my people" (Isa. 10:2), and "did not aid the poor and needy" (Ezek. 16:49).

---

4. Ezekiel similarly shows the development of the exodus narrative around this time. Ezekiel is a priest, and, if you recall from chapter three, the Priestly source of the Pentateuch was the last source to be written. Ezekiel therefore sees the earlier Pentateuchal traditions as being incorrect and presents God as condemning them: "Moreover I gave them statutes that were not good and ordinances by which they could not live" (Ezek. 20:25).

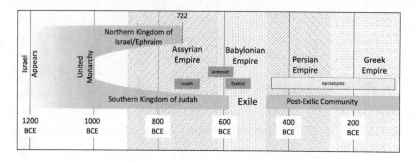

Apocalyptic

After the exile, with the disappearance of the monarchy, Israelite prophecy underwent a radical shift, bringing about a new genre of writing. In books such as Daniel, we are guided through bizarre visions of beasts, angels, battles, and destruction. The prophet's message is deliberately opaque, and the language is filled with symbolism and codes. This genre is known as apocalyptic prophecy.

The Old Testament preserves a few examples of apocalyptic prophecy, such as the books of Daniel and Zechariah. But dozens of apocalypses were written by both Jews and Christians during the centuries around the time of Christ, such as the Apocalypse of Elijah, 2 Baruch, the Shepherd of Hermas, the Ascension of Isaiah, the Book of Enoch, and the book of Revelation in the New Testament.

While each apocalyptic work has its own style, we see numerous points of continuity across the genre. They are usually written in the form of a dream or vision. A prophet or hero from ancient times is guided through a vision by an angel, and the angel has to explain each symbol to the prophet. World history unfolds in the vision as a series of great empires, with each empire usually represented by a beast. The succession of empires culminates in a final, terrible empire that oppresses the righteous and persecutes the saints; and though it rules for a time, in the final battle good triumphs. The prophet is often confused or distressed by what he sees, and the angel soothes his anxiety by revealing when the persecutions will end. At some point, the prophet is commanded to write the vision and hide it up so that it may come forth "on the day of tribulation" (1 Enoch 1:1) or when "the times are ended" (4 Ezra 14:9).[5]

---

5. All translations are taken from James H. Charlesworth, ed., *The Old Testament*

The persecution of the righteous pervades apocalyptic literature, so it is no coincidence that this genre became popular during times of intense religious persecution. When Antiochus Epiphanes IV outlawed Judaism in the second century BCE, when Jerusalem was destroyed in 70 CE, and when Roman emperors persecuted Jews or Christians, apocalyptic literature abounded. Apocalyptic authors almost universally believed that they were living in the final age, on the eve of the great last battle, when God would finally intervene to save his people. They believed they were about to witness "the apocalypse," the final terrible scene before the curtain closes.

Another convention of apocalyptic books is that they have a narrator other than the author. Much as F. Scott Fitzgerald assumes the persona of Nick Carraway to tell the story of Gatsby, so apocalyptic authors take on the persona of Adam, Abraham, Isaiah, or Moses to convey their visions, presenting history as if it were prophecy. These "prophecies" are all very specific up to a certain point—the time the author was composing his apocalypse—but then become general and vague.

1 Enoch, for example, "predicts" the persecutions under Antiochus Epiphanes in great detail, with animals standing for major characters or groups in this history. But when the account reaches the Jews' rebellion against these persecutions, the author suddenly resorts to broad statements and platitudes about what will happen. We read that the wicked will perish and the righteous prosper, but gone is the specificity that characterized the vision up to that point, which makes it quite easy to determine when the book was written.

Understanding apocalyptic literature as a genre can have a significant impact on how we interpret a book like Daniel, only half of which is written in the apocalyptic genre. In the non-apocalyptic portions, Daniel and his three friends go through various ordeals, such as the lion's den, the fiery furnace, and refusing to eat the king's meat. Throughout these episodes, Daniel is portrayed as a wise sage, able to interpret dreams and the writing on the wall, remaining ever calm in the face of danger.

In Daniel 7, however, the point of view switches from third-person

---

Pseudepigrapha: Apocalyptic Literature and Testaments (New Haven, CT: Yale University Press, 2009).

to first-person, and Daniel relates how he is guided through bizarre dreams of beasts and symbols. "Terrified" and "troubled" (Dan. 7:15) by what he sees, he can no longer interpret the dream, leaving it to his angelic guide. The dreams focus on persecution, specifically from a king who "shall wear out the holy ones of the Most High" (Dan. 7:25). The angel eventually reveals when the persecutions will cease and when God will save his people (Dan. 8:13–14; 9:24–17; 12:11–12). Daniel is then commanded to "keep the words secret and the book sealed until the time of the end" (Dan. 12:4; see also 8:26), as the vision is meant to comfort those who will undergo these tribulations.

Like most apocalyptic books, Daniel is quite specific up to a certain point in history. He describes Babylonia (Dan. 2:38), Persia (Dan. 8:20; 10:20; 11:2), and Greece (Dan. 8:21; 10:20; 11:2) by name, and the majority of the book is spent describing the persecutions that take place under the Greek king Antiochus Epiphanes IV. In thinly veiled language, Daniel describes how Antiochus outlaws Jewish practice (Dan. 7:25; 8:11; 9:27; 11:31), sets up an altar to Zeus in the Jerusalem temple (Dan. 8:13; 9:27; 11:31), and persecutes the Jews for roughly three and a half years (Dan. 7:25; 8:14; 9:27; 12:7, 11). Even his military campaigns are described in perfect detail (Dan. 11:20–35). But after this point, the author becomes vague: God will defeat Antiochus (Dan. 7:26; 9:27), he will give dominion to the saints (Dan. 7:27), and a new kingdom will be established that will rule the world and never be destroyed (Dan. 2:44; 7:27). But not a single detail is given about how this will happen.

All of this indicates that the book of Daniel was written not by Daniel, but by someone in the mid-160s BCE who lived during the throes of Antiochus's persecution. Other factors that point to a second-century composition date are the book's late temporal Hebrew dialect and its numerous historical problems.[6] In the Jewish

---

6. Daniel is written in a stage of Hebrew known as Late Biblical Hebrew, and it contains a few Greek loanwords. Though the date of the text should not be established solely based on these loanwords, it is unlikely that the text could have been written before the Greeks took over the land of Israel. Much of the book is also written in Aramaic, a language that did not become common in Israel until after exile. As for problems in the text, Michael Coogan writes, "the history and chronology are confused. Thus, Nebuchadnezzar assumed the throne in 605 BCE, and the first exile from Judah took place in 597, the seventh year of his reign (see Jer. 52:28), but his dream, interpreted by Daniel, one of the exiles, is dated to the second year of his reign (Dan. 2:1). The successors of

organization of the Old Testament, Daniel is not even included among the prophetic writings.

As prophecy morphed into this apocalyptic form, it became much more of a literary, rather than oral, phenomenon. Rather than old-time, street-corner prophets, the apocalypses were written by scribes, who were students of the scriptures. By the time Zechariah was written, a clear distinction had arisen between Zechariah and what he calls "the former prophets" (Zech. 1:4). Daniel explicitly references his study of "the books ... according to the word of Yahweh to Jeremiah" (Dan. 9:2). This shift shows Judaism developing into the biblical religion we now know (and which Christianity follows), where God's will is revealed through the study of scripture.

If we modern readers are unfamiliar with the norms of apocalyptic literature, we are in danger of incorrectly assuming that the book of Daniel contains the predictions of Daniel himself, and we are likely to take portions of Daniel's vision out of their historical context. For example, Latter-day Saints tend to read Daniel 11 as an account of the "wars, leagues, and conflicts that lead up to the Second Coming of Christ" (see the LDS chapter heading). But in its original context, this chapter quite clearly—and accurately—describes the wars, leagues, and conflicts under Antiochus Epiphanes in the second century BCE. This is not to say that Daniel cannot be read as describing the context of the Second Coming, but if we do so, we depart from how this book was originally understood.

Inspiration and Scholarship

When I present this kind of information, one of the reactions I get from non-scholars is a kind of brusque dismissal. They assume that secular scholars do not believe in revelation or inspiration, and that they are therefore biased against the scriptures. I myself used to hold this view, and it is an understandable sentiment. After all, I have

---

Nebuchadnezzar were Amel-Marduk (Evil-Merodach, 2 Kings 25:27) and Nabonidus, not Belshazzar, as Daniel 5:2 states. Belshazzar was Nabonidus's son and coregent. ... Darius the Mede is unknown and is probably a confusion with the Persian king Darius, who succeeded Cyrus in 522. These errors suggest that the book was written a considerable time after the events described, or they may be deliberate indications that it is not to be understood as historical" (*The Old Testament: A Historical and Literary Introduction to the Hebrew Scriptures*, 3rd ed. [New York: Oxford University Press, 2014], 533).

argued here that passages typically used to prove that Jesus was the Messiah do not, in fact, refer to Jesus, and that those passages used as proof of the Restoration do not, in fact, refer to Joseph Smith or the Book of Mormon. I have also argued that the prophecies in books such as Daniel are not prophecies at all; instead, they are history written down long after the fact and presented as if they were from an ancient author. This can look like an all-out attack against the inspiration of scripture, but it is actually just an indication of the differences between how scholars and believers tend to read the scriptures.

Scholars, when working as scholars, have one job: to use the tools of history, linguistics, and cultural studies to examine the text and present what we can know about it. It is true that these findings sometimes contradict how the text has traditionally been understood, and this can sometimes be disconcerting to believers, who often approach the scriptures for inspiration and comfort.

Consider the book of Daniel. It is written in an extremely late temporal dialect—one that is without question later than what Daniel could have possibly spoken. It is also written in a genre popular around the time of Jesus that relates in exact detail everything that happens up until the mid-160s BCE, after which the author essentially says that somehow good will triumph. Is it possible that the historical Daniel, a person living in the sixth century BCE, received the book through revelation and wrote it down? Yes, it is possible. But it is extremely unlikely, even if you do believe in revelation. It would be the equivalent of someone handing you a book written in a contemporary dialect that talks about COVID-19, the internet, and *The Simpsons*, and then claiming that it was written by Joseph Smith. Would it be possible that Joseph wrote such a book? Yes, but the language and cultural references make it much more likely that the book was written by someone else. If scholars analyzed this book, they would have nothing to say about whether Joseph Smith was a prophet or whether the book in question was inspired. Their only job would be to point out that words such as "social distancing," etc., did not come into vogue until well after Joseph Smith's time.

Need this mean that the book of Daniel is uninspired? If we accept revelation, or even inspiration, then we can easily believe that more people than just Daniel could receive either. In fact, we already do. With all the prophets we honor, it should be easy to believe that a second-century author could be directed by God to create something inspirational, even scriptural, using a popular genre. The value of Daniel lies not in its ability to predict the future, but rather in its message of God's ultimate triumph and of comfort for those who suffer. Similarly, as we look at Old Testament prophecies that are usually applied to Christ or the Restoration, our interpretation of their original meaning may shift, but this need not detract from their value. If Ezekiel did not intend the "stick of Ephraim" to represent the Book of Mormon, then we may need to change the way we talk about this prophecy, but it can still serve as an inspired description of how the Old Testament and Book of Mormon interact—even if we place the locus of that inspiration somewhere other than the prophet Ezekiel. With the knowledge Bible scholarship has given us, we have the opportunity to find other ways to reveal God in the scriptures.

The distinction between scholarship and devotional reading is especially important because the conflation of these two lies at the heart of what is likely the most controversial aspect of Old Testament scholarship for Latter-day Saints: the book of Isaiah.

8

ISAIAH

Arguably no book in the entire Bible—including books in the New Testament—has had a greater impact on Christian and LDS tradition than the book of Isaiah. This magisterial work spans sixty-six chapters, covering everything from judgment to condemnation, repentance to restoration. Isaiah's prophecies, such as the description of the future restored Zion or the king who would one day bring salvation to the people, form the foundation of subsequent Jewish and Christian thought. Later religious writings, such as the Dead Sea Scrolls from Qumran, the New Testament, and the Book of Mormon, all draw from Isaiah extensively. Jesus tells the Nephites, "Great are the words of Isaiah" (3 Ne. 23:1), and the Book of Mormon reproduces almost a third of Isaiah's writings. After only twenty-three verses, the New Testament starts quoting from Isaiah to show how Christ fulfills Old Testament prophecy. The Book of Mormon uses Isaiah's prophecies as a herald for the latter-day Restoration and proof of the Book of Mormon's divine origins. It describes the Nephites as fulfilling Isaiah 29: a people who "shall speak unto [the Gentiles] out of the ground, and their speech shall be low out of the dust, and their voice shall be as one that hath a familiar spirit" (2 Ne. 26:16). It interprets Isaiah's prophecy of the servant protected by God as foretelling Joseph Smith's ministry (3 Ne. 21:10). However, the inclusion of Isaiah in the Book of Mormon also presents one of the most difficult challenges to the Book of Mormon's historicity, and has thus become a fierce battleground in LDS scholarship.

The crux of the problem is this: the Book of Mormon claims to have been written by a group that left Jerusalem in 600 BCE, approximately fourteen years before the Babylonians destroyed Jerusalem and carried the Israelites into captivity. Isaiah lived in the eighth century, approximately a century before Lehi's time, so it would make sense that Lehi would have access to Isaiah's writings. But for reasons we will soon discuss, most scholars believe that the final third of the book of Isaiah was not written by Isaiah himself. It was instead composed during and after Babylonian exile—well after Lehi left Jerusalem. According to the academic consensus, Isaiah 40–55 was written toward the end of exile and is referred to as "Second Isaiah" or "Deutero-Isaiah," while Isaiah 56–66 was written in the early Persian period and is referred to as "Third Isaiah" or "Trito-Isaiah."

When Nephi quotes from Isaiah, he draws extensively from the chapters in Second Isaiah, claiming that they were "written upon the plates of brass" taken from Laban (1 Ne. 19:21), and he reproduces some of them in their entirety (see 1 Ne. 20–21 and 2 Ne. 7–8; cf. Isa. 48–51). If scholars are correct that chapters 40–66 were not written until after the Israelites were carried into exile, then they could not have been inscribed on the plates of brass. It would be as if a story claimed that Abraham Lincoln sat down one day to read his copy of *Harry Potter*. Such a glaring anachronism would make the historicity of the Book of Mormon implausible, if not impossible.

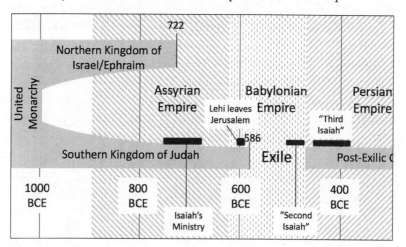

In this chapter we examine the process by which the prophetic books were created; then we look at the arguments for why the final third of Isaiah is an exilic and post-exilic document. Finally, we look at the implications of these arguments for the Book of Mormon.

Writing the Prophets

Modern readers often have a straightforward view of authorship, assuming that a book's listed author is in fact the person who wrote it. But authorship can be complex. In some cases, ghost writers interview a person and then write an autobiography as if they were the interviewee. If an author dies before finishing a series, other authors may write entire books hewing to the original author's voice and style. Indeed, Joseph Smith did not actually put pen to paper and write down everything attributed to him. Much of his words were recorded and edited by scribes. His sermons were often written down after the fact by his listeners.

Ancient views of authorship were considerably laxer than ours. As we saw with the book of Daniel, authorship could be ascribed to an individual simply if the book used that person as its main character. The Pentateuch came to be ascribed to Moses centuries after the first sources were written as a way to shore up its authority as law. Just because a book is named Ezekiel does not mean it was written by Ezekiel.

To understand how and when the book of Isaiah was written, we need to understand how prophetic books in the Old Testament were generally composed. There is no better example of this process than the book of Jeremiah. Even though the book bears Jeremiah's name, the text itself unquestionably comes from many different sources and authors. At times Jeremiah prophesies in the first person, as when he prefaces his revelations, "The word of Yahweh came to me, saying ..." (Jer. 2:1). At other times we can clearly see another author at work, such as when the text refers to Jeremiah in the third person: "The word of Yahweh that came to Jeremiah ..." (Jer. 14:1). Interspersed with these oracles are prose narratives, and once again we see some in first person (see Jer. 13:7) and others in third person (see Jer. 20:2). Some sections were not written by Jeremiah or his followers at all, but were copied directly from the Deuteronomistic

History, as with Jeremiah 52, which is a duplicate of 2 Kings 24–25. Jeremiah occasionally repeats itself, as in chapters 7 and 26, and 39 and 52. In other places the text incorporates parts of the book of Isaiah (see Jer. 48 and Isa. 15–16).

In short, the book of Jeremiah is a mosaic of different sources. Who put these sources together, and when? Two obvious candidates would be Jeremiah himself or Baruch, his scribe. But, historically speaking, they cannot have been the final editors. They were both carried off to Egypt before the final destruction of Jerusalem (Jer. 43:6–7), and we know that the group responsible for the creation and preservation of the Old Testament lived in Babylonia. The book of Jeremiah also incorporates 2 Kings 24–25, and we know the Deuteronomistic History was written in Babylonia during the exile. The book of Jeremiah could not, therefore, have been written until well after the prophet's time.

What makes the mystery even more intriguing is the fact that well into the post-exilic period there were not one, but two versions of the book of Jeremiah in circulation. One version is preserved in our Old Testaments today, but a second rearranges the chapters of the book—for example, taking chapters 46–51 and putting them right in the middle of chapter 25—and is roughly an eighth shorter than the version we have. (Both versions are preserved in the Dead Sea Scrolls.) When the Old Testament was translated into Greek, it was this second version that the translators based their text on. In other words, the compilation of the book of Jeremiah was not a one-time event, it was a process, and this process was not completed until roughly five centuries after Jeremiah's death.

These books are mosaics, incorporating many different sources written over hundreds of years. They were assembled during the exilic and post-exilic periods when Israel was struggling with its identity and transitioning to the book-centered religion we know today. The Pentateuch, the Deuteronomistic History, Chronicles, and practically every other book of the Old Testament emerged during exile and the Persian period. It would be shocking if Isaiah did not follow the same pattern.

Indeed, the book of Isaiah shows all the same characteristics as books such as Jeremiah. It has the same blend of oracles in the first and third person (see Isa. 21:16 and 13:1) as well as some narratives written in Isaiah's voice and some in the voice of another (see Isa. 6:1 and 20:2). Just like Jeremiah, Isaiah reproduces entire sections of the Deuteronomistic History, which was not written until the exile—more than a hundred years after Isaiah's time (see Isa. 37–39 and 2 Kgs. 19–20). The question is not whether Isaiah wrote the entire book of Isaiah. It is clearly a composite of many sources, and the fact that it incorporates part of the Deuteronomistic History means that the final form of the book could not have been written before the exile. The real question is whether the prophecies in chapters 40–66 can be traced back to the prophet Isaiah himself or whether these chapters were composed in their entirety after Lehi left Jerusalem.

The Case for Second Isaiah[1]

Most scholars are convinced that Second Isaiah (Isa. 40–55) was written in its entirety at least a century after Isaiah lived—after the Israelites went into exile. Consider the fact that while Isaiah was active, Assyria was the dominant world power, and every prophet active during that time—including Isaiah—prophesied about the Assyrian threat. All through chapters 1–39, Isaiah prophesies about how Yahweh will bring the Assyrians in judgment against his people (Isa. 7:17–20) and how Assyria will destroy the northern kingdom of Israel (Isa. 8:4). When God has pity and restores his people, Isaiah says God will build up "a highway from Assyria for the remnant that is left of his people" (Isa. 11:16). When God ultimately brings peace to the world, Isaiah says he will do so by pacifying the Assyrians: "On that day there will be a highway from Egypt to Assyria, and the Assyrian will come into Egypt, and the Egyptian into Assyria, and the Egyptians will worship with the Assyrians" (Isa. 19:23). All throughout these chapters, Israel's punishment and salvation are presented with reference to the Assyrians.

But beginning in Isaiah 40, the Assyrians are suddenly nowhere to be found; they're only mentioned in a single verse that deals with

---

1. The Book of Mormon does not quote from Third Isaiah (Isa. 56–66), so in this section I focus only on the arguments for seeing Second Isaiah (Isa. 40–55) as an independent unit composed after exile. Many of these same arguments could be applied, *mutatis mutandis*, to Third Isaiah, and if you are interested, I highly recommend picking up a good academic commentary on Isaiah or on the Old Testament as a whole.

happenings from "long ago" (Isa. 52:4). Now the people are in Babylon, and the author is told to "comfort my people ... and cry to her that she has served her term, that her penalty is paid, that she has received from Yahweh's hand double for all her sins" (Isa. 40:1–2). The people are commanded, "Go out from Babylon, flee from Chaldea" (Isa. 48:20). And while First Isaiah presents salvation in terms of the people returning on a highway "from Assyria" (Isa. 19:23), now the highway comes from Babylon (Isa. 40:3). Cyrus, the Persian king who would capture Babylon in 539 BCE and allow the Jews to return to the land of Israel, is mentioned by name twice (Isa. 44:28; 45:1) as a savior who would humble Babylon and redeem God's people (Isa. 47). The audience for Second Isaiah is thus best described as the exiles at the end of Babylonian captivity.

Does a different context necessarily imply different authorship? After all, if Isaiah could see the future, could he not have predicted the Babylonian captivity and the coming of the Persian king Cyrus? Such prediction is theoretically possible, and if you recall from the previous chapter, scholars do not take a position on whether prophets could see the future or not. The problem is that Isaiah 40–55 is not presented as prophecy. Isaiah does not say, "One day you will go into captivity in a faraway land, and a foreign king named Cyrus will arise to save you." Instead, the author assumes his audience already knows all this. When he does refer to the conquest of Jerusalem, he always describes it as having happened in the past (e.g., Isa. 50:1), while the return to the land of Israel is predicted as still to come. It is this assumed knowledge that marks Second Isaiah as having been composed during the exile.

Think about every prophecy in the Old and New Testaments, as well as any prophecy given by LDS leaders, from Joseph Smith to the present. In every single case, from the ancient world to today, the prophecy is never addressed to a future audience, nor are the prophesied events presented as having already passed. Not a single section of the Doctrine and Covenants takes this form. Joseph Smith never says something like, "Now that the Cold War is over, you must move to make amends between East and West in order to establish a truly global church; but beware of Putin's designs against religious tolerance!" This prophecy would have made as much sense to a nineteenth-century LDS audience as Second Isaiah's prophecies would have made to the people living during the time of First Isaiah. For First Isaiah to prophesy of Babylon and Persia would also fall well outside the social role we know prophets played in the ancient world—dealing only with the near future.

This is enough to convince most scholars that Isaiah 40–55 was composed during the time of the exile, but it is further supported by the fact that, unlike First Isaiah, Second Isaiah extensively quotes from and alludes to other parts of the Old Testament. Most of the Old Testament was not written until the exile, so First Isaiah would not have had access to it, but Second Isaiah uses these later writings profusely. It refers to Abraham and Sarah (Isa. 41:8; 51:1–3), Noah (54:9), Jacob (43:27), and the suffering servant whose life is patterned after Moses's.[2]

Second Isaiah also takes prophecies from other parts of the Old Testament and reapplies them to Babylonian captivity. For example, Zephaniah condemns Assyria for its pride, for it "said to itself, 'I am, and there is no one else'" (Zeph. 2:15), and then predicts the downfall of Assyria. Second Isaiah uses this same wording to condemn the Babylonians, "who say in your heart, 'I am, and there is no one besides me'" (Isa. 47:8), and then predicts the downfall of Babylon. Similarly, Isaiah 45:12–13 describes God's choosing of Cyrus in the same terms that Jeremiah had used to describe God's choosing of Nebuchadnezzar decades earlier (Jer. 27:5–6). Second Isaiah is dense with allusions and quotations from Psalms, Nahum, Zephaniah, Jeremiah, Micah, Hosea, Deuteronomy, Genesis, and many others. Nothing like this shows up in First Isaiah. As we saw in the previous chapter, after the exile, prophecy became more of a literary phenomenon. No longer was the prophet someone who preached on the street, rather he pored over and interacted with written scripture—just as we see in Second Isaiah.

---

2. To give only a few of many examples, in Numbers 11:11–12 Moses complains, "Why have you treated your servant so badly? Why have I not found favor in your sight, that you lay the burden of all this people on me? Did I conceive all this people? Did I give birth to them, that you should say to me, 'Carry them in your bosom, as a nurse carries a sucking child,' to the land that you promised on oath to their ancestors?" In Second Isaiah, the suffering servant is despised (Isa. 53:3), bears the burden of the people (53:4), and is tasked with bringing Israel back to the promised land (49:6).

The language[3] and themes of Second Isaiah also fit best within an exilic context. Before the exile, God was thought of as a king, but just as there is more than one king in the world, so the Israelites believed in the reality of more than one god. We saw this earlier in verses such as Deuteronomy 32:8, where God "fixed the boundaries of the peoples according to the number of the gods," as well as in Psalm 82:1, 2 Kings 3:5, and Judges 11:24. The prophets before the exile condemned the people for idolatry, but their primary concern was how the worship of these gods impacted Israel's faithfulness to their covenant with Yahweh.

Yahweh was Israel's national god, and while other gods existed, Yahweh demanded that the people have "no other gods *before me*" (Ex. 20:2, emphasis mine). But with the destruction of Israel as a nation, a national god no longer made sense. If kings could be vanquished by other kings, did the destruction of Jerusalem mean that Yahweh had been conquered by Marduk, a stronger god? Such thinking was common in the ancient Near East, which was one reason why the destruction of the temple was just as traumatic for ancient Israel as the destruction of Jerusalem itself. Israel needed either to let go of Yahweh or to reconceptualize him. So during the exile Israel came to think of Yahweh as the only God in existence, an emperor to whom "every knee shall bow, every tongue shall swear" (Isa. 45:23). It was during exile that a true monotheism first emerged in Israel.

Second Isaiah contains the Old Testament's most outspoken arguments for monotheism, and its polemic is directed primarily against Marduk, the chief god of Babylon. Every year, the Babylonians staged a reenactment of *Enuma Elish*, the creation myth that celebrated Marduk's victory over the sea goddess Tiamat and the creation of the world. In counterpoint to this celebration, Second Isaiah insists that it was Yahweh who performed these feats. "Was it

---

3. Linguistic analysis here is tricky. Second Isaiah does show some signs of a later temporal dialect than First Isaiah, and it additionally uses some Aramaic loanwords, which would not have entered Hebrew until the time of the exile, but the amount of material we have for analysis is fairly sparse. Further complicating matters is that Second Isaiah is written as poetry, which is more difficult for linguistic analysis than prose (cf. the prayers used in the church today, which deliberately use words such as "thou" and "thine" even though these words fell out of common usage centuries ago). These arguments are also fairly technical, so I will not plumb them here.

not you," he asks, "who dried up the sea, the waters of the great deep [Hebrew: *Tehom/Tiamat*]?" (Isa. 51:10). God affirms that no one else was involved in creating the world: "I am Yahweh, who made all things, who alone stretched out the heavens, who by myself spread out the earth" (Isa. 44:24).

While Marduk was one of many gods, born from the union of the primeval deities, Yahweh announces, "Before me no god was formed, nor shall there be any after me" (Isa. 43:10). During the reenactment of *Enuma Elish*, Marduk's statue was physically carried through the streets of Babylon, and Second Isaiah uses this to show how gods other than Yahweh are not real: "they hire a goldsmith, who makes it into a god; then they fall down and worship! They lift it to their shoulders, they carry it, they set it in its place, and it stands there; it cannot move from its place. If one cries out to it, it does not answer or save anyone from trouble" (Isa. 46:6–7). In short, Second Isaiah claims, there is only one God: "I am the first and I am the last; besides me there is no god" (Isa. 44:6).[4] This belief in a strict monotheism did not emerge until the exile, which lines up exactly with the context of Second Isaiah.

Finally, Second Isaiah's late composition date can be seen in the book's overall structure. Isaiah 1–39 look like a patchwork quilt, composed of oracles and stories about Isaiah that are drawn from many sources and then sewn together. But beginning with Isaiah 40, that composite nature disappears. No longer do we see prophecies with superscriptions such as "The word that Isaiah son of Amoz saw" (Isa 2:1) or "Thus Yahweh said to me" (Isa. 18:4), and gone are the narratives by or about Isaiah. In fact, the character of Isaiah is never mentioned after chapter 39. Rather than the patchwork of oracles, we find essentially one continuous poem whose major divisions are left to the reader to discern.

Isaiah 1–39 are even structured as an independent book. Just as the book of Jeremiah begins with Jeremiah's call as a prophet and ends with an excerpt from the Deuteronomistic History, so Isaiah begins

---

4. It is no coincidence that the Priestly creation story in Genesis 1 uses imagery from the Babylonian creation myth to depict God as the sole creator of the world. The Priestly source and Second Isaiah were both written during the exile, and they show numerous other parallels (see, for example, God's creation of light and darkness in Isa. 45:7; cf. Gen. 1:3–4).

with his call as a prophet (Isa. 6) and ends with an excerpt from that same history (Isa. 36–39). And the same thing happens when Isaiah 40 opens. The anonymous author is commanded by a heavenly voice, "Cry out!" and he responds with confusion, just as we see in First Isaiah (Isa. 6:11), Jeremiah (Jer. 1:6), and Exodus (Ex. 3:11).

Taken together, the evidence for Second Isaiah as a separate work from First Isaiah is substantial. We know that prophetic books in general were expanded and edited for centuries after their initial composition. We also know that prophets in ancient Israel focused on the near-term, which would make the prophecies of Second Isaiah a poor fit for the historical Isaiah. Second Isaiah presupposes—rather than predicts—an exilic context, and for a prophecy to presuppose a future context is unlike any other prophecy from ancient to modern times. The problems and themes Second Isaiah focuses on are exilic, it draws extensively from Babylonian myth, and its literary character matches precisely other works created around this time. That Second Isaiah was composed during exile seems inescapable.

This is not to say that Second Isaiah is a random composition that has no relationship to the first part of the book. First Isaiah mentions a group of followers who preserve Isaiah's teachings (Isa. 8:16); any from that group could be among Second Isaiah's possible authors. Such disciples would have felt comfortable expanding the original prophet's words. There are also numerous links evident between First and Second Isaiah that bind these two sections together into their final form.

Second Isaiah and the Book of Mormon

The academic consensus around the exilic origin of Second Isaiah poses a problem for the historicity of the Book of Mormon. Regardless of whether Second Isaiah was composed in its entirety during the exile, the final form of the book of Isaiah would not have come about until quite late. Yet 2 Nephi 12–24 quotes the entirety of Isaiah chapters 2–14 almost exactly, which would mean that Nephi had these chapters in practically the same form we have them today. For such a collection to exist so early would be highly unlikely, particularly since the words of Second and Third Isaiah do not appear exclusively in the final third of the book. When these sections were added, the later authors shaped the entire book of Isaiah—including the prophecies of First Isaiah—to give the book greater coherence. For example, Second Isaiah begins in Isaiah 40:1, but Isaiah 36–39 had to have been added after the exile since it quotes from the Deuteronomistic History.

Even in the sections quoted in the Book of Mormon we see clear examples of post-exilic editing. For instance, Isaiah 6:13 describes Israel as the stump left behind after a tree is cut down. Questions arose in post-exilic Israel as to whom exactly this stump (symbolizing the chosen people) referred to. Were they the people who were left behind in Israel during Babylonian captivity, or were they those who were taken to Babylon but preserved the Old Testament's traditions? The group that was taken to Babylon came to be referred to as "the holy seed" (e.g., Ezra 9:2). A later editor came back to Isaiah 6:13 and clarified that the Babylonian captives were indeed the chosen people by inserting the phrase, "The holy seed is its stump" (Isa. 6:13). We can tell that this addition is late not only because it refers to a post-exilic debate that took place well after Isaiah's time, but also because one of our earliest witnesses to the book of Isaiah—the Greek translation made in the second century BCE—does not include the addition at all. Even though it was added well after Nephi left Jerusalem, the addition appears in Nephi's quotation (2 Ne. 16:13), which should be impossible.

One way some LDS authors have addressed this controversy has been to deny that the book of Isaiah was written by multiple authors.[5] Kent Jackson writes, "The fundamental issue that underlies the idea of multiple authors within the book of Isaiah ... is centered on this basic question: Can a prophet see beyond his own time?"[6] If

---

5. See, for example, Avraham Gileadi, John Welch, Sidney Sperry, Kent Jackson, and others.

6. Kent P. Jackson, "Isaiah in the Book of Mormon," in *A Reason for Faith: Navigating LDS Doctrine and Church History*, ed. Laura Harris Hales (Salt Lake City: Deseret Book Co., 2016), 74–75. Much has been made by scholars in this camp of wordprint or stylometric studies, where computer analysis of the Hebrew text is used to determine authorship, but these studies are notoriously problematic. Such studies depend on having both a large block of text that is known to come from a particular author and a large block of text to be analyzed to see if it matches the original author's style. Isaiah is difficult in this regard for several reasons. First, the criteria for identifying an authentic block of text in Isaiah is highly subjective. Should researchers use all of Isaiah 1–39, or

you believe in prophecy, so the thinking goes, then there is no reason to think Isaiah 40–55 was written by a separate author, even if the prophetic style of those chapters breaks with the prophetic style of every other biblical and modern prophet. This approach is roughly the equivalent of claiming that Adam wrote the book of Isaiah and that anyone who disagrees simply does not believe that Adam was a prophet who could see the future and write to a future audience from a future perspective. In my view, this line of thinking either ignores or misrepresents the majority of evidence in favor of Second Isaiah.

A second line of reasoning accepts that Second Isaiah is an exilic text but claims that Nephi could have had access to it or to some version of it. The first wave of exiles went to Babylon just before King Zedekiah's reign, which is when Nephi places his family's flight from Jerusalem (1 Ne. 1:4). Thus, it is theoretically possible that within the span of a few months an exilic prophet could have written parts of Second Isaiah and sent them back to Jerusalem where they were engraved on the plates of brass, but such a timeline strains credulity. This theory also fails to account for the fact that Second Isaiah was written toward the end of exile, not the beginning. Another theory is that Nephi could have received the chapters in Second Isaiah through revelation, but that does not square with the fact that Nephi presents these chapters as being "written upon the plates of brass" (1 Ne. 19:21).

A third approach is taken by scholars who accept that the Book of Mormon is, at its core, an ancient text, and—as with the anachronistic "five books of Moses" in 1 Nephi 5:11 and the Book of Mormon's use of the Tower of Babel—use it to better understand how the Book of Mormon was produced. Perhaps Joseph Smith knew that Nephi quoted from Isaiah and then took liberties from there, inserting entire chapters that Nephi could not have known but

just the oracles written in first person? Should the first-person narratives be included and the third-person oracles left out? Second, the amount of text in Second Isaiah is fairly small—only sixteen chapters. This is further complicated by the fact that wordprints change depending on the style a text is written in; poetry and prose from the same author will often manifest differently, and styles can also change depending on the type of poetry. On top of all that, scholars have long recognized that First Isaiah had a profound influence on the author(s) of Second Isaiah, which makes distinguishing authors even more difficult. Given these challenges and the subjective nature of determining the original text, it is unsurprising that one can find wordprint studies supporting any side of the authorship debate.

which nevertheless conveyed Nephi's message. Or maybe Nephi did not quote from Isaiah at all; perhaps Joseph Smith inserted the Isaiah chapters because quoting from Isaiah at length was what books about the inhabitants of ancient America traditionally did, as we see in Ethan Smith's 1823 work, *View of the Hebrews*.

Still others see the inclusion of Second Isaiah as evidence that the Book of Mormon is not an ancient text at all, but rather a nineteenth-century composition. Such a view does not necessarily imply that Joseph was not a prophet or that the Book of Mormon is uninspired, but it does force us to reimagine what Joseph's role as a prophet was and how the Book of Mormon might be best understood.

The problem of Second Isaiah in the Book of Mormon is part of a broader problem: Why does so much of the Bible—including quotations from the New Testament—appear in the Book of Mormon when these sources could not possibly have been accessible to the Nephites? For example, how could Abinadi use phrases from Paul's letter to the Corinthians (1 Cor. 15:54–55) to describe Christ's victory over death (Mosiah 16:7–8)? How could Alma quote from John the Baptist (Matt. 3:2) and Jesus' conversation with Nicodemus (John 3:3) while preaching to the people of Gideon (Alma 7:9, 14)? Was the exact wording of the King James Bible given to the Nephites through revelation? Or did Joseph Smith find these ancient ideas and render them using wording he knew from the New Testament? These issues provide an invitation to think deeply about the book at the center of the LDS Church.

9

THE
OLD TESTAMENT
AS ADVICE

(Ezra–Song of Solomon)

In this chapter, we look at how the Old Testament may be read not as law, prediction, or story, but rather as a repository of advice for living a good life. As we will see, the Old Testament does not contain one single view on how best to live; instead, it offers various answers—and these answers change, both between authors and over time. Some Old Testament authors felt strongly that intermarriage with foreigners was evil; others saw nothing wrong with it. Some felt sacrifice was ordained by God; others disagreed. Some believed that Israel's survival depended on adherence to its distinctive religious laws; others felt assimilation was the only viable path forward.

Reading the Old Testament as advice entails taking what it offers and weighing it, deciding what is useful and what is not, what is universal and what is bound to Israel's particular culture and time. For believers, this approach locates the source of inspiration not in the Old Testament, but in the Spirit as it guides modern readers.

In my mind, the Old Testament as advice is best exemplified by the book of Proverbs, which tells the reader, "Do not answer fools according to their folly, or you will be a fool yourself" (Prov. 26:4) and then, in the very next verse, says, "Answer fools according to their folly, or they will be wise in their own eyes" (Prov. 26:5). So, which is it? Should we answer fools according to their folly or not? These two verses encapsulate the many and varied worldviews that appear throughout the Old Testament. The Old Testament does not tell us

141

the one way to respond to fools. Instead, we are left to figure out how each approach might fit in the various circumstances of our lives.

Wisdom Literature: Job, Proverbs, and Ecclesiastes

One strand of Israelite religion is made up of prophets—the individuals who received God's messages and conveyed them to the people. But alongside the prophets, another branch of Israelite religion emerged that came to be known as the "Wisdom tradition." Unlike the prophets, who received their messages directly from God, those who produced the Wisdom tradition believed that they could discover the underlying laws governing the world through their own observation. God granted humans wisdom, and he expected them to use it to uncover nature's divine pattern.

There was no antagonism between prophets and Wisdom tradition adherents, but they do represent two distinct ways of thinking about God and religion. While the prophets' trademark phrase was "Thus saith Yahweh," those in the Wisdom tradition were much more likely to say "go to the ant ... consider its ways, and be wise" (Prov. 6:6). Following the precepts of Wisdom was a way to prosper, earn riches, and be at peace with God and the world.

The Wisdom tradition was actually an international affair. Scholars have unearthed numerous Wisdom texts from throughout the ancient Near East, many of which are quoted in the Old Testament.[1] Thus, biblical Wisdom texts are decidedly non-Israelite in character. Never is the reader encouraged to offer sacrifice or follow Israel's dietary restrictions, and not once do Wisdom authors refer to Moses, Sinai, the Davidic covenant, or the patriarchs. They had a different way of conceptualizing Israel's God and religion than we see in the rest of the Old Testament.

While Wisdom influences may be found throughout the Old Testament, the three main works in this tradition are Job, Proverbs, and Ecclesiastes. Proverbs contains collections of sayings: advice ranging from proper courtly manners to how to be a good neighbor and spouse, and it presents the classic Wisdom outlook on life. For example, Proverbs repeatedly claims that people always get what

---

1. See, for example, the Egyptian text *The Teaching of Amenemope*, which is quoted extensively in Proverbs 22–24.

they deserve. "Yahweh's curse is on the house of the wicked, but he blesses the abode of the righteous" (Prov. 3:33); "Yahweh does not let the righteous go hungry, but he thwarts the craving of the wicked" (10:3); "All those who are arrogant … will not go unpunished" (16:5); "The reward for humility and fear of Yahweh is riches and honor and life" (22:4). The list goes on. Proverbs is full of advice on how to keep God's commandments, followed with descriptions of the blessings the righteous will receive in this life. Notice, by the way, how temporal these promises are. Proverbs does not claim that you will live forever with God or that you will inherit mansions after this life; the righteous are instead promised that God will bless their houses, keep them fed, and give them wealth and honor. Similarly, not once are the disobedient told of the punishment that awaits them after this life. Instead, they are told how their actions will lead to their destruction and ruin in the here-and-now.

Even when evil seems to triumph in Proverbs, the victory is only temporary; eventually "sin overthrows the wicked" (Prov. 13:6). Alternative scenarios are never even considered. Never does the author concede that God may abandon those who keep his commandments; never does he address those who do not receive God's blessings before they die, for such scenarios are impossible. As Proverbs reminds us, "The righteous will never be removed" (Prov. 10:30), and "the desire of the righteous will be granted" (Prov. 10:24).

This undeviating view of God's justice is not embraced by all authors in the Wisdom tradition, however. According to Ecclesiastes, life does not always fit into such neat categories. Sometimes the righteous suffer and die; sometimes the wicked prosper. "The race is not to the swift, nor the battle to the strong, nor bread to the wise, nor riches to the intelligent, nor favor to the skillful; but time and chance happen to them all" (Eccl. 9:11). The idea that riches do not go to the intelligent almost seems a deliberate contradiction of Proverbs, which repeatedly claims that "riches and honor" are the reward of the wise (Prov. 3:16; 8:18; 22:4).

The reality of life is that bad things happen to good people, so Ecclesiastes concludes that life is filled with "vanity," and—contra Proverbs—even obeying God could be considered worthless. "There are righteous people who are treated according to the conduct of the

143

wicked," the author observes, "and there are wicked people who are treated according to the conduct of the righteous. I said that this also is vanity" (Eccl. 8:14).

Ecclesiastes continues: "There are righteous people who perish in their righteousness, and there are wicked people who prolong their life in their evildoing" (Eccl. 7:15)—another indictment of Proverbs, which states: "The fear of Yahweh prolongs life, but the years of the wicked will be short" (Prov. 10:27). The author recommends against striving excessively after a righteousness that might not pay off: "Do not be too righteous, and do not act too wise; why should you destroy yourself?" (Eccl. 7:16). Instead, one should enjoy life, for "there is nothing better for mortals than to eat and drink, and find enjoyment in their toil" (Eccl. 2:24).

The book of Job is an extended argument about whether righteousness in fact leads to blessings. The opening chapter presents us with the Proverbial view of the world, where Job "was blameless and upright" (Job 1:1) and therefore blessed with astounding wealth. In the heavenly court, the adversary points out that this immediate connection between righteousness and prosperity essentially amounts to God's bribing Job into obedience. The adversary asks: "Does Job fear God for nothing? ... You have blessed the work of his hands" (Job 1:9–10). So, to prove Job's loyalty, God breaks the obedience-blessing pattern and afflicts this blameless man.

As hardships come to Job, his friends draw the Proverbial conclusion: bad things happen to bad people, and bad things are happening to Job, therefore Job must be bad. Eliphaz would fit right into the world of Proverbs, for he reminds Job, "Who that was innocent ever perished? Or where were the upright cut off? As I have seen, those who plow iniquity and sow trouble reap the same" (Job 4:7–8). Job rejects this view, arguing that God must be unjust, for "he destroys both the blameless and the wicked" (Job 9:22), and "the tents of robbers are at peace, and those who provoke God are secure" (Job 12:6). His friends respond by repeating the party line, that Job's great misfortune must indicate the magnitude of his wickedness: "Is not your wickedness great? There is no end to your iniquities" (Job 22:5). And the argument goes on.

Job's friends insist that the worldview of Proverbs is correct. Job

144

takes the position of Ecclesiastes. His innocent suffering has shown him that the righteous are not always blessed.

What is particularly interesting about this debate is that neither Job nor his interlocutors bring up what might seem like the most obvious solution to this problem: the afterlife. Today, when we see the innocent wronged or the guilty go free, we do not accuse God of injustice as Job and Ecclesiastes do. We usually assume that everyone will get what they deserve in the afterlife. But nowhere in these books' combined 85 chapters is the afterlife ever mentioned as a place where blessing or punishment might be meted out. In fact, Job explicitly says, "mortals lie down and do not rise again; until the heavens are no more, they will not awake or be roused out of their sleep" (Job 14:12). Then he asks rhetorically, "If mortals die, will they live again?" (14:14)—the implied answer being "no." Proverbs lists the many ways that God rewards the righteous, but never does it mention blessings after this life; keeping the commandments brings "length of days and years of life and abundant welfare" (Prov. 3:2), "riches and honor" (Prov. 3:16), and the peace of mind to "live at ease, without dread of disaster" (Prov. 1:33), but not a reward in heaven.

Why do these authors never mention heaven or hell? Why do Job's friends never argue that while sometimes life is not fair, all will be made right in the afterlife? As it turns out, they do not say these things because they do not believe them. In fact, as best we can tell, no one in ancient Israel did. Have you ever noticed that both heaven and hell are entirely absent in the Old Testament? Nowhere is heaven talked about as a place of eternal reward or hell as a place of eternal punishment. The only eternal bliss the Old Testament talks about takes place during the Millennium, but the prophets insist that it will come in this world, not the next.

Of course, the Old Testament does mention "the heavens" (roughly 400 times across more than 23,000 verses), but "the heavens" practically always means either "the sky" or "the dwelling place of God," with little distinction between the two. Nowhere is it said that the righteous will one day go there. In fact, the only person who is taken to the heavens—Elijah—is still alive. Compare this with the New Testament, Book of Mormon, and Doctrine and Covenants where heaven is spoken of frequently. Jesus and John the Baptist preach of it, people debate over who will get in, the righteous are guaranteed heavenly rest, and practically every exhortation to do good is tied directly or indirectly with "your reward ... in heaven" (Matt. 5:12).

During Old Testament times, people believed in an afterlife that looked much like what the rest of the ancient Near East believed in. The gods had their abodes—Olympus, Mt. Zaphon, Anu—but humans did not go there after death. Instead, they went to the underworld—Kurnugi, Hades, Ki—usually a dreary place. As one Babylonian myth describes it: "Those who enter are deprived of light, where dust is their food, clay their bread. They see no light, they dwell in darkness."[2] Rarely does the underworld make any distinction between the righteous and the wicked. All end up in death's grasp, and generally the best you can hope for is that your descendants will continue to place food and drink in your grave so that you may eat—a practice attested to in the Old Testament (see Deut. 26:14).

The Old Testament's name for the underworld is Sheol, and it does not get good reviews. People there subsist "in darkness and in gloom, prisoners in misery and in irons" (Ps. 107:10). The Psalmist compares his own state to those in Sheol: "I am counted among those who go down to the Pit; I am like those who have no help, like those forsaken among the dead, like the slain that lie in the grave, like those whom you remember no more, for they are cut off from your hand ... in the regions dark and deep" (Ps. 88:4–6). Those in Sheol are bound in affliction, kept in darkness, forgotten by God, and at the bottom of the deep. The righteous actually pray for God to keep them alive, "For in death there is no remembrance of you; in Sheol who can give you praise?" (Ps. 6:5).

Though these descriptions sound like modern Protestant conceptions of hell, Sheol is quite different, mostly because *everyone* ends up in Sheol. "The same fate comes to all," Ecclesiastes preaches, "to the righteous and the wicked, to the good and the evil. ... The dead know nothing; they have no more reward, and even the memory of them is lost" (Eccl. 9:2–6). Psalm 89 likewise laments, "Who can escape the power of Sheol?" (Ps. 89:48).

---

2. Staphanie Dalley, *Myths from Mesopotamia: Creation, the Flood, Gilgamesh, and Others* (New York: Oxford University Press, 2008), 155.

Sheol shows up in a story about Saul, who needs a revelation about how to conduct the war against the Philistines. Since God no longer speaks to him, he disguises himself and goes to a witch. The story reads:

> Then the woman said, "Whom shall I bring up for you?" He answered, "Bring up Samuel for me." When the woman saw Samuel, she cried out with a loud voice; and the woman said to Saul, "Why have you deceived me? You are Saul!" The king said to her, "Have no fear; what do you see?" The woman said to Saul, "I see a divine being coming up out of the ground." He said to her, "What is his appearance?" She said, "An old man is coming up; he is wrapped in a robe." So Saul knew that it was Samuel, and he bowed with his face to the ground, and did obeisance. Then Samuel said to Saul, "Why have you disturbed me by bringing me up?" (1 Sam. 28:11–15)

According to the narrator, this is no illusion. The woman indeed sees "a divine being" coming out of the ground. Samuel, apparently none too happy about having his spirit brought "up" from the underworld, delivers a doom-laden prophecy to Saul, which is fulfilled shortly thereafter. Even though he was righteous, Samuel would have gone to Sheol just as everyone else did.

Modern Latter-day Saints do not usually know about Sheol due to an odd quirk of the Christian translators of the King James Version. The descriptions of Sheol sounded much like their view of hell, and they were evidently uncomfortable with the idea that both the righteous and wicked end up there. So whenever they came across a reference to the wicked in Sheol, they translated it as "hell": "The wicked shall be turned into hell [*Sheol*]" (Ps. 9:17), the prostitute's house "is the way to hell [*Sheol*]" (Prov. 7:27), the king of Babylon "shalt be brought down to hell [*Sheol*]" (Isa. 14:15). But whenever the righteous are spoken of, these translators rendered Sheol as "the grave." Thus, Jacob mourns that his sons will "bring down my gray hairs with sorrow to the grave [*Sheol*]" (Gen. 42:38), and David hopes that Joab will not "go down to the grave [*Sheol*] in peace" (1 Kgs. 2:6).

However, by the end of the Old Testament period, Israelites had begun to leave their former notions of Sheol behind and embrace a binary view of the afterlife where the righteous are rewarded and the wicked punished. Only in Daniel, the latest book in the Old

Testament, do we see something resembling Christian notions of the afterlife, where, for example, "many of those who sleep in the dust of the earth shall awake, some to everlasting life, and some to shame and everlasting contempt" (Dan. 12:2). By New Testament times, this belief in heaven and hell had gained a central place. One cannot read the Gospels or the letters of Paul without being struck by how deeply ingrained this belief had become. This binary notion of the afterlife dominated LDS discourse until the revelation recorded in Doctrine and Covenants 76 regarding the three degrees of glory.

Psalms

Psalms has proven to be one of the most timeless and enduring compositions in the Bible. But while modern readers gravitate toward these poems, the book itself defies easy categorization. Some psalms are pleas for forgiveness, others exult in triumph; some are ancient, dating from well before the monarchial period, others reflect the life of exile in Babylon. Wisdom psalms may be found interspersed with psalms celebrating the monarchy. Some psalms praise the study of Torah; others draw heavily from the mythology of the ancient Near East. Themes and ideas from the entire spectrum of Old Testament religion populate this book, leading scholars to refer to it as the "hymnbook of the Second Temple."

In the book of Samuel, David is portrayed as particularly skilled with the lyre, and this musical talent, along with David's central role in establishing the temple, eventually led people to believe that he was Psalms' author. We can actually trace this process. In the Hebrew Bible, seventy-three psalms are explicitly attributed to David, but in the Greek translation, which was made a few centuries later, that number climbs to 84. By the time of the New Testament, the entire book seems to be ascribed to David (e.g., Acts 4:25). But while a few psalms do appear to be ancient enough to come from the time of David, the vast majority were composed significantly later, such as Psalm 137, which describes life in exile "by the rivers of Babylon" (Ps. 137:1).

While Psalms appears to be randomly organized, it actually exhibits a thoughtful and deliberate arrangement. Divided into five different "books" (Ps. 1–41, 42–72, 73–89, 90–106, and 107–150), each concludes with a short statement praising God. Book I, for example, concludes with the words, "Blessed be Yahweh, the God of Israel, from everlasting to everlasting. Amen and Amen" (Ps. 41:3). Book II concludes similarly: "Blessed be his glorious name forever; may his glory fill the whole earth. Amen and Amen" (Ps. 72:19). The final book concludes with five different psalms dedicated entirely to the praise of the Lord, each beginning and ending with the command, "Praise Yahweh!" (Ps. 146–150). This five-fold division seems to be a deliberate reflection of the five books of Moses in the Pentateuch.

In their final form, the five books of the psalter contain a microcosm of the Old Testament. The first book of Psalms introduces the covenant God makes with David, with God proclaiming, "You are my son; today I have begotten you" (Ps. 2:7). Through the rest of Books I and II, the titles of many of the psalms are connected with David's life. Songs are sung "when he fled from his son Absalom" (Ps. 3), "on the day when Yahweh delivered him … from the hand of Saul" (Ps. 18), "when he feigned madness before Abimelech" (Ps. 34), or "when he was in the Wilderness of Judah" (Ps. 63). At the conclusion of Book II, David speaks "in the time of my old age" (71:9), after which Book II's final psalm presents Solomon as having taken over for his father.[3]

The psalms of Book III cover Israel's history from the time of Solomon until the exile. The later psalms in this book reflect the existential crisis Israel was going through during the exile. Had God forgotten the Davidic covenant and the promises associated with it? How could God have let Jerusalem be captured by the Babylonians? In the final psalm of Book III, the author accuses God of failing to honor his promise to David: "But now you have spurned and rejected him … you have defiled his crown in the dust" (Ps. 89:38–39). "Lord, where is your steadfast love of old, which by your faithfulness you swore to David?" (Ps. 89:49).

Book IV deals with Israel's time in exile when Judaism reoriented itself around the law of Moses and the covenant at Sinai. Thus, Book IV opens with "A Prayer of Moses" (Ps. 90), where Moses stresses

---

3. At one point this psalm seems to have been the conclusion for the entire psalter, for the final verse reads, "The prayers of David son of Jesse are ended" (Ps. 72:20), despite the fact that other psalms attributed to David occur after this point (e.g., Ps. 86, which is titled, "A Prayer of David").

the faithfulness of God. Israel needs no king, he says, for Yahweh has always been the true king of Israel. Book IV ends with a plea for God to end the exile and "gather us from among the nations" (Ps. 106:47).

Book V deals with life after the Israelites return from exile, beginning with thanksgiving for all the people God "redeemed from trouble, and gathered in from the lands" (Ps. 107:2–3). Some of the most joyous poetry in the Bible is found here, much of it taken from a series of earlier psalms called the "Songs of Ascents" (Ps. 120–134), which were probably sung by the Israelites as they traveled to Jerusalem for yearly festivals such as Passover. By placing these songs in Book V, the compiler imagines them as being sung by the Israelites as they return to Jerusalem from Babylon. "Too long have I had my dwelling among those who hate peace" (Ps. 120:6); "I was glad when they said to me, 'Let us go to the house of Yahweh!'" (Ps. 122:1). The reader can almost feel the Israelites' awe as they finally arrive: "Our feet are standing within your gates, O Jerusalem" (Ps. 122:2). In Hebrew, the book of Psalms is known as תהלים [tehillim], "praises," and the book's final verse, "Praise Yahweh!" (Ps. 150:6) encapsulates a spirit of joy and thanksgiving as Israel is redeemed.

Judaism as Religion: Intermarriage and Cultural Distinctiveness

One of the most heated debates in post-exilic Israel broke out over a tectonic shift in the way people understood religion. In the modern world, nationality, language, ethnicity, and religion are usually understood as being distinct categories. I am a white, LDS-raised, English-speaking American, but being white does not necessarily mean I must be LDS, nor does being American guarantee that I will speak English. Since people can convert to another religion, change their citizenship, and learn new languages, we have grown comfortable with a high degree of fluidity in these categories.

In the ancient world, however, these categories were generally bound together and fixed for life. A peasant in rural Israel would most likely spend her entire life within the confines of her village. The notion that she could become Babylonian or worship the god of Babylon would have made about as much sense as a white person today trying to become ethnically East Asian. In this pre-exilic world, religion did not exist as a separate category; the worship of Yahweh was part of what it meant to be Israelite, for Yahweh was the god of Israel. To call yourself an Israelite implied that you lived in the land of Israel, spoke the Israelite language, worshiped the Israelite god, and subjected yourself to the Israelite king. This is why there was no concept of religious "conversion" before the exile. The closest the Old Testament comes to the idea is in the story of Naaman, who recognizes the power of Yahweh when the prophet Elisha heals him. But he is so confused about how a foreigner could pay respect to the god of Israel that he offers to carry "two mule-loads of earth" back to Aram, as if Israel's god could be worshiped only on Israelite soil (2 Kgs. 5:17).

With exile, however, Israel's concept of religion shifted radically. Now that the Israelites were living in the land of Babylonia, was it even possible to worship the god of Israel? Ezekiel thought so. He implores the people to stay faithful to Yahweh and goes to great lengths to show that the divine presence is not confined only to Israel. The throne of Yahweh is carried about by "wings" (Ezek. 1:6) and "wheels" (1:16), following the exiles east to Babylonia (11:22). Though the Israelites had to live in the land of Babylonia, be subject to its rulers, and speak its language, they could still worship the god of Israel. This is how the Israelites came to embrace the idea that religion could exist separately from nationality, language, and culture. While a person before the exile could not convert to being Israelite, a person after exile could convert to being Jewish.

This innovation solved one problem but created others. Aside from revering Yahweh in their hearts, how exactly were the Israelites supposed to worship him? Did not the Babylonians expect them to participate in Babylonian religion, since it was an integral part of Babylonian society? A fierce debate erupted about how Israelites should worship Yahweh and the extent to which they should assimilate into Babylonian society.

One side of this debate may be seen in the Priestly source of the Pentateuch, which was written during exile. According to this source, God had "separated [Israel] from the other peoples" and expected them to be "holy to me" (Lev. 20:26). This holiness was demonstrated by keeping the Sabbath, adhering to Israel's traditional diet, and maintaining ritual purity—in other words, by maintaining as distinct a cultural identity as possible. We see this approach in the post-exilic book of Daniel. The stories in Daniel all revolve around the mortal threats Daniel and his friends face as they maintain their dedication to the outward signs of Judaism. In none of the stories is Daniel tempted with adultery, theft, or lying; instead, he and his friends are portrayed as willing to risk death as they maintain their distinctive diet (Dan. 1), refuse to honor the emperor as divine (Dan. 3), and continue praying to Yahweh in a foreign land (Dan. 6). These stories were meant to encourage Jewish readers to hold fast to their separate cultural identity under foreign domination.

Distinctively Jewish religious practices, such as eating kosher food and observing the Sabbath, served to keep the Jewish people from completely assimilating into the surrounding culture, much as the Word of Wisdom acts as a social marker for LDS members to-day. Refusing to drink at a party or to get coffee with an associate limits the degree to which one can be "covertly Mormon." Every re-fusal keeps your membership in the church salient for you and those around you. The biblical authors who advocated for these practices most likely saw them as a way to ensure that the Jews did not assim-ilate to the broader culture so much that they disappeared entirely.

But not all biblical authors thought that such radical separation was the best course of action. The book of Esther, for example, stands in direct counterpoint to Daniel. Both Esther and Daniel are Jews living in a foreign land, but while Daniel refuses to eat the king's food, Esther regularly dines with the king, even having a banquet named after her (Esth. 2:18). While Daniel's friends refuse to bow to the emperor's statue, Esther falls at the feet of the king to beg his mercy (Esth. 8:3). Daniel prays by the window so that everyone may see his devotion to Yahweh, but Esther deliberately hides the fact that she is Jewish (Esth. 2:10) so that she may join the king's ha-rem. No mention in Esther is made of Jewish dietary laws, Sabbath observance, marriage restrictions, religious worship, or anything else distinctively Jewish. Not even Yahweh is mentioned. It would be difficult to find an approach more diametrically opposed to Daniel's.

In Esther, it is the very fact that the Jews live "separated among the peoples in all the provinces" with laws "different from those of every other people" that provokes the king to decree their destruction (Esth. 3:8). The Jews are saved from literal annihilation not by holding to their laws, but by covertly moving people into positions of power. It is Esther, the woman whose husband does not even know she is Jewish, that intercedes with him and saves the people. The moral of the story seems to be that if the Jews are to survive, they have to fly under the radar—something that can only be hindered by the kind of defiance and separation advocated in the book of Daniel.

Marriage

Before the exile, marriage to non-Israelites was a negligible issue, primarily because so few foreigners lived in the land of Israel. Later in Israelite history, however, such intermarriage became more common. Ezra in particular was concerned about this trend. "The people of Israel, the priests, and the Levites have not separated themselves from the peoples of the lands," he rails. "For they have taken some of their daughters as wives for themselves and for their sons," and "in this faithlessness the officials and leaders have led the way" (Ezra 9:1–2). Both Ezra and Nehemiah are quick to put an end to such unions. Nehemiah uses an obscure passage from the Exodus story to claim that intermarriage is forbidden by the law of Moses. "When the people heard the law, they separated from Israel all those of foreign descent" (Neh. 13:3).

While Ezra and Nehemiah interpreted the law to mean that marriage to non-Israelites was forbidden, a sizable contingent disagreed. Notice, for example, how in the verse from Ezra above it is the priests, Levites, officials, and leaders—prominent members of the community who took their religion seriously enough to leave their former lives in Babylon and return to Jerusalem—who are leading the way in marrying foreigners. This was a pervasive practice carried out by religious leaders, and one could reasonably interpret many biblical passages as supporting these marriages.

One author who disagreed with Ezra and Nehemiah was the creator of the book of Ruth, a story that seems to have been written around their time.[4] The book of Ruth is written as a kind of fable,

---

4. An indication of how late Ruth was written is that the narrator has to explain former customs the audience would no longer be familiar with: "Now this was the custom

as can be seen in the way the author plays with words and names. The story begins "in the days when the judges ruled," meaning there was no king (Ruth 1:1), and into this scene steps Elimelech, a man whose name means "God is king." A famine depletes the bread in Bethlehem (a city whose name means "the house of bread"), and Elimelech is forced to take his family to Moab. He has two sons with the unfortunate names of Mahlon ("sickly") and Chilion ("destruction"), who, of course, die after only a few verses. Naomi—whose name in Hebrew means "sweetness"—then returns to Bethlehem with her two daughters-in-law, Ruth ("friendly") and Orpah ("backish"). We are hardly surprised when Orpah turns her back on Naomi while Ruth remains friendly.[5]

Ruth is not just a foreigner but a Moabite—one of the nations expressly condemned in the Exodus story Nehemiah cited to dissolve mixed marriages—but she is portrayed as having unwavering integrity as well as devotion to Israel and its God. Rather than abandon her widowed mother-in-law, Ruth stays with her, proclaiming, "Your people shall be my people, and your God my God" (Ruth 1:16). Over and over the author praises Ruth's character and her decision to join the Israelites. Boaz tells her, "You left your father and mother and your native land and came to a people that you did not know before. May Yahweh reward you for your deeds, and may you have a full reward from Yahweh, the God of Israel, under whose wings you have come for refuge!" (Ruth 2:11–12), and "all the assembly of my people know that you are a worthy woman" (Ruth 3:11). At the end of the story, all the women of the city bless Ruth to become like the Israelite matriarchs: "May Yahweh make the woman who is coming

---

in former times in Israel concerning redeeming and exchanging: to confirm a transaction, the one took off a sandal and gave it to the other; this was the manner of attesting in Israel" (Ruth 4:7). The temporal dialect of Ruth is also late, and while the exact dating of the book is debated, the most reasonable setting seems to be after the exile.

5. The stereotypical portrayal of the characters and the high literary style of Ruth further clue us in that the story is not meant to be taken literally. Ruth and Orpah are written as literary foils. The story is full of "leading words," alliteration, reversals, and deliberate ambiguity. In addition to its own tightly woven plot, the story also interweaves complex allusions to other biblical texts, such as the Judah and Tamar story, the story of Lot and his daughters, and the stories of the matriarchs. Of course, such literary features do not preclude the book from being non-fiction, but these are the characteristics we would expect more from *The Red Badge of Courage* than from *A History of the Civil War*.

into your house like Rachel and Leah, who together built up the house of Israel" (Ruth 4:11). They tell Naomi that Ruth "is more to you than seven sons" (Ruth 4:15). And, as the last verse of the book says, Ruth is no mere Moabite convert; she is the great-grandmother of none other than King David.

The events in the book of Ruth are relatively unremarkable; but the fact that the story was written with these emphases shows a different approach to intermarriage than that taken by Ezra and Nehemiah.

One reason the Bible is so fascinating is that both these books were included in the Old Testament. Just as Proverbs contains verses that tell you both to answer and not to answer fools according to their folly, so the Bible also contains books that promote separatism and assimilation. The Bible does not have a unified position on whether intermarriage is good or whether God always rewards the righteous; instead, it contains an array of views, many of which directly contradict each other. The author of Proverbs, for example, would probably have been none too happy to discover that Job was also included in the Bible.

The Bible brings multiple viewpoints together without harmonizing them. The Priestly creation story in Genesis 1 directly contradicts the J source's creation story in Genesis 2–3, both in details and in its broader conception of God. Yet Genesis moves from one story to the next without comment. The Pentateuch contains four sets of stories along with multiple law codes, all of which contradict each other. The Deuteronomistic History stands alongside Chronicles, both claiming to be the definitive story of Israel from Moses to exile. Then the Bible goes directly from 2 Kings 25 to 1 Chronicles 1, leaving the reader to sort out these competing histories. As we saw earlier, the original word that we get "Bible" from, βιβλία [biblia], literally means "books."

I once had a professor in graduate school joke that if we come across two biblical statements that directly contradict each other, we should not call the statements contradictory; instead, we should say that they are "in tension." If the two statements are so contradictory that they are mutually exclusive, then we should say that they are in "creative tension." As we have seen, many parts of the Bible exist in creative tension, but it is in these "creative tensions" that theological innovation is born. The contradiction between the Davidic covenant and the destruction of the Davidic monarchy led to the reframing of God's promises to refer to a future Davidic Messiah. The tension between Yahweh as a national god and the destruction of his temple by the Babylonians led to the emergence of strict monotheism. The contradiction between the two creation stories in Genesis 1 and 2–3 led Joseph Smith (in the book of Moses) to frame Genesis 1 as describing the creation of all things "spiritually, before they were naturally upon the face of the earth" (Moses 3:5) and then Genesis 2–3 as their physical creation. A little later, in the book of Abraham, Smith framed Genesis 1 as being the plans which "the Gods counseled among themselves to form" (Abr. 5:3). All of these arose from the Bible's creative tensions.

Old Testament scholar David Bokovoy compares the Bible to our experience at church. He writes, "In our worship services and Sunday meetings we listen to fellow members who all experience God in different and varying ways. And while we may not always fully agree with them, we are still able to appreciate and even learn from their testimonies. Rather than being persons who we completely depend on for worship, they are persons whom we worship *with*.[6]"

In a similar vein, the various voices of the Bible do not tell us the One True Way to understand God, justice, marriage—or anything, really. Instead, they offer their perspectives. Certainly, the Bible's authors believed in the correctness of their approach, but it is left to us to figure out how—or even whether—to incorporate what they say into our own belief system. Latter-day Saints do not worship the Bible. In Bovokoy's words, they worship *with* the Bible.

Personally, I find this approach quite liberating. To treat the Old Testament as advice means that I take what it says seriously, for it represents the distilled wisdom of many people as they wrote about their experience with God. But that does not mean that I am bound to follow everything I read within its pages. I know that its authors were influenced by their own culture and time, so when I see a disagreement, I remember that the Old Testament has room for both authors. If the Old Testament itself can accommodate

---

6. David Bokovoy, *Authoring the Old Testament: Genesis–Deuteronomy* (Salt Lake City: Greg Kofford Books, 2014), 133.

contradictory opinions, then surely my own ward can extend that same grace to its members.

Latter-day Saints are often counseled to treat general conference talks as scripture. As we have seen, there are many ways to read scripture. When I come across statements from church leaders that I disagree with, I think of what it means to read the Old Testament as advice—to take seriously the competing claims of Ezra and Ruth, or Daniel and Esther. I know that our current leaders are no freer from the influences of time and culture than the authors of the Old Testament were. If the Old Testament can be understood as either myth or history, either law or advice, then surely there is room for many ways of understanding the words of any scripture, be it modern or ancient.

10

THE
OLD TESTAMENT
AS SCRIPTURE

For most of this book, I have focused on why the Old Testament was written, what its authors cared about, and what historical circumstances led to the production of these texts. But for most modern readers, these subjects are secondary—important only insofar as they help them understand what the Bible can and should mean for us today. You presumably chose to read this book, as opposed to a book about *The Odyssey*, because the Old Testament has more value to you than Greek mythology. So, in this final chapter, we look at what the Old Testament means for three of the groups that call the Old Testament scripture: Christians, Jews, and Latter-day Saints.

What Makes a Book Scripture?

Religious communities all have books they treasure. For Latter-day Saints, such books might include James E. Talmage's *Jesus the Christ*, Gerald Lund's *The Work and the Glory* series, or Richard Lyman Bushman's *Joseph Smith: Rough Stone Rolling*. But to call a book scripture is to put it in a category of its own, both in terms of how it functions within the community and how the community understands the text itself.

When it comes to reading the Old Testament as scripture, believers from most religious traditions share a set of assumptions about how to interpret the text. These assumptions are often unspoken, and therefore operate without readers even being aware of them. Thus, they exert a profound influence on the way scripture is read. James Kugel, a Jewish biblical scholar, identifies four of these assumptions:

Scripture is relevant

Scripture is cryptic

Scripture is perfect

Scripture is divine[1]

For example, one of the most fundamental differences between reading the prophecies of Isaiah as an ancient collection of Israelite oracles and reading them as scripture is the assumption that, as scripture, these oracles are relevant to the modern world. For those who read the Bible as scripture, the words of Isaiah are not simply God's word to ancient Israel; they are God's word to us, no matter our present circumstances. In this view, the stories of Abraham are meant to teach us how to live righteously in a wicked world; the law of Moses contains principles for governing today; and the Psalms give us a pattern for praying to and praising God.

The assumption of scriptural relevance gives new life and meaning to all parts of the Old Testament. Isaiah's words are no longer seen as historically bound to the eighth century; in fact believers feel that, through careful study, they can find prophecies of events yet to come. The significance of Genesis does not lie in how its stories functioned for ancient Israel; instead, its characters serve as paragons of faith in a faithless world. The Deuteronomistic History is not valued so much for its warnings about exile as for what it can teach us about the dangers of ignoring prophets today.

Believers also value scripture for being cryptic. In other words, they see it as being filled with ciphers and codes that the faithful may discern. Even when the meaning of a passage is plain, it might have additional meanings hidden beneath the surface. In the New Testament, for example, Jesus tells the disciples, "I have other sheep that do not belong to this fold" (John 10:16). In the context of the Gospel of John, Jesus appears to be referring to the Gentiles. Latterday Saints, however, believe that Jesus is also speaking cryptically about the Book of Mormon's Nephites.

---

1. James Kugel, *The Bible as it Was* (Cambridge, MA: Harvard University Press, 1997), 17–23.

Latter-day Saints are not the only ones who value scripture for being cryptic—such a view is found in both Jewish midrash and Christian allegorical interpretation. The Old Testament, however, is the site of the most frequent cryptic interpretations since it was written by ancient authors who did not share our current worldview. Modern readers "decode" the Old Testament in an effort to make it more relevant. For example, the assumption that scripture is cryptic has led Latter-day Saints to believe that Gog is not a literal kingdom, but a cipher for the wicked (Ezek. 39); that Shiloh is code for the Messiah (Gen. 49:10); that the serpent in Eden represents Satan (Gen. 2–3); that turning the hearts of the children to the fathers refers to temple work (Mal. 4:6); that when God says "day," he really means a thousand years (Gen. 2:17); that Babylon is a "type" for the wickedness of the world before the Second Coming (Isa. 13); and that Elias actually refers to John the Baptist (Mal. 4:5, Matt. 11:14).

The third assumption, that scripture is perfect, asserts that nothing in the Bible is factually inaccurate. If the book of Joshua says that Joshua destroyed Jericho, then there is no doubt that he did so. If scholars claim to have evidence to the contrary, then these scholars must be misinterpreting the facts. Similarly, a perfect Bible implies that the Bible does not contradict itself. If Paul claims that we are saved by faith (Eph. 2:8–9) and James claims that we are saved by works (James 2:24), then they must be describing two sides of the same coin. The contradictions we see when the sources of the Pentateuch are spliced together—such as the dissonance between the two creation stories—present challenges for harmonization, resulting in, for example, the doctrines of the premortal council of the gods (Abr. 4) and the spiritual creation (Moses 3).

Finally, the assumption that scripture is divine leads readers to wrestle with its contents. In the book of Joshua, God commands the Israelites to completely wipe out the inhabitants of Canaan, including men, women, and children. We already know the academic view of this story, namely, that it never happened. But for those who read the text as scripture, the story poses a major question: did God actually endorse genocide? If so, what does that tell us about God? If not, how should we understand the divinity of this text?

In short, when you read the Old Testament as scripture, the text

161

contains an entirely new meaning. It becomes a source of guidance, a code to be unlocked, and a glimpse into the divine realm. Believers must grapple with what it means to say that these stories come from God.

Reading the Old Testament as scripture also violates some of the basic tenets of academic inquiry. It ignores or stretches the authors' original meaning, and historical context becomes secondary to present-day application. But reading the Old Testament as scripture brings ancient texts to life for believers around the world, and it develops new meanings that would otherwise never be born were academia our only interpretive lens. Nor does reading the Old Testament as scripture mean that one cannot read it in other ways. I find that I read the Old Testament differently between Sunday and Monday.

But, beyond this basic set of shared assumptions, Jews, Christians, and Latter-day Saints have their own ways of using the Old Testament as scripture.

The Old Testament as Christian Scripture

Christianity comes in a staggering variety of forms, from Southern Baptists to Unitarians, from the cathedrals of Catholicism to the tent revivals of the Great Awakening, from African Pentecostalism to the secularized Christianity of Europe. Yet these different manifestations share a common approach to reading the Old Testament, for they all share a common origin. Every Christian denomination traces its roots back to Jews, specifically the Jews who followed Jesus.

Peter, Paul, and the other early church leaders were not Christians as we usually think of the term; they were Jews who happened to believe that Jesus was the Jewish Messiah—or Christ (Christ and Messiah are simply two different ways of saying "anointed," one from Greek [χριστός, *christos*] and one from Hebrew [מָשִׁיחַ, *mashiah*]). They saw themselves as the vanguard of a new movement within Judaism, not as the founders of a new religion. The split between Judaism and Christianity would not happen until decades after Jesus' death and well after Paul delivered his last sermon. For these early leaders, the Old Testament was not old, nor had it been superseded by the coming of Jesus. Rather, the Hebrew Bible was the only scripture they had, and they used and valued it much as modern Latter-day Saints use and value the Book of Mormon.

These early church leaders believed that Jesus was the Jewish Messiah, but there were no clear expectations about what the Messiah would actually do. Some Jews thought God's salvation would come through an angelic figure, what the Dead Sea Scrolls refer to as the "Prince of Light," while others thought it would come through a Davidic king. Some actually looked for two different Messiahs, one priestly and one royal. Others did not expect a Messiah at all. But no one thought that the Messiah would be a local preacher who would be executed by the Romans and then rise from the dead.

Leaders such as Peter and Paul had experienced something miraculous with Jesus, and they looked for a reflection of that miracle in the Bible. They wanted to find that Jesus' ministry, execution, and resurrection were not only compatible with, but predicted by, the Old Testament. They wanted to "Christianize," or "Messianize," the Old Testament. Thus, Matthew takes Isaiah's prophecy of the child Immanuel being born during the reign of King Ahaz and applies it to Jesus, claiming that the virgin birth "took place to fulfill what had been spoken by the Lord through the prophet" (Matt. 1:22). Mark takes the opening line of Psalm 22, "My God, my God, why have you forsaken me?" (Ps. 22:1) and "Messianizes" it by implying that the Messiah was prophesied to be forsaken by God (Mark 15:34). The author of Acts uses Psalm 2:7, where God declares how the Davidic monarch will be a son to him, to claim that the Messiah was supposed to be the Son of God (Acts 13:33). It must be said that these interpretations were outliers. We have access to many Jewish writings from before and after the time of Jesus, and in none of them are any of these verses used in reference to a coming Messiah. It was only the New Testament authors who applied them to Jesus.

This process of Christianizing the Old Testament has continued through to today. For most Christians, the Old Testament's Wisdom tradition or the covenant at Sinai may be interesting, but their primary value lies in how they prophesy of, or point to, Christ.

Indeed, Christianity came to embrace what is known as replacement theology, or supersessionism. This line of belief holds that the old covenants between God and his people have been replaced by the "new covenant" of Christ (Luke 22:20). Eventually the old covenants even came to be viewed as inferior, the law of Moses being interpreted as a lesser law given to the Israelites because of their rebelliousness—"a yoke that neither our ancestors nor we have been able to bear" (Acts 15:10).

The Mosaic covenant was not the only part of the Old Testament Christianity rejected. The Israelites themselves came to be viewed as especially wicked, constantly persecuting the prophets and turning to idolatry—a view reinforced by the many anti-Jewish passages in the New Testament. Christians even came to view the God of the Old Testament in a negative light, seeing him as vindictive and harsh while seeing the God of the New Testament as compassionate and kind.

With this rejection of all things Jewish, Christians began to focus on the part of the Old Testament that deals with life before Moses and Sinai: the book Genesis. Think about the Old Testament stories you hear most about: Adam and Eve, Cain and Abel, Noah and the flood, the Tower of Babel, Abraham and Isaac, Sodom and Gomorrah, Jacob and Esau, Jacob tricking his uncle Laban to marry Rachel, Jacob's ladder, Jacob's twelve sons, and Joseph being sold into Egypt. These stories all come from Genesis. How many stories can you recount from Numbers? Or 2 Kings? For the LDS Sunday school curriculum for 2022, the *Come Follow Me* manual devoted almost a quarter of the year to the book of Genesis. Much of the rest of the year was devoted to prophecies of Christ.

The Old Testament as Jewish Scripture

Christians often consider the Old Testament to be a Jewish text. But this is not true. Biblical prophets such as Hezekiah, Isaiah, Jehoshaphat, et al., were not Jewish; they were Israelite. Judaism is not the parent religion from which Christianity spawned; rather, Judaism and Christianity are sister religions descended from the religion of the Old Testament. Almost everything we typically associate with Judaism, such as synagogues, yarmulkes, rabbis, Pharisees, and Hanukkah, are nowhere to be found in the Old Testament; none of them developed until after the Old Testament was written.

Jews refer to what we call the Old Testament as the Tanak—an acronym derived from the words *Torah*, *Nevi'im*, and *Ketuvim*, Hebrew words meaning Law/Instruction, Prophets, and Writings respectively. The Tanak arranges these books differently than we do. While both versions begin with Genesis–Deuteronomy, the Tanak then includes the "former prophets": Joshua, Judges, 1–2 Samuel, and 1–2 Kings, followed by the "latter prophets": Isaiah, Jeremiah, Ezekiel, and the twelve minor prophets of Hosea–Malachi. The Writings includes Psalms, Proverbs, Job, Song of Solomon, Ruth, Lamentations, Ecclesiastes, Esther, Daniel, Ezra, Nehemiah, and Chronicles. Ruth, however, is not placed between Judges and 1 Samuel since Ruth is not part of the Deuteronomistic History. Daniel is listed among the Writings rather than among the Prophets, reflecting its late date of composition and its apocalyptic (rather than prophetic) genre. While the Old Testament ends with prophecies about the future, providing a bridge to the New Testament, the Tanak ends with the decree of Cyrus that the Babylonian captivity has ended and that "whoever is among you of all his people, may Yahweh his God be with him! Let him go up …" (2 Chr. 36:23). Yes, the book ends with a literal ellipsis; it is an unfinished history of a people being called back to Jerusalem.

The way Jews understand the Tanak differs radically from how Christians understand the Old Testament. Most Jews have little interest in the Messianic prophecies that enthrall Christians. Neither do they see the ancient Israelites as being particularly rebellious, nor the God of the Bible as especially harsh. The seeming contrast between a harsh Old Testament God and a loving New Testament God can mostly be chalked up to genre. The Hebrew Bible is dominated by histories created to explain where the people went wrong and how the prophets called them to repentance, so the most common themes are rebellion and judgment. By contrast, the New Testament is dominated by gospels (a word that literally means "good news") and Paul's letters of encouragement to his congregations.

But if you read closely, the God of the New Testament can appear to be just as harsh as the God of the Old Testament. See, for example, the book of Revelation where God's enemies are "tormented with fire and sulfur in the presence of the holy angels and in the presence of the Lamb" (14:10) until their blood fills the land (Rev. 14:19–20). Christ appears "clothed in a robe dipped in blood" (19:13). Even the parables can take a dark turn, as in the parable of the wedding feast, where the king (God) "was enraged. He sent his troops, destroyed those murderers, and burned their city" (Matt. 22:7). In the parable of the ten pounds, the king commands, "as for these enemies of mine who did not want me to be king over them—bring them here and slaughter them in my presence" (Luke 19:27). If you contrast these with the tender verses from Psalms or Isaiah, you can see why Jews might bristle at the suggestion that the Old Testament God compares unfavorably with the New Testament God.

Of course, Jews do not see the Hebrew Bible as being superseded by the New Testament, but they still face the challenge of applying a book written over two thousand years ago to their own lives. This is what rabbinic interpretation is for. Its two pillars are the Mishnah and Talmud. The Mishnah is a collection of oral rabbinic teachings dealing with the Torah, compiled sometime in the early third century CE. Here, the sages debate how various points of law should be interpreted and applied. Many Jews believe that some of these teachings extend back to the time of Moses. The Talmud is a multi-volume commentary on the Mishnah. It spans thousands of pages and touches on almost every aspect of Jewish law and theology. The Talmud was compiled in the centuries immediately after the completion of the Mishnah, and it stands as the centerpiece of almost every denomination of Judaism to this day. These commentaries are valuable enough that, for many Jews, the Talmud has replaced the Hebrew Bible as the focal point of their study. Rabbinic interpretation thus serves a similar role for Jews that the New Testament serves for Christians. It gives them a way to apply an ancient text to contemporary life.

Jews wrestle with many of the same issues and divisions Christians do. Orthodox Jews take a conservative approach to religion and scripture, while Reform congregations largely disregard the dietary restrictions and gender roles of traditional Judaism. Most Jewish denominations consider the Talmud to be an inspired document, but Karaite Jews do not accept the rabbinic tradition at all. Some Jews believe in a traditional heaven and hell, while others do not. Some branches look forward to the day when the Messiah will return. But among all these groups, the Hebrew Bible serves as the primary text for approaching a religious life.

The Old Testament as Mormon Scripture

Latter-day Saints take a unique approach to the Old Testament, and if we want to understand it, we have to come to terms with the way Jews, Judaism, and Jewish scripture are treated in the Book of Mormon.

The Book of Mormon is decidedly anti-Semitic in character. It anachronistically refers to the Israelites in Jerusalem as "Jews," and Nephi refuses to teach his people "concerning the manner of the Jews; for their works were works of darkness, and their doings were doings of abominations" (2 Ne. 25:2). Jacob refers to the Jews as "a stiffnecked people" who "despised the words of plainness, and killed the prophets, and sought for things that they could not understand" (Jacob 4:14). He also asserts that they constitute "the more wicked part of the world" (2 Ne. 10:3). In a description of their ultimate salvation, Nephi prophesies that "the Jews which are scattered also shall begin to believe in Christ ... and as many as shall believe in Christ shall also become a delightsome people" (2 Ne. 30:7)—implying that the Jews are not so delightsome at the moment.

Jews in the Book of Mormon serve as a foil against which the righteous are contrasted. When describing a particularly wicked people, the Book of Mormon often refers to their place of worship as a synagogue, even though synagogues did not exist until centuries after Lehi would have left Jerusalem. Thus, the wicked Amalekites "built synagogues after the order of the Nehors" (Alma 21:4). In the Zoramites' synagogue, someone would ascend the platform every week and declare, "Holy God, we believe that thou hast separated us from our brethren; and ... we believe that thou hast elected us to be thy holy children; and also thou hast made it known unto us that there shall be no Christ" (Alma 31:16). The prayer seems to be a direct reference to the New Testament stereotype of Jews who believe in their own election but refuse to believe in Christ.

Being a product of the "Jews," the Old Testament is often viewed in the Book of Mormon with suspicion. Though Book of Mormon characters refer to Old Testament scriptures frequently, such as when Nephi quotes Isaiah at length, they see the current form of the Old Testament as fundamentally lacking. Nephi reports that while the Bible was originally an inspired document, it is now missing its most important parts, for the wicked "have taken away from the gospel of the Lamb many parts which are plain and most precious; and also many covenants of the Lord have they taken away" (1 Ne. 13:26). This is why Book of Mormon prophets often prefer to quote authors and prophecies that were allegedly "taken away" from the Old Testament, such as Zenos (Jacob 5), Zenock (Alma 33:15–16), Ezias (Hel. 8:20), and the lost prophecies of Joseph in Egypt (2 Ne. 3).

Latter-day Saints thus interact with two different Old Testaments. The first is an idealized Old Testament that was inspired by God and contained the fulness of the gospel; the second is the Old Testament we actually have.

The Eighth Article of Faith allows Latter-day Saints to further dismiss the Old Testament, asserting that we believe the Old Testament/Bible to be the word of God only "as far as it is translated correctly" (A of F 1:8)—a sweeping statement often used to disregard anything disagreeable or to explain a lack of Christ-centric prophecies. Latter-day Saints generally love this first, idealized, Old Testament. The second—the Old Testament we actually have—can only be trusted if it can be Mormonized.

Latter-day Saints Mormonize the Old Testament by adopting Christian interpretation strategies, such as supersessionism, and giving them an extra twist. So while most Christians interpret Isaiah as prophesying of Christ, Latter-day Saints go one step farther and find prophecies of Joseph Smith and the Restoration as well. We interpret Ezekiel's prophecy of the sticks as predicting the coming forth of the Book of Mormon. Daniel's vision of the "stone ... cut out, not by human hands" that "filled the whole earth" (Dan. 2:34–35) is taken to refer to the spread of the LDS Church.

The LDS conception of gospel dispensations serves to further Mormonize the Old Testament by turning ancient Israelite prophets into believers in and preachers of the LDS gospel. In this view, every prophet, from Adam to Jesus, preached the same basic tenets that lie at the core of the LDS gospel as it is understood today, including priesthood, the Atonement of Christ, and the Restoration. (Not coincidentally, every dispensation listed in the LDS Bible Dictionary is associated with a figure from the book of Genesis, with the exception of Moses and Jesus.)

The concept of dispensations, together with the idea that plain and precious truths have been taken from the Old Testament, often lead Latter-day Saints to read the Old Testament primarily to find cryptic allusions to LDS beliefs. For example, when Job says, "I know that my redeemer liveth, and that he shall stand at the latter day upon the earth" (Job 19:25, KJV), Latter-day Saints tend to interpret this to mean that Job believed both in the resurrection of Jesus and in his Second Coming, despite the fact that such concepts are completely foreign to the rest of Job. When 1 Kings describes a wash basin in the temple mounted on twelve oxen, Latter-day Saints generally assume it to be a baptismal font, possibly for baptisms for the dead. Mormons also see the Israelite temple as an analogue to modern LDS temples.

The Hebrew Bible or the Old Testament?

Reading the Old Testament as LDS scripture means, in a very real sense, to fundamentally misread the text. When we read Ezekiel's prophecy of the two sticks as predicting the coming forth of the Book of Mormon, we have to read against the plain-sense meaning of the text, and we have to assume that Ezekiel was actually speaking in code, on the surface teaching the Israelites about the coming together of two kingdoms when really he was prophesying to latter-day readers about the Restoration. We also have to ignore all the evidence that Israelite prophets dealt exclusively with near-term predictions. If we assume that there was more to this prophecy that was taken out by wicked scribes, then we are rejecting the Old Testament we have in favor of one that does not actually exist. Using the four assumptions associated with scripture further obscures the message that the historical Ezekiel tried to convey. Of course, Latter-day Saints have no monopoly on misreading the Old Testament; reading the Old Testament as Christian scripture, or even as Jewish scripture, is equally problematic.

No matter what our religion, if we use the four assumptions of reading scripture, we run a real risk of studying the Old Testament and not learning anything about what the book itself has to say. Any passage, no matter what it says or how surprising it may be, can be interpreted to fit a Jewish, Christian, or Latter-day Saint worldview. The assumption of scriptural perfection allows us to harmonize difficult passages with the more comfortable teachings of Sunday school manuals and modern prophets. The assumption that the text is cryptic allows us to read against the plain-sense meaning of the text and interpret it any way we want. If we take the assumption of scriptural divinity too far, we risk believing that aspects of Israelite culture represent God's will about the way things should always be. One of the greatest challenges for believers, then, is walking that fine line between approaching the Old Testament as familiar and as other, between allowing the Old Testament to confirm truth we already know and allowing it to teach us something new.

The Old Testament is not a Mormon book. Nor is it a Christian or Jewish book. The Old Testament is an ancient Israelite book. If we want to take it seriously, we need to recognize the gulf that divides its world from ours. The authors of the Old Testament had questions they were trying to answer. They experienced God in a way that modern readers do not. They had theological disputes that have long since lost their edge. If we pretend that Israelites were essentially modern Mormons who happened to live a long time ago, we will blindly walk right into that gulf dividing our world from theirs.

But it is also important to note that we *will* read the Old Testament as Jews, Christians, and Mormons. We have chosen the Old Testament as scripture, as a source through which we interpret our lives and beliefs. Though reading the Old Testament as scripture means to fundamentally *mis*read it, such misreading is an essential part of building our collective worldview. Like the US Constitution, the Old Testament needs to be interpreted in new contexts, and often in ways that its original authors may never have foreseen or agreed with. As thoughtful readers, our job is to misread with our eyes open, to know where the boundary lies between the Israelite and Mormon Old Testaments.

If you have learned anything from the past chapters, I hope it is that no single approach to the Old Testament can possibly circumscribe it. The Old Testament is myth and story, law and history, advice and prophecy. It is a Jewish, Christian, Mormon, and ancient Israelite book. It is scripture that has unified believers across the world and it is also a record of divisions and arguments that arose in a changing world. It is a univocal text to those who read it as scripture, and a mosaic of sources to those who study its history. It more than lives up to the plural title: *Biblia*, "Bibles." The next time someone tells you that the Bible is boring, just ask: Which one?

THE
OLD TESTAMENT
AND THE
BOOK OF MORMON

Over the course of this book, we have seen how the Old Testament may be read through many different lenses: myth, advice, law, and history. For LDS readers, mentioning this final classification almost invariably draws forth the question: What about the Book of Mormon? Can we understand the Book of Mormon to be history—an accurate account of events that actually took place?

Before answering this question, I should clarify that Book of Mormon historicity is not my area of expertise. I am trained as a biblical scholar, and so my knowledge of Mesoamerican archaeology, for example, is limited to non-existent. Scholars' conclusions are also limited by the quality and quantity of the available evidence. The Bible may tell us a great deal about the world of the Bible, but it becomes less relevant when we move into the Book of Mormon.

With these limitations in mind, in my opinion, the findings of biblical scholarship do not bode well for the Book of Mormon's historicity. The reasons for this conclusion break down into four main categories: text-based problems, anachronisms, ideas we would expect to find but do not, and lack of change. Let us briefly consider each of these.

Text-Based Problems

One of the most problematic pieces of evidence against the Book of

Mormon's historicity is the way it quotes from the Old Testament. The evidence is overwhelming that Isaiah 40–66 was written by a separate author during the exile, thus making it impossible for Book of Mormon authors to quote from these chapters—as happens in 1 Nephi 20–21, 2 Nephi 6–9, and Mosiah 12–15. Some LDS writers have tried for decades to prove that the entire book was written by Isaiah himself, thus solving the anachronism, but their arguments are roundly rejected outside of LDS circles.

Even if we set Isaiah aside, the Book of Mormon still refers to Old Testament texts in a way that is impossible given what we know about the Old Testament's development. For example, when Lehi leaves Jerusalem in 600 BCE, he sends his children back to get the brass plates. Upon receiving them, he finds

> that they did contain the five books of Moses, which gave an account of the creation of the world, and also of Adam and Eve, who were our first parents; And also a record of the Jews from the beginning, even down to the commencement of the reign of Zedekiah, king of Judah; And also the prophecies of the holy prophets, from the beginning, even down to the commencement of the reign of Zedekiah; and also many prophecies which have been spoken by the mouth of Jeremiah. (1 Ne. 5:11–13)

The "five books of Moses" clearly refer to the Pentateuch, but the Pentateuch was not compiled—nor indeed was the Priestly source even written—until well after Lehi would have left Jerusalem (see chapter three). There could not, therefore, have been "five books." Further, the earliest indication that these books were ascribed to Moses does not surface until after exile.

"A record of the Jews from the beginning, even down to the commencement of the reign of Zedekiah," seems to refer to the Deuteronomistic History, and while there most likely were editions of this history created before the exile, the idea that it would have been continually updated through the currently reigning king runs counter to everything we know about how and why this history was created (see chapter five).

"The prophecies of the holy prophets" being included on the brass plates is equally problematic. The Deuteronomistic History quotes and borrows extensively from dozens of sources, but not once does it quote from Isaiah, Jeremiah, Ezekiel, Amos, or any of the other prophets whose books are now in the Old Testament. Isaiah and Jeremiah, however, quote entire chapters from the Deuteronomistic History, meaning that they were written *after* the Deuteronomistic History—during exile. In fact, as we saw in chapter seven, different configurations of the book of Jeremiah circulated for centuries after Jeremiah's death, which suggests that the book was written quite late. In contrast to the Deuteronomistic History, Chronicles, which was written after the exile, quotes from these prophets extensively. All of this suggests that the prophetic books were not compiled until well into the exile, which means they could not have been included on the brass plates.[1]

The Book of Mormon supposes that a kind of proto-Old Testament—a compilation of everything dealing with life before the exile—existed in 600 BCE, but over and over again modern scholarship shows this supposition to be highly unlikely, if not impossible. Consider the fact that Lehi, Nephi, and Jacob are familiar with essentially the entire story of Genesis through Joshua: the seven-day creation story (Jacob 4:9); the Garden of Eden, including the later interpretive tradition that the serpent was the devil (2 Ne. 2:18); covenants with Abraham, Isaac, and Jacob (1 Ne. 17:40); the selling of Joseph into Egypt (1 Ne. 5:14); Moses delivering the people from Pharaoh and crossing the Red Sea (1 Ne. 17:25–27); Moses receiving the law (2 Ne. 3:17); the miraculous provision of food and water in the wilderness (1 Ne. 17:28–29); the wilderness rebellions against God (1 Ne. 17:30); and the conquest of Canaan (1 Ne. 17:32–33).

The first difficulty here is that some of these narratives, such as the seven-day creation story, come from the Priestly source, which was not written until exile (see chapter three). Not only had some pieces of this story not yet been written, the continuous narrative

---

1. While the prophetic books were not compiled until quite late, the prophecies themselves were most likely written during the time of the prophets. Thus the prophecies in Isaiah 2, for example, were probably written down in the time of Isaiah, but they would have been preserved and passed down by his disciples (see Isa. 8:16), not by some central authority that kept "the prophecies of the holy prophets, from the beginning, even down to the commencement of the reign of Zedekiah; and also many prophecies which have been spoken by the mouth of Jeremiah" (1 Ne. 5:13). If they had been kept by some central authority, we would expect the Deuteronomistic History to have known and quoted from them, particularly when covering the time when these prophets were active.

itself—the story that moves from creation to conquest—did not exist either. Bits and pieces of this tradition circulated for a long time (see chapters one and two), but no one would bring it together into one coherent story until exile when the Israelites compiled their traditions into the grand narratives we know today. To see this, you need look no further than Jeremiah, who was contemporaneous with Lehi and yet who claims that "in the day that [God] brought your ancestors out of the land of Egypt, [he] did not speak to them or command them concerning burnt offerings and sacrifices" (Jer. 7:22; see also Amos 5:25 and the discussion in chapter seven). While Jeremiah talks frequently about the law that God gave the people (see Jer. 2:8; 5:4–5; 8:8; 9:13; etc.), he never mentions Moses in connection with it—because that story had not yet been formulated. In every writing we have from before the exile, the traditions from the primeval history and the patriarchal narratives are practically never mentioned. No one talks about Adam and the Garden of Eden, no one mentions the Tower of Babel, and no one talks about Joseph's sojourn in Egypt. The traditions existed, but they were not part of a larger salvation history that people could draw from.

Scholars do not know everything about the world of the Old Testament, but everything they do know indicates that the brass plates could not have existed as Nephi describes them. Even their form is anachronistic. In the ancient world, any text longer than a few lines was written on scrolls that were rolled up. The idea of writing a text on separate pages and binding them together into a codex did not come about until the Roman period, around the first century CE. But the Book of Mormon describes the text taken from Laban not as a scroll, but as metal "plates."

The fact that these texts were written on metal makes the story even more implausible. Literacy was rare in the ancient world, and before the age of printing, creating and writing a scroll by hand was mind-bogglingly time-consuming and expensive. To get a sense of how difficult the process was, try copying out the first chapter of Isaiah by hand; but first make a long piece of "paper" by killing a sheep, removing all the hair, drying out its skin, and smoothing the surface as best you can. Then use a pen that you constantly have to dip in ink—and make the ink yourself. Of course, they did not have pristine, computer-printed texts to work from, so try copying the text from a faded, handwritten document. And do not work too fast; any mistakes you make are essentially permanent. Now time yourself, multiply that by 929, and you can start to get a sense of how long it would take to copy out the entire Old Testament. If that sounds expensive and difficult, just imagine how long it would take—and thus how expensive it would be—to carve the text into metal sheets thin enough that, together, they could contain the entire Old Testament story without being too heavy to carry.[2] And all this would be to preserve a set of stories that Jeremiah barely seems to even know exists. In short, the idea of a codex containing the biblical stories—much less a codex made of metal—is so unlikely as to be practically impossible.

Anachronisms

The textual issues described above, such as Nephi quoting Second Isaiah and having access to an anachronistic form of the Old Testament, pose a significant problem for the ancient historicity of the Book of Mormon. But these issues are relatively minor when compared with the other anachronisms spread throughout the book. By anachronisms, I am not referring to minor issues such as Nephi's "steel" bow or the presence of horses and sheep in the Americas; I am talking about anachronistic beliefs. From an academic perspective, it is these that place the Book of Mormon unquestionably outside the realm of history.

The basic problem may be summed up as follows: the theological worldview of the Book of Mormon is entirely that of nineteenth-century Christians, not that of ancient Israelites 600 years before Christ. To cite the most obvious example, Book of Mormon prophets focus on the expectation of a Messiah, but such a belief did not exist in Lehi's time. A Davidic monarch still ruled in Jerusalem and the Kingdom of Judah was independent. Why, in

---

2. The brass plates would have probably been the single most expensive item in Israel—the kind of thing that kings would brag about having created during their reign—yet no mention is made of them in either the archeological or literary record. Israel is also home to more archaeological digs than any other place in the world, yet not a single other example of metal plates has been found. The only item even remotely similar is the so-called "copper scroll" from Qumran, which (1) comes from the first century CE, (2) is a scroll, not a codex, and (3) is not a biblical text at all, but rather a kind of treasure map.

these circumstances, would people hope for a future Davidic king to restore the throne and deliver Israel? It was only after the Babylonian captivity that such a hope even began to take shape—and even then, it took centuries before that expectation developed into the full-blown Messianism of the first century CE. If you look through the King James translation of the Old Testament, you notice that the word "Messiah" is conspicuously absent, only appearing twice in the book of Daniel, which is the Old Testament's latest book. In the New Revised Standard translation, the word "Messiah" does not appear at all. Yet before Lehi has even arrived at the promised land, he is teaching his family about "a Messiah, or, in other words, a Savior of the world" (1 Ne. 10:4).

Not only do the Nephites expect a Messiah, they expect a particular kind of Messiah. As we saw in chapter ten, during the first century CE there were many ideas about who the Messiah would be—a king or a priest, an angel or a human, a political or religious leader—or even whether there would be more than one Messiah. Yet the Nephites believe in a Messiah who would be the Son of God (1 Ne. 11:7), who would offer himself as sacrifice (Alma 34:10) to atone for the sins of the world (Alma 33:22), and who would rise from the dead after three days (Mosiah 3:10).

Their view of the Messiah is also decidedly trinitarian. Abinadi teaches: "And because [Christ] dwelleth in flesh he shall be called the Son of God, and having subjected the flesh to the will of the Father, being the Father and the Son—The Father, because he was conceived by the power of God; and the Son, because of the flesh; thus becoming the Father and Son—And they are one God, yea, the very Eternal Father of heaven and of earth" (Mosiah 15:2–4).[3] This idea of Christ being both Father and Son, as "one God," was common in nineteenth-century Christianity but completely absent in sixth century BCE Israel.

The Nephites also believe in the existence of Satan, though, as we saw in chapter six, the concept of Satan did not arise until the

---

3. A trinitarian view of God may also be seen in Mosiah 3:8, Mosiah 16:15, and Alma 11:38–39. It showed up in numerous Book of Mormon passages that were subsequently changed to reflect a non-trinitarian view. For example, in the first printing of the Book of Mormon, in 1830, Mary is referred to as "the mother of God" (1 Ne. 11:18), but in later editions this was changed to read, "the mother of the Son of God."

Persian period (sixth to fourth centuries BCE), most likely under the influence of Zoroastrianism. The Nephites further believe that the afterlife is divided into two kingdoms: the righteous "inherit the kingdom of heaven" (Alma 5:51) while the wicked go "down to hell—yea, that great pit which hath been digged for the destruction of men" (1 Ne. 14:3), "an endless torment" (Moro. 8:21), "that lake of fire and brimstone" (2 Ne. 9:19). This view certainly was not Israelite. If you recall from chapter nine, the Israelites during Lehi's time believed that everyone ended up in Sheol. The concept of heaven and hell do not appear until near the end of the Old Testament period, the earliest indication being in the book of Daniel, likely written in the second century BCE. This view lines up precisely, however, with a nineteenth-century Christian view of the afterlife.

Similarly, baptism did not emerge until the end of the Old Testament period. As we saw in chapter nine, before the Babylonian captivity, Judaism was not conceptualized as a religion to which a person could convert, so there were no conversion rituals such as baptism. No one in the Old Testament is said to be baptized, and archeological evidence of "fonts" for ritual washing do not appear until close to the time of Jesus. Yet Nephi preaches "repentance and baptism by water" (2 Ne. 31:17). He even inserts baptism into Isaiah 48:1, which is more anachronistic still (2 Ne. 20:1). The Book of Mormon assumes that baptism was a regular part of Israelite religion at the time that Lehi left Jerusalem, in contradiction to every piece of evidence we have from that period as well as everything we know about Israelite religion at that time.

The Book of Mormon further presumes that the Jews worshiped in synagogues. As early as Nephi, we hear how Christ has not "commanded any that they should depart out of the synagogues" (2 Ne. 26:26). The Zoramites likewise have synagogues; they even "gather themselves together on one day of the week, which day they did call the day of the Lord" to worship (Alma 31:12). But this kind of communal worship did not evolve in Judaism until the end of the Old Testament period. Synagogues themselves do not appear in either the archeological or the literary record until shortly before the time of Christ.

The theological issues debated in the Book of Mormon would

have made no sense to an ancient Israelite audience. For example, universalism, the idea that God will ultimately save all his children in heaven, rears its head frequently. Nehor preaches "that all mankind should be saved at the last day, and that they need not fear nor tremble, but that they might lift up their heads and rejoice; for the Lord had created all men, and had also redeemed all men; and, in the end, all men should have eternal life" (Alma 1:4). Zeezrom and Amulek debate whether you can "be saved in your sins" (Alma 11:37), and Alma's son Corianton is chastised for his belief "that it is injustice that the sinner should be consigned to a state of misery" (Alma 42:1).

This entire debate is predicated on a view of heaven, hell, repentance, and judgment that is completely foreign to the Israelites. In ancient Israel, salvation was a matter of God protecting the community in this life. There was no concept of someone going to heaven in the next life. Individuals did not repent by confessing their sins or having faith in a Son of God. This debate better fits in a nineteenth-century context when Christians were clashing over the universalist movement that had emerged a few decades earlier.

Christians during Joseph Smith's time also wanted to know whether, or how, a just God could condemn unbaptized children and righteous unbaptized adults to an eternity of suffering. (See, for example, the reaction Joseph Smith's family had upon the death of Joseph's oldest brother, Alvin.) Israelites would not have even understood the terms of this debate, much less its underlying assumptions, yet Mormon writes to a community that is supposedly having "disputations ... concerning the baptism of your little children" (Moro. 8:5).

The Book of Mormon's anachronistic beliefs would take an entire book to list. Nephites believe in a "high priesthood of the holy order of God" (Alma 13:6) though even early Christians did not distinguish between two priesthoods. They also believe in both a first and a second resurrection (Alma 40:17–25) though the concept of communal rebirth does not appear until Ezekiel (Ezek. 37)—and the idea of an individual's body and soul coming back together does not appear until close to the time of Christ. They believe that faith is a power through which a person can perform miracles (Alma 44:3) though "faith" in the Old Testament is used exclusively in the sense of "faithfulness" or "fidelity." The idea of faith as a power only came about during the New Testament period, as seen in Jesus' statements that faith could move a mountain (Matt. 17:20). They advance the notion that those cursed by God are given a "skin of blackness" (2 Ne. 5:21). This idea, based on an interpretation of Ham's curse in Genesis 9:25–27, did not come about until at least the Middle Ages and did not become prominent until the advent of slavery. The Nephites further believe that Adam and Eve's actions in Eden resulted in a fall, "which was the cause of all mankind becoming carnal, sensual, [and] devilish" (Mosiah 16:3). The Brother of Jared believes that "because of the fall our natures have become evil continually" (Ether 3:2). But the concept of a fall, along with the idea that Adam's sin let death into the world and that the serpent was actually the devil, did not develop until the time of Christianity.

Book of Mormon characters, in short, share every major aspect of their theological worldview with nineteenth-century Christians. Their ideas, assumptions, and debates presuppose developments that would not take place for centuries, if not millennia, after Lehi left Jerusalem.

One common apologetic response to this evidence is that the Nephites received their Christian worldview through revelation. But revelation cannot resolve these difficulties for two reasons. First, if the Nephites received their doctrine through revelation, why does this revelation always mirror nineteenth-century Christian beliefs rather than twenty-first-century Latter-day Saint beliefs? For example, if Lehi previously believed in Sheol but was taught by an angel about the true nature of the afterlife, why should he be taught about heaven and hell instead of the three degrees of glory? Why should the Nephites believe that God curses people with black skin—a common belief among Christians of Joseph Smith's time—when the LDS Church now "disavows the theories advanced in the past that black skin is a sign of divine disfavor or curse"?[4] Why should they believe that Jesus Christ and God the Father are "one eternal God" (Alma 11:44; see also 2 Ne. 31:21, Mosiah 15:4, 3 Ne. 11:27, and Morm. 7:7) rather than the later LDS view that God the Father and Jesus Christ are separate beings? If the Book of Mormon prophets received their beliefs through revelation, then they received

---

4. "Race and the Priesthood," Gospel Topics Essays, The Church of Jesus Christ of Latter-day Saints, accessed Dec. 2, 2021, churchofjesuschrist.org.

a very specific iteration of Christian belief that is no longer accurate considering subsequent LDS revelation.

The second reason an appeal to revelation cannot adequately address these anachronistic beliefs is that, generally, the Book of Mormon does not present this knowledge as coming through revelation. It is true that Book of Mormon characters often talk about their belief in Christ as coming from angels and the Spirit, but the vast majority of these anachronisms are simply presented as part of the Israelite religion from whence the Nephites came (see, for example, worship in synagogues or the attribution of baptism to Isaiah).

Simply put, according to the best scholarship we have, the theology presented in the Book of Mormon does not fit the state of Israelite theology in 600 BCE.

Ideas We Would Expect to Find but Do Not

The Book of Mormon has nothing to say about any traits or practices we would expect to find among sixth-century Israelites. Take, for example, observing the law of Moses.[5] Upon his arrival in the Americas, Nephi writes that "we did observe to keep the judgments, and the statutes, and the commandments of the Lord in all things, according to the law of Moses" (2 Ne. 5:10), yet aside from occasional mentions of the law, there is nothing distinctively Mosaic or even Israelite about what the Nephites observe. Aside from the Ten Commandments, not a single law is quoted or appealed to, including any mention of dietary considerations or how purity laws might apply to animals in the new world. Indeed, the Israelite concept of purity and the annual pilgrimage feasts of Booths, Weeks, and Passover—all central pillars of Israelite religion before exile—are never even mentioned.

If you recall from chapter four, the single most important command in Deuteronomy (which Lehi would likely have had access to) was to centralize worship, prohibiting all sacrifice outside the temple. But Lehi offers sacrifice in the wilderness outside Jerusalem (1 Ne. 7:22). Nephi builds an entirely new temple (2 Ne. 5:16) without

---

5. Mosaic law did not reach its final form until after the exile, but many of the statutes written in the Pentateuch, such as the prohibition against eating pork, would most likely have been observed by earlier Israelites.

mentioning that they would need a priest or Levite to officiate in the temple—a real problem since Lehi's family was descended from Manasseh. The law regarding centralization of worship was so important that every king in 1–2 Kings is judged on the extent to which he follows it. Thus, it seems very strange that upright Nephi would make no mention of why they repeatedly violated this commandment.

The Davidic covenant was likewise central to early Israelite religion; in many ways it eclipsed the Mosaic covenant at Sinai. But aside from Nephi's quotation of Isaiah, the Davidic covenant is never even mentioned in the Book of Mormon. Indeed, the only reference to David occurs in the book of Jacob, where David is condemned for his "many wives and concubines" (Jacob 2:24). Otherwise, this central piece of Israel's religion and culture is entirely missing.

The transition from judges to monarchy was a pivotal moment for Israel because, as we saw in chapter five, kings became the de facto head of the temple cult. Israel's salvation came to be imagined in terms of a future king, and God came to be understood as a king reigning over Israel. The king became God's adopted son and stood as a mediator between God and the people (unlike the Mosaic covenant at Sinai, which conceptualized Israel itself as God's son). When the Nephites make the reverse transition, from kings to judges, beyond a passing mention that bad kings could lead the people to wickedness, there is no acknowledgement of how central kings were within Israelite religion, nor is there talk of any religious realignment as the Nephites move from monarchy to judges. In over 500 years, from the beginning of the reign of the judges to the end of the Book of Mormon, the transition to judges has no discernible impact on the Nephites' concept of God, salvation, or any other aspect of their theology.

None of this is to say that the various authors and editors of the Book of Mormon could not have left those parts out, but doing so would be akin to, for example, a group of Mormons isolated on Mars deciding to ignore the Word of Wisdom, abandon temple worship, and restructure top church leadership without leaving anything in their official record about why they did so or without leaving any later evidence of how those changes affected their theology and religious practice.

Lack of Change

The fact that the shift from kings to judges had no impact on Nephite theology brings up one of the Book of Mormon's most problematic issues: the lack of theological change over time.

Biblical scholarship has uncovered huge amounts of change over the history of ancient Israelite religion. The early Israelite worship of El and the patterning of the patriarchal stories after the myths of Ugarit (see chapter two) contrast sharply with the strong condemnation of Canaanite religion that arose during the monarchic period. The laws regarding slavery, rape, and manslaughter show significant differences as we move through time, from the Covenant Code in Exodus to the Holiness Code in Leviticus (see chapter four). The very nature of Israelite religion changed with the exile, with Judaism becoming separate from nationality and political affiliation. Then, after the exile, we see the emergence of Satan, a budding belief in heaven and hell, the advent of Messianism, and the reimagining of the Davidic covenant along Messianic lines. The Israelite religion of 1000 BCE bears only passing resemblance to the Jewish religion of 1 CE.

Such significant change over a thousand years is not strange at all. The theology of both Judaism and Christianity changed drastically from the year 1 CE to 1000 CE, and similarly from the year 1000 CE to now. Even the LDS Church has changed profoundly since 1830. It reimagined polygamy; instituted and then revoked a temple-priesthood ban on those of African descent; dropped glossolalia; corporatized the institutional church; implemented correlation; ceased the law of consecration; emphasized temple work as part of regular worship; codified the Word of Wisdom; and largely dispensed with rituals such as women's blessings, the second anointing, baptism for health, and anointing before childbirth. The church of the early nineteenth century differed drastically from the church today.

However, the religion described in the Book of Mormon exhibits no such shifts. The theologies of Nephi and Moroni are indistinguishable, even though the two characters are separated by more than *one thousand years*. Think about that for a moment; not a single Nephite belief shows significant change from 600 BCE to 400 CE. Heaven and hell, resurrection, the final judgment, the Atonement, faith as power, the Godhead, baptism, angels, the structure of the church, the Millennium, the requirements for salvation, the fall— every single one of these beliefs remains unchanged.

The Book of Mormon's historicity also hinges on the historicity of stories such as the Tower of Babel. If there were no actual Tower of Babel where God confounded humankind's languages, then Jared and his family could not have prayed to be spared or ultimately made their way across the sea to found the Jaredite civilization. But as we saw in chapter one, the Tower of Babel story is a myth, inspired by the towering temples of Babylon. The stories from the primeval history (Gen. 1–11) are not history in the same way that the Deuteronomistic History is. These stories are similar to the myths passed down by any ancient civilization.

Mormonism without Mormon

It is true that Old Testament scholarship is not flawless; it cannot give us a 100 percent definitive verdict on the Book of Mormon's historicity. However, everything we know about the Old Testament undermines the idea that the Book of Mormon recounts the lives of historical people. From its reliance on an actual Tower of Babel to its many anachronistic beliefs, from the difficulties involved with the brass plates to its unchanging nineteenth-century Christian theology, every indication is that the Book of Mormon story is not ancient history.

Latter-day Saints often talk about the Book of Mormon as the keystone of our religion, that if we take the Book of Mormon out, the entire arch will crumble. If the Book of Mormon is not a historical text, does that then leave us with no religion? Does Mormonism depend on a historical Mormon, Moroni, and Nephi?

Imagine that question framed this way: Did Israelite religion depend on the truthfulness of the stories in Genesis through Deuteronomy? The Pentateuch, after all, gives the account of how Yahweh created the world and chose Israel from among all the nations. If that foundational story had turned out to be untrue, would that have negated the Israelite religion?

In modern times, we tend to judge religions based on the reliability of their truth-claims: if Mohammed spoke to God, then Islam must be true; if Jesus rose from the dead, then Christianity must be true. Israelite religion turns out to be based upon some shaky truth-claims. As we saw in chapters two and five, the evidence that Israel actually emerged from an Egyptian Exodus and conquered the Canaanites is problematic, to say the least, and the farther back before the Exodus we go, the more their history blends into myth and legend. But does that mean that the Israelites never experienced God's presence in their lives? I think they would vehemently disagree, considering the hundreds upon hundreds of pages in the Old Testament that recount their religious experiences. Countless millions of believers in this tradition—Israelites, and later Jews and Christians—have experienced God, and no analysis of the Bible's truth-claims will change that fact.

If the purpose of religion is to convey facts, then, yes, the reliability of a religion's truth-claims is of utmost importance. But if the purpose of religion is something else, such as bringing people closer to God or binding communities together, then truth claims ultimately do not matter.

Does a non-historical Book of Mormon mean that Mormonism is untrue? I cannot deny the problems I see when I examine the Book of Mormon through the lens of biblical scholarship, but I also cannot deny the experiences of millions of Latter-day Saints as they experience God in their lives. What a non-historical Book of Mormon does mean, however, is that Latter-day Saints need to reevaluate how we think and talk about it. Maybe the value of our religion lies not in how many facts we have about God, but in how much good it prompts us to do in the world. Or maybe it lies in the comfort that the plan of salvation can bring to those who mourn, or in the way it brings us closer to God, or in the strength of the community we build together. In the King James Version of the New Testament, James describes "pure religion" as "to visit the fatherless and widows in their affliction, and to keep himself unspotted from the world" (James 1:27). I may be in the minority of Latter-day Saints by holding this opinion, but I wonder if letting go of the historicity of the Book of Mormon may be exactly what is needed to more closely approach the "pure religion" spoken of by James.

RESOURCES FOR FURTHER STUDY

If you want to understand the Old Testament better, two resources are indispensable. The first is a good translation with academic footnotes. This will allow you to really dig into passages you have questions about. My personal favorite is the *New Oxford Annotated Bible*, which uses the New Revised Standard Version (NRSV) translation as its base and contains footnotes from some of the field's leading scholars. There are many editions and versions of the *New Oxford Annotated Bible*, but they are all outstanding.

The second necessity is a good introduction to the Hebrew Bible/ Old Testament. Any introduction from an academic press will work, but I love Michael Coogan's *The Old Testament: A Historical and Literary Introduction to the Hebrew Scriptures*. It treats every major topic of biblical scholarship, and Coogan is a world-renowned scholar who writes in a way non-professionals may easily understand.

However, if you want something a little more accessible, James Kugel has a phenomenal book titled *How to Read the Bible: A Guide to Scripture, Then and Now*. Kugel is a Jewish scholar who goes through the entire Old Testament juxtaposing believers' and scholars' perspectives on each story, attempting to find a common ground between scholarship and belief. I must warn you, though: Kugel's book is long, at over 800 pages. You have to be really invested to get all the way through it. You can find a similar, and shorter, approach in Marc Brettler's *How to Read the Jewish Bible*.

If you want to dig deeper into any aspect of the Bible, such as Isaiah, the Documentary Hypothesis, prophecy, etc., any good academic introduction to the Old Testament will have an abundance of resources for further reading. For how Old Testament scholarship impacts Latter-day Saints and our understanding of Restoration scripture, David Bokovoy's *Authoring the Old Testament: Genesis–Deuteronomy* is fantastic.

BIBLIOGRAPHY

Bokovoy, David. *Authoring the Old Testament: Genesis–Deuteronomy*. Salt Lake City: Greg Kofford Books, 2014.

Charlesworth, James H. ed. *The Old Testament Pseudepigrapha: Apocalyptic Literature and Testaments*. 2 vols. New Haven: Yale University Press, 2009.

Coogan, Michael D. *The Old Testament: A Historical and Literary Introduction to the Hebrew Scriptures*. 3rd ed. New York: Oxford University Press, 2014.

Cross, Frank Moore. *From Epic to Canon: History and Literature in Ancient Israel*. Baltimore: Johns Hopkins University Press, 1998.

Dalley, Stephanie. *Myths from Mesopotamia: Creation, the Flood, Gilgamesh, and Others*. New York: Oxford University Press, 2008.

Fishbane, Michael. *Biblical Text and Texture: A Literary Reading of Selected Texts*. Oxford: Oneworld Publications, 1998.

Friedman, Richard Elliott. *Who Wrote the Bible?* New York: Harper Collins, 1997.

Hallo, William W. and K. Lawson Younger. *The Context of Scripture*. 3 vols. Leiden: Brill, 1997.

Jackson, Kent P. "Isaiah in the Book of Mormon." In *A Reason for Faith: Navigating LDS Doctrine and Church History*, edited by Laura Harris Hales, 69–78. Salt Lake City: Deseret Book Company, 2016.

Journal of Discourses. 26 vols. Liverpool: Latter-day Saints' Book Depot, 1854–86.

Kugel, James L. *The Bible as it Was*. Cambridge, MA: Harvard University Press, 1997.

————. *How to Read the Bible: A Guide to Scripture, Then and Now*. New York: Free Press, 2008.

Levenson, Jon D. *The Death and Resurrection of the Beloved Son: The Transformation of Child Sacrifice in Judaism and Christianity*. New Haven: Yale University Press, 1993.

McConkie, Bruce R. "Christ and the Creation." *Ensign*, June 1982.

Nissinen, Marti. *Prophets and Prophecy in the Ancient Near East*, edited by Peter Machinist. Atlanta, GA: Society of Biblical Literature, 2003.

Roth, Martha T. *Law Collections from Mesopotamia and Asia Minor*. 2nd ed. Atlanta, GA: Scholars Press, 1995.

INDEX